Crafting the Infosec Playbook

Jeff Bollinger, Brandon Enright & Matthew Valites

Beijing · Cambridge · Farnham · Köln · Sebastopol · Tokyo

Crafting the InfoSec Playbook

by Jeff Bollinger, Brandon Enright, and Matthew Valites

Printed in the United States of America.

Published by O'Reilly Media, Inc., 1005 Gravenstein Highway North, Sebastopol, CA 95472.

O'Reilly books may be purchased for educational, business, or sales promotional use. Online editions are also available for most titles (*http://safaribooksonline.com*). For more information, contact our corporate/institutional sales department: 800-998-9938 or *corporate@oreilly.com*.

Editors: Mike Loukides, Katie Schooling, and Amy Jollymore	**Indexer:** Wendy Catalano
	Interior Designer: David Futato
Production Editor: Kristen Brown	**Cover Designer:** Karen Montgomery
Copyeditor: Jasmine Kwityn	**Illustrator:** Rebecca Demarest
Proofreader: Marta Justak	

June 2015:   First Edition

Revision History for the First Edition
2015-05-06:   First Release

See *http://oreilly.com/catalog/errata.csp?isbn=9781491949405* for release details.

978-1-491-94940-5

[LSI]

Table of Contents

Foreword

Over the past decade, Cisco's Computer Security Incident Response Team (CSIRT) has participated in countless customer meetings where we sat down and explained how we had protected one of the most attacked and interconnected companies in the world. As we reviewed the tools, people, and process for protecting large organizations, the "playbook" featured heavily. At the end of each one of these sessions, the group we were sharing with always asked, "Can I have a copy of this playbook?" We initially distributed some early sanitized versions—but soon it got too big, too company specific, and too full of things that were impossible to sanitize to share. Now, with this book, we can finally answer "yes, you can!"

When I started the Cisco CSIRT at the beginning of this century, I had always hoped we could do something that had more relevance than protecting one company. Cisco has benefited from the interconnectivity it has provided, and I felt we had a responsibility to use some of those resources to help protect the same people we had connected. More specifically, I wanted to help groups that may not be able to afford a large CSIRT. Cisco has been very supportive of the team's efforts to share cybersecurity information and has provided resources and time to allow us to realize my hope.

At the time this book was written in 2014, the world witnessed a cataclysmic failure of cybersecurity efforts across the board, with large organizations seemingly hacked at will. Extremely damaging hacks to large retailers, entertainment companies, restaurant chains, and hundreds of others have ushered in the end of reliance on automated incident detection tools like security information and event management (SIEM) systems.

The Cisco CSIRT was at the forefront of the idea that people, not tools, were the answer to protecting organizations. This book details what some of the smartest people in this field have done to detect, identify, isolate, and mitigate cyber security threats. It started simply enough—if we had an incident that we didn't detect, we would look and see if there was any commonality about the attack that we could detect with normally available detection tools (intrusion detection systems, packet capture, logs, etc.). If there was, we would string together a detection method, or "play," to look for it. If the play was useful, we would keep it. If not, we would drop it. Then it would eventually be added to the daily work of our security operations center. So the body of work this book represents was baked in the crucible of ongoing attacks and response over a very busy decade.

I am more proud of the work that this team has done than anything else in my professional career. I am really excited they took the time and effort to share the work at this level and depth. The information provided here can be used as a baseline for both new and old teams facing similar challenges. I hope that sharing like this can signal another watershed in the history of cybersecurity—when the good guys started hitting back.

—Gavin Reid
Vice President of Threat Intelligence
Lancope

Preface

If you are reading this, chances are you are looking to enhance your threat detection capabilities and techniques, and up your game as an InfoSec, incident response, and network defender or manager. Threats both in scale, complexity, and profile have evolved dramatically over the last several years and continue to increase. Proper detection and response require a lot more effort and sophistication to remain effective. Building, maturing, and maintaining an effective incident response team is no easy task. We have talked with hundreds of security teams of all types and sizes who are waging the same war between the attackers and their organizations' networks, users, and information. Few have done it well, but with a solid strategy, the right expertise, and the right infrastructure, you can compete with the bad guys.

Any good attacker will tell you—your expensive security monitoring and prevention tools are not enough to keep you secure. Successful computer security incident response teams (CSIRTs) realize that intrusions are inevitable, and the best plan is a combination of cultivated threat intelligence, vigilant monitoring for early detection, and rapid and thorough response. Having the right data available in the right tools doesn't mean that the right people are looking at it and responding properly. Operational experience is invaluable and cannot be replaced by a magic black box or a single threat feed.

Our strategy focuses on collecting, organizing, mining, enhancing, and analyzing as many relevant data sources as possible in the hunt for intrusions and security breaches. We call our strategy, this bundle of detection and response methods, the *playbook*. We have developed a fundamental approach to building a successful incident response program that will detect the inevitable security incidents, minimize damage, yield enough information to share with the incident response community, and prevent successful attacks from recurring.

This book demonstrates how to boil down complex security monitoring, incident response, and threat analysis ideas into their most basic elements. Using a data-centric approach, we share how to create or refine your own unique incident detection strategy, how to keep your ideas and methods fresh, how to discover and develop your own threat intelligence, and how to compete against the malicious actors already attacking your network.

Should You Read This Book?

This book is for IT and information security (InfoSec) professionals, particularly incident or emergency response teams, InfoSec managers or directors, and IT architects, who want to either develop a nascent security monitoring and incident response program or evolve their existing program to a modern, more effective approach.

We wrote this book with InfoSec and incident response teams in mind, yet concepts such as log and data mining using a metadata-centric approach can certainly be applied to other fields as well, including system administration, threat research, and other data analytics. In the end, it is a strategy for organizing data, developing the right questions to ask, searching through the data, and then responding. Each chapter includes our observations and advice, based on real incidents and evidence, on how you can create a successful incident detection system.

This book will help you to answer common questions:

- How do I find bad actors on my network?
- How do I find persistent attackers?
- How can I deal with the pervasive malware threat?
- How do I detect system compromises?
- How do I find an owner or responsible parties for systems under my protection?
- How can I practically use and develop threat intelligence?
- How can I possibly manage all my log data from all my systems?
- How will I benefit from increased logging—and not drown in all the noise?
- How can I use metadata for detection?

Why We Wrote This Book

We wrote this book to help security professionals develop a unique and custom methodology, including broad data analysis and metadata extraction. Many of the basic concepts within incident response haven't changed over the years. However, our do-it-yourself technology and data-centric approach is unique, and has evolved to compete with today's extant threats. We've discovered and discuss the principal ideas that any team can automate high-fidelity security incident and breach detection with technology and preparation, as well as using basic information science to inform the human analyst for everything else. We stress the importance of investment in human intelligence and analytical skills. Effective and modern security monitoring requires metadata analysis, data organization, and information retrieval.

We've read plenty of InfoSec books. Generally, most have a few core ideas, and in some cases, some interesting and novel approaches. Yet many tend to fall into the same trap of spending page after page describing how to configure open source security software packages, or drone on about various configuration options replete with screenshots. Although inescapable, this book does describe some of the toolkits available for modern incident response, but the focus remains on strategy, technique, and informed decision making. We expect that readers already have some of their favorite tools deployed, and have some experience doing incident detection. We wrote this book to give those in the know, as well as those just getting started, practical advice and examples of not just how to install and configure tools, but how to strategically use them in real-world settings.

Cut to the Chase

Everyone wants to know how to find "bad stuff." We've had many discussions with a diverse set of incident response teams around the world, and it's clear there's a need within the industry to formalize the methods to discover malicious hacking and policy violations in a structured and organized way.

In our day jobs for Cisco Systems' world-class incident response team, we actively plan, deploy, and develop monitoring strategies and incident response techniques for many unique networks globally. We have formalized our approach and made it generic, yet applicable enough that we know we can teach other organizations how to best build their own playbooks while being specific enough to solve real-world problems. It's also important to note that each organization may face different types of threats that may not be covered in our team's specific playbook (the healthcare industry, for example, has substantially different concerns than we do in information technology). Therefore, it's clear that a methodical and tested approach is what people need to hear.

It seems like there's a product for every possible aspect of computer and network security. For years, security engineers have been promised and sold "silver bullet" security solutions that "correlate" all their events, and their security problems are "solved." In our experience, these solutions often fall short of providing long-term value. We believe we have a solid approach that we will lay out in detail for any InfoSec professional.

How to Navigate This Book

Generically, the concepts cover the basic ideas of what a security incident response team should do, along with a well-reasoned approached for how they can do it best. The book attempts to cover these aspects in a strictly technology-agnostic manner so that regardless of any technology investments already in place, an organization can pick up the book and apply its principles to their own infrastructure.

If you are new to incident response and unfamiliar with how to build an effective monitoring program, begin with Chapter 1. If you're missing out on some fundamental concepts (like understanding incident response and security monitoring), start with Chapter 2. If you are a salty InfoSec or incident response veteran like us, you can probably jump in at Chapter 4.

In any case, we've laid the book out as follows, for those nonlinear types:

- Chapter 1 introduces the incident response fundamentals: why it's important to get back to basics, and how an understanding of the classic incident response model will inform your detection strategy.

- Chapters 2 and 3 help you to understand and answer the fundamental questions: What should you be protecting? What are the threats you face?

- Chapter 4 introduces the data-centric approach to security monitoring. It details how to work with the data you're collecting and how to understand and use metadata.

- Chapter 5 discusses how to develop and structure incident detection logic into your own playbook.

- Chapter 6 takes the data-centric concept theory from Chapter 4 and turns it into operational practice. Additionally, it details how to effectively use your human resources, improve and demonstrate efficiency, and build the required systems to make your plan work.

- Chapter 7 details the different types of tools and technology available for security monitoring and incident detection, options for threat intelligence consumption and management, and how best to select and implement them.

- Chapters 8 and 9 detail techniques and strategies for developing detection logic using queries to put your data to work. These chapters build on the previous chapters and get into the core of developing your own threat detection. This chapter is all about plowing through the data to get the most out of your tools.

- Chapter 10 addresses the response phase of the incident response cycle, and what actions to take when events fire.

- Chapter 11 closes the book with a discussion of keeping your incident response plan and playbook relevant, and the challenges faced by next-generation network and host security.

Additional Resources

This book builds upon and draws inspiration from the previous literature discussing log management, InfoSec, incident response, and network security monitoring. Our recommended reading includes:

- Anton A. Chuvakin, Kevin J. Schmidt, and Christopher Phillips, *Logging and Log Management* (Waltham, MA: Syngress, 2013).
- Richard Bejtlich, *Practice of Network Security Monitoring: Understanding Incident Detection and Response* (San Francisco: No Starch Press, 2013).
- Chris Fry and Martin Nystrom, *Security Monitoring: Proven Methods for Incident Detection on Enterprise Networks* (Sebastopol, CA: O'Reilly, 2009).
- Richard Bejtlich, *Extrusion Detection: Security Monitoring for Internal Intrusions* (Boston, MA: Addison-Wesley Professional, 2005).
- Kenneth R. van Wyk and Richard Forno, *Incident Response* (Sebastopol, CA: O'Reilly, 2001).
- Karen Kent and Murugiah Souppaya, *NIST 800-92: Guide to Computer Security Log Management*.
- Chris Sanders, and Jason Smith, *Applied Network Security Monitoring* (Waltham, MA: Syngress, 2013).

Conventions Used in This Book

The following typographical conventions are used in this book:

Italic
> Indicates new terms, URLs, email addresses, filenames, and file extensions.

`Constant width`
> Used for program listings, as well as within paragraphs to refer to program elements such as variable or function names, databases, data types, environment variables, statements, and keywords.

`Constant width bold`
> Shows commands or other text that should be typed literally by the user.

Constant width italic

Shows text that should be replaced with user-supplied values or by values determined by context.

This icon signifies a tip, suggestion, or general note.

This icon indicates a warning or caution.

Safari Books Online

Safari Books Online is an on-demand digital library that delivers expert content in both book and video form from the world's leading authors in technology and business.

Technology professionals, software developers, web designers, and business and creative professionals use Safari Books Online as their primary resource for research, problem solving, learning, and certification training.

Safari Books Online offers a range of plans and pricing for enterprise, government, education, and individuals.

Members have access to thousands of books, training videos, and prepublication manuscripts in one fully searchable database from publishers like Maker Media, O'Reilly Media, Prentice Hall Professional, Addison-Wesley Professional, Microsoft Press, Sams, Que, Peachpit Press, Focal Press, Cisco Press, John Wiley & Sons, Syngress, Morgan Kaufmann, IBM Redbooks, Packt, Adobe Press, FT Press, Apress, Manning, New Riders, McGraw-Hill, Jones & Bartlett, Course Technology, and hundreds more. For more information about Safari Books Online, please visit us online.

How to Contact Us

Please address comments and questions concerning this book to the publisher:

O'Reilly Media, Inc.
1005 Gravenstein Highway North
Sebastopol, CA 95472
800-998-9938 (in the United States or Canada)

707-829-0515 (international or local)
707-829-0104 (fax)

We have a web page for this book, where we list errata, examples, and any additional information. You can access this page at: *http://bit.ly/crafting-infosec-playbook*.

To comment or ask technical questions about this book, send email to: *bookquestions@oreilly.com*.

For more information about our books, courses, conferences, and news, see our website at *http://www.oreilly.com*.

Find us on Facebook: *http://facebook.com/oreilly*

Follow us on Twitter: *http://twitter.com/oreillymedia*

Watch us on YouTube: *http://www.youtube.com/oreillymedia*

Acknowledgments

It took a lot of effort from a lot of talented people to pull off our playbook at Cisco. The entire CSIRT works in some way or another with the playbook or its supporting systems, although we'd specifically like to extend thanks to the following people from CSIRT present and past for their explicit support and collaboration: Gavin Reid, Michael Scheck, Chris Fry, Martin Nystrom, Lawrence Dsouza, Dustin Schieber, Ray Espinoza, James Sheppard, Joseph McCauley, David Schwartzburg, Imran Islam, Tammy Nguyen, Jayson Mondala, Darryl Delacruz, Marianela Morales, Juan Gabriel Arce, Julian Umana, Ashwin Patil, Archana Mendon, and Chad Ruhle.

The incredibly talented technical reviewers and editors took our incomplete thoughts, ill-defined phrases, and occasionally our taboo and embarrassing grammar failures and turned them around on us. Their insight and help really took this book to the next level. A hearty thanks to everyone: Devin Hilldale, Sonya Badigian, Chris Fry, Scott McIntyre, Matt Carothers, Seth Hanford, and Robert Sheehy.

A very special thank you to the folks at O'Reilly for agreeing to let us write a book for them, and helping us turn our thoughts and writings into a cohesive and comprehensive package. Many thanks to Mike Loukides, Amy Jollymore, Katie Schooling, Rebecca Demarest, Jasmine Kwityn, Kristen Brown, and Dan Fauxsmith.

CHAPTER 1

Incident Response Fundamentals

"In tranquillo esse quisque gubernator potest."
(Anyone can hold the helm when the sea is calm.)

—Publilius Syrus

This book is about building a playbook or a concrete set of strategies so your InfoSec team or Computer Security Incident Response Team (CSIRT) can be efficient and effective. However, before you can develop a playbook, you need a team to run it and the policy backing to enforce it. If you are reading this book, chances are you are in some way involved with InfoSec and are looking to implement or improve a solid incident response plan, or are at least interested in how to develop effective security data mining queries. But before diving in, it's important to cover a few essential foundations of security monitoring and incident response. You cannot create a useful playbook without understanding the basics. Crafting it well assumes an understanding of a few principles and some prerequisite capabilities.

In this first chapter, we'll cover the following concepts:

Characteristics of a successful CSIRT
There are a few key components needed for an efficient team.

Relationship building
Successful teams develop and maintain active relationships with internal teams and external organizations, and communicate constantly and effectively within the CSIRT.

Sharing
Mature CSIRTs are responsible for engaging both customers and industry partners to share best practices, and collaborate on and research threat intelligence.

Trusting your tools

CSIRTs are responsible for managing detection and prevention tools that provide either actionable security events or detailed, historical information, as well as a myriad of other tools and services to support investigation and analysis efforts.

Policy backbone

A clear, supported policy allows you to create the CSIRT charter (authority), scope, mission, responsibilities, and obligations.

If you already have a mature CSIRT, these steps may seem obvious. However, it's worth recognizing that relationships, tools, policies, and techniques change over time. Predicting future security threats and attack techniques is very difficult, and about as accurate as predicting the weather. Researching, staying updated, and being agile with your monitoring and response capabilities will deliver success and improve your efficacy.

The Incident Response Team

Incident response teams clean up after intruders break in, deface, steal, disrupt, knock over, or just mess with hosts or networks. They will find out where the perpetrators came from, how they did it, and most of the time know exactly why. They will try to know when it happened and for how long. They'll know what was affected, and will figure out how to stop it from happening again. They will also share all this information with their friends. Intruders only need to be right just once, no matter how many times they try; *incident response teams need to be right every time.*

Without a dedicated team of security professionals to protect an organization, it will be impacted, and in some cases, devastated by security threats and intrusions. Inevitably, investing in InfoSec and incident response will justify itself once a serious incident is revealed. Think of the response team as a type of insurance policy. Investing in an incident response team up front pays off in faster restoration of business and ongoing preventative measures when there are no active incidents. Although an incident response team is unlikely to provide a revenue stream, they minimize the ultimate impact and cost to an organization during and after a critical incident. Organizations concerned with protecting their data and IT systems need to have a team and a plan ready to respond. Computer Security Incident Response Teams (with any acronym: CSIRTs, CIRTs, CERTs, SIRTs, or IRTs) get business back online quickly after a security incident, and then investigate and document exactly what happened. They provide a detailed understanding of how the incident occurred, why it occurred, who was responsible, how it can be prevented from happening again, and hopefully refine future detection, mitigation, and investigation techniques.

In the event that an incident goes public, an organization's leaders and public-facing figures must be well informed and confident about every detail. When handling the incident and taking responsibility, trust is on the line, affecting reputation and bringing potentially unwanted attention to your organization's InfoSec problems. The public element of an incident aside, there are other fires to put out, in some cases including financial loss or significant downtime. A good incident response team and proper InfoSec controls can help determine how it happened and how to fix it—and can communicate the details to anyone that needs them.

Justify Your Existence

Incident response teams have often been compared to the network security equivalent of firefighters. Actual firefighters are responsible for putting out fires, saving lives, enforcing fire safety codes, and promoting fire safety awareness. When they're not actively rescuing people from burning buildings and putting out fires, firefighters practice their skills, maintain equipment, and audit buildings and structures for fire safety based on established codes. All of this makes future fires less intense and easier to control and extinguish quickly.

Similar to the firefighters' approach, CSIRTs respond to security incidents, salvage and protect data, enforce security policy, and evangelize security best practices and development. When they are not responding to incidents, they are designing better detection techniques and strategies, while researching and preparing for the latest threats. CSIRTs are an integral part of an overall InfoSec strategy. A functional InfoSec strategy specifically includes multifaceted teams tasked with risk assessment and analysis, policy development, and security operations and controls. Response teams fill the gap of responding to computer emergencies and intrusions, while working to prevent future attacks. Cleaning up after a major incident requires real work and a response team that's capable of:

- Managing and triaging a large problem
- Understanding computer systems, networks, web applications, and databases
- Knowing how and when to execute mitigation techniques
- Engaging relevant stakeholders
- Developing short-term fixes as necessary
- Working with business, host, and application owners on long-term fixes
- Participating in incident postmortems and after-action reviews
- Determining the root cause of an issue and how to prevent a reoccurrence
- Creating detailed incident write-ups and presenting to broad audiences

When not actively investigating an incident, CSIRTs work to improve and document their detection and response techniques. Teams improve by developing additional prevention methods and maintaining an updated playbook. While an incident response playbook helps you discover incident details hiding in your data, an incident response handbook tells you how to handle them.

A good handbook provides a compendium of directives for handling cases, current links to documentation, contact information for various groups, and specific procedures to follow for any number of incident types. Combining a handbook and an incident tracking system goes a long way to help satisfy audit requirements, as you can deliver precise detail on how any incident should be handled, complete with supporting evidence in the incident tracking records. It's also very helpful when bringing new team members into the fold because it provides a guide on how to handle common cases.

Along with an effective playbook, an incident response handbook, and a mandate to protect the organization, great teams will also possess:

- Adequate resources, tooling, and training availabilities for the team to remain relevant and effective
- Proper documentation and understanding of what must be protected, including information like host or user identity, and logical diagrams for systems and networks
- Documented and reliable relationships with other groups in the organization

Good teams don't necessarily have all these requirements and "nice-to-haves," but will find creative ways to protect their organization with the resources available to them. At minimum, a team needs ample log data and methods to analyze it, and accepted techniques for shutting down attackers.

Measure Up

Measuring performance of an incident response team depends on many subjective factors. Because of a deep understanding of security and hopefully broad experience, CSIRTs fill numerous small niches in an organization, and generally work to positively influence overall security posture. There are several ways to measure a team's detection efficacy with a few simple metrics such as the following:

- How long it takes to detect an incident after it initially occurred (which should be revealed in its investigation)
- How long it takes to contain an incident once it has been detected
- How long it takes to analyze an alert or solve an incident
- How well playbook reports are performing
- How many infections are blocked or avoided

Keeping track of incident cases, application or host vulnerabilities, and a historical record of incidents helps tremendously and is invaluable for proper long-term incident response. Data garnered from these tools can help to calculate the metrics just listed and measure incident response teams over time.

Who's Got My Back?

An incident response team cannot exist in a vacuum. Just like a firefighter doesn't rebuild a burned-out house or calculate the possible insurance payout, an incident response team can't bring a return to normalcy without depending on their preexisting relationships with other groups. Cultivating these relationships early, and keeping them strong, will ensure the CSIRT's confidence in pragmatically responding to any InfoSec situation. Because there are so many other tasks to own during a serious incident, it's not practical for one team to do it all. The response team needs to have active engagements with many groups, including:

IT, networking services, hosting/application, and database teams
> Having a solid relationship with IT is the most significant factor of a CSIRT's success. To respond properly, you need to understand the network and its architecture, as well as how complex IT systems perform their operations and the inner workings of custom software. It's therefore imperative to partner with IT teams that work on these systems daily and have a more detailed understanding of their operating environments. IT teams such as network operations, DNS management, directory administrators, and others should be able to provide logical diagrams, details about logging, any known issues or potential vulnerabilities, attribution, and reasonable answers when it comes to questions about potentially malicious behavior on their systems. Earning the trust of the IT teams enables a better response to incidents and mitigation, and also encourages good support of your security monitoring infrastructure and its impact on IT operations.

Other InfoSec teams and management
> CSIRTs can't possibly own all the aspects of InfoSec for an organization, and because the fallout from many incidents provides fodder to drive architectural changes, it's important to stay close with other teams that have a stake in overall security. Maintain active relationships with risk and vulnerability assessment teams, security architects, security operations teams (e.g., access control list [ACL] or firewall changers/approvers, authentication masters, public key infrastructure (PKI) groups, etc.), and security-focused executives and leadership. These will be the teams responsible for driving the long-term fixes.

> Handing off the responsibility for long-term fixes from security incidents should be inevitable, and you need the expertise of architecture teams to address the current failings that may have precipitated the incident and to help develop future protections from harm so that you can continue to focus on fighting fires. For

quick remediation, having the operations teams on standby will make it easier to insert an ACL, firewall rule, or other blocking technique as necessary. Having regular contact with security-focused executives instills their trust in the response team's capabilities, as well as providing a direct channel for communicating situational awareness, impact, and progress upward.

Internal technical support services

In the event of an incident (say, for example, a mass worm outbreak), internal technical support staff needs to be updated on the current situation and armed with the proper information to respond to calls for support. If there are internal applications down as a result of an incident, technical support should be aware of the outage and, if necessary, aware of the security implications involved. There might be incidents where mass password resets are required, in which case the incident response team must rely on technical support services to properly handle the volume of potential questions and support requests. Externally facing technical support teams are often the biggest public facing part of an organization, and if there's a published security incident, it's certainly possible that the technical support services will be called for details, and will have to respond according to the relevant local disclosure laws. Ensuring that support teams understand what's appropriate to share about an incident is a major component in the incident containment process and could have legal ramifications without the guidance of the organization's legal group. This will help prevent unnecessary or possibly damaging information from being disclosed about an incident. Technical support services should have documented and tested procedures for engaging with internal incident response, legal, and InfoSec teams in the event that a major incident occurs that impacts a broad group of their customers. In some cases, the incident response team might advise of alternative remediation procedures. An example might be if a developing play indicated a new infection that required additional forensics. The incident response team may not want a system reinstalled or tampered with until it can be investigated.

Human resources (HR) and employee relations

In most cases, CSIRTs don't just focus on external threats—they handle internal threats as well. They are often the go-to group for internal investigations, if only because they generally have logs useful for troubleshooting and investigation. When it comes to insider threats like disgruntled employees, sabotage, abuse, or harassment, log data often comes into play as evidence. Depending on the type of incident, human resources may be involved as either the entity that initiated the investigation, or as the recipient of any employee wrongdoing uncovered as the case progresses. Many security event and log data sources can be useful to both develop a timeline of activity for an incident and to profile a user's behavior. As HR builds a case, they may request log evidence to confirm or deny a user's behavior. CSIRT teams are well suited to search for evidence supporting HR investigations, particularly when armed with rich log data sources, such as DHCP and VPN logs that can show an employee connecting to the network, web proxy logs showing where they browsed, or NetFlow logs showing any outbound connections.

Mature CSIRTs will consider possible insider threats and ways to detect them, involving HR as appropriate. CSIRTs support investigation efforts involved in incidents like disgruntled system administrators backdooring critical devices, a departing software developer downloading many times the normal volume of company source code, or fraudulent accounting activities and embezzling. Improperly handling an employee investigation can result in lawsuits or affect the livelihood of an individual. Therefore, monitoring for and taking action on malign employee behavior should not be done without proper authorization and oversight from HR and in some cases the legal departments. Notifying HR or employee relations about an incident allows them to take action based on company policy or legal regulations.

Public relations (PR) and corporate communications

It's happened. Your customers' personally identifiable information (PII) data was stolen. You have evidence of the hack. Perhaps you've mitigated the threat, perhaps you haven't. Who's going to break the news to customers, inquisitive reporters, or corporate executives? Like incident response, the art of public relations is a unique skill unto itself. A balance must be struck between the amount and quality of information divulged through the proper channels, the commitments made by your organizations, and the subsequent impact of any information disclosure upon your organization. A good PR relationship will allow you to directly provide an update on the details, scope, and impact of an incident. PR, in turn, can create the necessary language and disseminate information to appropriate internal or external parties. Face it—incidents happen. The sooner you can notify PR of something that may get press coverage, reflect poorly on the company, or affect your customers, the easier to diffuse and responsibly handle the situation. Having a solid relationship with PR also means you can keep each other updated on issues that might require a joint response, or that might affect each other's teams.

Legal departments

Rules and regulations abound describing things that can or cannot be done with data, who can view that data, how long data must be kept, how long data must not be kept, and how to properly manage and maintain data as evidence. Even more confusing, sometimes regulations differ from region to region, or customer to customer. As a CSIRT, it's your job to understand that you may need legal approval for how you interact with data that you collect and where you collect it from. Your data retention policy needs the stamp of approval from your company's legal counsel, in the event of a customer request for information (RFI), compliance audit, or lawsuit demanding old log data. Your legal counsel is not likely to be technical, nor understand in detail the data or systems involved. Ensure they're aware of your use cases, as opposed to them determining for you how you may use data. This helps legal not define a policy from scratch, but rather simply determine if for any reason what you're doing is acceptable or not. After you've received approval, ensure that legal's statements are documented in an accessible and referenceable location.

Product security or development teams' support (if applicable)

If your organization develops software (or hardware) for internal or external use, you're susceptible to security vulnerabilities. These may be found via external notification of a product vulnerability (security researchers), by investigating an incident where a vulnerability allowed ingress for an attacker, or by penetration testers (aka *pentesters*) scoped to test your products. Regardless of how they're disclosed, the vulnerabilities require patching. If you have teams that focus on product security (as opposed to infrastructure, network, and system security), they should have a direct relationship with development teams to understand what a secure fix requires and to prioritize the development, testing, and deployment of that fix. Without a dedicated product security team, you'll need to establish a relationship with the development org to build processes for dealing with product vulnerabilities yourself.

Also consider what value, as an investigative entity, your CSIRT can provide to the organization when a vulnerability is discovered. Can you help to determine risk by scanning all affected products for susceptibility? Do you have any log evidence showing signs of compromise prior to disclosure? Can you build a playbook item to detect abuse of the vulnerability until the product security group is able to deploy a patch?

Additionally, if you lack a robust centralized logging infrastructure where developers can send their app logs, or a well-defined logging policy requiring generated events suitable for security monitoring, you may need to contact the development teams directly to acquire evidence to support an investigation. You should understand the process, be it a helpdesk ticket, bug submission, or email, to request investigative support data prior to that data actually being needed.

In organizations with no product development or product security teams, earning the trust and understanding the capabilities of other investigative groups can prove mutually valuable.

Friends on the Outside

Having solid relationships external to your organization will also go a long way toward improving the capabilities and expertise of the incident response team, not to mention the opportunities for best practice sharing and good "netizenship." These are some of the organizations you'll need to work with:

Internet service providers (ISPs) and other networked peers

In lieu of in-house detection and mitigation capabilities, your last resort in distributed denial of service (DDoS) defense is working with your upstream provider(s) to identify and block the source of possibly spoofed traffic. During a denial of service incident, you, your network administrators, and your ISP must work together to isolate and contain or redirect the abusive traffic.

Local and national law enforcement

Only in (hopefully) rare cases will an incident response team need to interact with law enforcement. However, there are plenty of incident types where the two paths will cross. In some cases, national law enforcement groups will request additional information about potential victims or attackers possibly engaged in activities on your organization's network. National law enforcement agencies may also release information to help detect criminal attacks by sharing indicators of compromise.

In the event of a crime involving computer evidence related to your organization, local law enforcement may request data, systems, or statements from IT staff on any pertinent details from their investigation. Having at least a relationship with a contact in local law enforcement can be helpful for having someone to reach out to when illegal activity is discovered during a CSIRT investigation.

In some ways, law enforcement teams face similar challenges to an incident response team. Both perform forensics, person of interest investigations, and correlate data from disparate systems. Though applied differently, these commonalities provide opportunities for sharing best practices.

Product vendors and technical support

The larger your toolset, the more potential product vulnerabilities and ensuing security patches to keep up with. Vendor support can also provide an avenue to file bugs or request feature improvements. Further, on a contract basis, a vendor's professional service group (PSGs) will integrate their vendor offerings within your environment. Keeping track of vulnerabilities in your systems as well as the overall organization ensures a readiness when major flaws are found and exposed. Subscribing to mailing lists such as Full Disclosure and others provide the CSIRT with early warning for any future incidents related to exploitation of newly released vulnerabilities.

When working with your own tools, it's also great to have a reliable relationship with technical support. You don't want to discover a new bug and have to wade through Sisyphean escalation chains during the middle of an incident when you really need them to work.

Industry experts and other incident response teams

Security conferences provide multiple avenues to establish and maintain beneficial relationships. Attending talks and interacting with speakers, participating in birds-of-a-feather or meet-the-engineer sessions, vendor events, or drinks at the bar all provide opportunities to connect with like-minded individuals with techniques and ideas to share. Somebody might be looking to deploy the same systems that you just deployed, or may provide a service you never knew existed, or perhaps has approached a shared security problem in an entirely different way.

CSIRTs can certainly exist without any external relationships, but their operations are only enhanced by outside perspectives. Internal relationships are absolutely critical, however, and all successful teams must cultivate them.

The Tool Maketh the Team

To create an incident response playbook to respond to security threats, you need an existing monitoring infrastructure or the intention/knowledge to build one, data retention long enough to alert or investigate, and repositories to collect, store, analyze, and present data. Assuming you have the infrastructure already, or a plan in the works, don't forget that running a network of systems, logs, and monitors means plenty of IT work has to be done both at the outset of a deployment and ongoing maintenance, documentation, and tuning.

Even the smallest-scale enterprise system has many moving parts. The smallest and worst case is a nonredundant single machine performing all of your dependent tasks. The largest systems will have hundreds or thousands of hosts, disks, processors, applications, and a network connecting them all. In either case, to ensure availability, you need to be able to both detect if any part of the system breaks and have a process to get it fixed. This is especially important for systems on which other users depend. Got a broken inline intrusion prevention system (IPS)? Web proxy failed? If you didn't build in redundancy or fail-open measures, you can be sure your users will let you know.

Any system administrator can rattle off the necessary components of a system that need to be monitored—ensuring your hosts are online, that the correct processes are running with the correct arguments, that you receive the intended data, have adequate disk storage, efficient disk operations, and efficient query processing. The supporting infrastructure for security monitoring—large or small—is no different than any other enterprise system. You must be able to identify when these key performance indicators are nearing or actually failing. Beyond detecting problems, you must also have a support infrastructure in place to quickly address the failure point and to do so in a reasonable amount of time. Don't count on hackers to wait for you until you've replaced a failed disk.

Selecting the right tools for the job is also critically important. Ensuring that you have the capacity to collect, store, and analyze data requires an understanding of your network, devices, and potential data volume and rate. Chapter 6 goes into much deeper detail on how to make the best choices for your environment.

Choose Your Own Adventure

CSIRTs need proper tooling, relationships, and a solid technical background. However, to have any kind of authority, teams need to be recognized within an organization's InfoSec or computing policies. Having a CSIRT internally means an expectation of network monitoring, as well as possible investigations into activity performed on an organization's assets. Policies accepted by everyone in the organization must include language indicating the role and obligation of the CSIRT.

Company policies specifically stipulate (dis)allowed behaviors, requirements, processes, and standards. Rules are made to be broken, so policies must be enforced. These policies will serve as the basis for your charter. A solid charter will help you identify roles and responsibilities that your CSIRT will require to be successful in your own environment. For instance, if you provide a paid service to customers, what level of detection capabilities (if any) do your clients expect? Who is responsible for physical security at your organization? Are PC rebuilds mandatory to fix malware infections? Ideally, your charter should be documented, accessible, and approved by your management and senior management, as well as third-party groups such as legal or HR. It is from this charter that you will draw your enforcement powers.

Not every possible activity a CSIRT might perform necessarily has to be enshrined in policy; however, it can be beneficial to explicitly mention a few directives. Remember that all policy development should be closely aligned with an organization's overall strategy and operations. Not every CSIRT will enforce identical policies; however, fundamentally they should be expected and explicitly permitted to:

- Monitor and audit equipment, systems, and network traffic for security event monitoring, incident detection, and intrusion detection.
- Execute efficient incident management procedures, including, but not limited to, disabling network access, revoking access rights and credentials, or seizure and forensic examination of electronic and computing devices.
- Maintain exhaustive and exclusive control over detecting, capturing, storing, analyzing, or mitigating computer security incidents.

Again, policies are totally dependent on a business and the role a CSIRT plays, whether internal or external. Having a defined constituency can also clear up any gray areas about a CSIRT's span of control. For example, a CSIRT might be charged with protecting corporate or organizational data, but not customer data. On the other hand, a team might be responsible for monitoring corporate networks, customer networks and data, and partner interconnections. Understanding the scope of a CSIRT's mission helps ensure proper resourcing and expectations.

An example policy establishing a charter might look something like:

> The incident response team has the authority to implement necessary actions for incident management, including but not limited to, removal of network access, revocation of access rights, or seizure and forensic examination of electronic and computing devices owned by [organization] or devices communicating on internal networks and business systems, whether owned or leased by [organization], a third party, or the employee. Data collected or analyzed during the course of an investigation will be handled according to the procedures described in the Incident Response Handbook.

> In adherence to event logging, intrusion detection, incident handling, and monitoring standards, the incident response team must monitor the [organization's] network and any networks owned by [organization], including all interconnections and points of egress and ingress.

Buy or Build?

The decision to develop an internal CSIRT or hire professional incident response services can be a difficult one. On one hand, you are absolving your organization from the overhead of hiring full-time employees onto the payroll, yet on the other hand, you are paying for a subscription service that can never replicate the contextual knowledge necessary for really good incident response. There are numerous offerings in this space, like managed security services of all types, consultants that help with one-time security incidents, or hired professional services from security companies to help you with your own response.

Even with an outsourced incident response service, it's still just as important to establish policies that define the scope of their access and authority. Some organizations hire clean-up incident response teams post-hoc to triage and remove any remaining problems and investigate and deliver a detailed incident write-up. Other teams offer ongoing externally hosted security monitoring and response services by deploying sensors to your network and managing/monitoring them remotely. In both cases, third-party companies are working with your organization's data and networks and should adhere to similar policies an internal incident response team might use.

Because we advocate for developing your own playbook and response capabilities, it follows that we are proponents of the homegrown CSIRT. Contextual knowledge, and a sense of ownership and domain over an organization, give an in-house incident response team the edge when it comes to overall efficacy and efficiency. Also remember that it's difficult for computers to understand context. There is no algorithm yet possible that can factor in some aspects of a security incident.

Run the Playbook!

There are any number of ways to protect your organization, and what works for one company might not work for another. Culture, priority, risk tolerance, and investment all influence how well an organization protects itself from computer security threats.

Whatever path your organization takes, understand that to craft an effective playbook backed by human intelligence, you must understand more than how to detect computer viruses. There's a broad variety of threats, attacks, incidents, and investigations that come up during the course of business, and it's great to have a skilled team to own and manage them all. Having a solid team in place is the first step to executing an effective playbook. Having a solid understanding of your network, threats, and detection techniques will help you craft your own tailored incident response playbook that can repeatedly adjust to business, cultural, and environmental changes, as well as to the organization's risk acceptance levels.

Chapter Summary

- Keeping an organization safe from attack, as well as having a talented team available to respond quickly, minimizes damage to your reputation and business.
- Fostering and developing relationships with IT, HR, legal, executives, and others is critical to the success of a CSIRT.
- Sharing incident and threat data with external groups improves everyone's security and gives your organization credibility and trust with groups that might be able to help in the future.
- A good team relies on good tools, and a great team optimizes their operations.
- A solid and well-socialized InfoSec policy gives the incident response team the authority and charter to protect networks and data.

What Are You Trying to Protect?

"You better check yourself before you wreck yourself."
—Ice Cube

Only when you know, and can describe, exactly what you are trying to protect can you develop an effective playbook and incident response program. You must have a solid understanding of what needs protecting. Starting with tools and technology is truly putting the cart before the horse. Remember that as defenders, we do not have the luxury of defining the attacks used against us. We can only decide what we believe is most important to protect and react when it is threatened. The attackers have their own ideas as to what's valuable, but it's up to us to determine where they are most likely to strike, and what's at stake if we lose.

When we originally developed our playbook, some of our earliest requirements demanded that it enabled us to:

- Detect malware-infected machines
- Detect advanced and sophisticated attacks
- Detect suspicious network activity
- Detect anomalous authentication attempts
- Detect unauthorized changes and services
- Describe and understand inbound *and* outbound traffic
- Provide custom views into critical environments

It's impossible to determine your risk (and subsequently how to manage it) if you are not aware of what you have and what you have to lose. The risk of an unknown system, with no log information and not even a reasonable way to trace back to the host, presents a significant risk to the organization. Imagine a datacenter filled with a mishmash of servers and services, some potentially orphaned by erstwhile sysadmins and projects. If they are unknown to the IT and security teams, they are the perfect jumping-off point for attackers—whether there is valuable data on these systems or not. What better way to access internal secrets than through an unknown box on the same network as the target? If the security teams ever do catch onto the scent, how will they find out who owns it, and most importantly, will they be able to shut it down without adversely affecting some business process?

Whether it be crown jewels, government mandate, or simply basic situational awareness, the point here is that a failure to understand your own assets and risks is a recipe for a security disaster. When someone compromises a host and you cannot respond properly, nor report as to why the host's information and ownership were unknown, you will be faced with hard questions to answer.

This chapter will cover what you can and should protect and what you're obligated to protect. We'll broadly discuss the basic risk management essentials as they apply to security monitoring, and provide solid examples to help you get started in developing your plan.

The Four Core Questions

When we set out to modernize our incident management process, we took a high-level view at what was and was not working in our operations. Rather than diving right in to solve the fun technical problems, we instead went back to the basics to ensure we had properly defined the problems we were trying to solve, and that we had answers for the most basic requirements of our charter to protect the security of our company. We distilled these problems and goals into the following four questions:

- What are we trying to protect?
- What are the threats?
- How do we detect them?
- How do we respond?

Answers to these four questions provide the core foundation to security monitoring and incident response. Ask yourself these questions now, and repeat them often. Throughout this book, we will help you answer these questions, but you must at least start with an understanding of what it is you are protecting. If you don't know what to protect, you will most certainly suffer the consequences of successful attacks. While you can prevent some attacks some of the time, you can't prevent all attacks all of the time. Understanding that there will always be a place for incident prevention, while also recognizing that not every threat can be blocked, ensures a pragmatic approach to detection and response.

There Used to Be a Doorway Here

The larger and more complex an organization's network, the more overhead required to inventory, assess, and attribute assets on that network. Take the example of the company (most companies) that only has a general idea of what systems, applications, and networks they own, much less how they interoperate. In some cases, outsourced hosting or application providers may be overlooked or unknown if procured outside of approved protocol or policy, creating an even larger attack surface. A small startup grows larger and larger, eventually reaching the point of acquiring additional companies. Throughout the growth periods, there's little time or tolerance to properly document the network changes and new systems and services, as leadership believes it impedes progress and doesn't contribute to the overall bottom line. So although the company and profits grow, the network becomes so complex that understanding who owns what hosts and where they are located becomes insurmountable, invariably leading to problems in the future.

Why does this even matter? If the company is doing well, does it really make a difference if you don't know where all the servers are? The fact remains that there is no perfect security. There are a finite number of resources available to protect your organization and its assets, and often it's a battle to get what you need to simply cover the basics.

No one can protect everything and everyone all the time. It is called *incident response* after all. Certainly there are ways to prevent attacks, but there will never be a perfect defense for everything. We believe it's all about finding a balance and prioritizing what's most critical first with the resources available, and then adding additional layers as your monitoring program matures. Beyond that, it's important not only to understand what's most important to your organization, but also how to access it and who owns it. Some organizations are keen on delivering attribution details on successful attackers. However, it's also important to attribute the victims of attacks as well for proper response and remediation. We're fond of saying that detection without subsequent attribution is worthless. That is, if you find compromised systems and data but no owners, mitigating the threat quickly will be challenging, if not impossible.

InfomationWeek.com once published an article entitled "Server 54, Where Are You?" (*http://www.informationweek.com/server-54-where-are-you/d/d-id/1010340*), which reported that a University of North Carolina server had been "lost." Not only lost, but also literally concealed by drywall after a remodeling project. According to the article, "IT workers tracked it down by meticulously following cable until they literally ran into a wall." Similarly, the University of California in San Diego found a long abandoned server in the physics department hidden above drop-down false-ceiling tiles. There are likely countless true tales of misplaced, unknown, rogue, or otherwise ambiguous servers and systems, not to mention pluggable computers designed for pentesting hiding in plain sight. Although these comical errors are easy to chalk up to poorly managed, under-resourced universities, these types of issues happen everywhere. Many organizations have experienced the more mundane issues of misattributed servers, abandoned IP addresses, unused segments, and geographical or physical layer challenges. How does this kind of thing happen, and what would happen if the lost hosts had been compromised? A hidden server hosting malware, a DoS attack, or worse, would be serious trouble for an incident response team—particularly if it was impossible, or nearly impossible to trace. There are logical solutions to cutting off attacks (e.g., ACLs, null IP routes, or MAC address isolation), but at some point the physical box needs to be located and remediated to get things under control again.

In short, whether it's mom-and-pop small, a nascent startup, or enterprise size, every network has a history and an expansion story. If you plan to succeed, you need a fundamental lay of the land for any network you're protecting.

Host Attribution

So how do you determine where a host is located? Without some type of host or network management system, it's very difficult to track every useful attribute about your hosts and networks. Knowing what metadata to collect, how to keep it updated, and how to perform checks against it makes running any large network easier, with the added benefit of quick error or outage detection. The first step is to look for clues.

The more clues, or context, you have to help identify an asset on your network and understand its purpose, the better your chances of successful identification. "Tribal knowledge," or simply having a history working at an organization can go a long way toward knowing the location and function of hosts. However, attribution data must be perpetually available to all analysts in the event that someone departs with the tribal knowledge and without leaving documentation for remaining staff. It's important to have reliable systems of record available for your network. Useful attributes you should seek to collect include the following:

Location (Theater/Building/Rack)	State (On/Off/Retired)	IP Address
DNS Hostname	Priority	Description
MAC Address	NetBIOS/Directory Domain	Compliance Record
OS Name/Version	Priority	Applications
Network Address Translation (NAT)	Business Impact	Business Owner
Network Location/Zone	SNMP Strings	Emergency Pager
Address Lease History	Escalation Contact	Lab ID
Primary Contact	Function	Registration Date

Possibly the easiest place to find some of this information is in the inventory systems maintained by your network and system administrators. Centralized solutions like Nagios, IBM Tivoli, HP OpenView, and many other products or custom solutions can offer these types of host information and monitoring databases. These systems can often store names or contact information for the asset owner, information on the running system, or a description of the host's purpose. Network, system, and lab administrators along with application developers might all maintain separate inventory systems. For every inventory system, the data must be reliable at any given point in time. An Excel spreadsheet, tediously and periodically updated by hand, will inevitably give way to stale data of no use during investigations. Getting a one-time dump of all known host information is only useful until something changes. Some of the concepts covered in Chapter 4 discussing data best practices apply equally as well to asset inventory systems. Getting the CSIRT access to these inventory systems, or at least the data in the systems, provides a gold mine of attribution information necessary for incident response and advanced event querying.

Bring Your Own Metadata

Some of the clues you can discover on your own. Additional attribute information and context come from infrastructure logs. Hosts with DHCP IP address reservations, VPN and authentication services (RADIUS, 802.1x, etc.), or network or port translation records (NAT/PAT) all include transient network and host addresses. Mining logs from these services can tie a host, and potentially a user, to a network address at a given point in time—a difficult requirement for investigating events. We've experienced entire investigations come to a dead end because we were unable to precisely attribute hosts at various points in time due to a lack of transient network logs, or more embarrassingly, because the timestamps were incorrect or in an unexpected time zone. The importance of standard time zones and proper time synchronization cannot be overstated, and the use of accurate Network Time Protocol (NTP) is highly recommended.

Network Address Translation (NAT) is of particular concern due to its prevalence and its masking effects on the "true" client source IP. Administrators rarely enable NAT logging either due to configuration complexity, log churn (i.e., too much data), or performance issues. Similarly, log data from a web proxy often contains only the source IP address of the web proxy itself and not the true client address. Fortunately, for most proxies, however, there are additional headers like `Via:` and `X-Forwarded-For` that you can append to all proxied requests to include both proxy and originating IP.

VPN and DHCP logging present their own challenges (although can also yield a great deal of reward) simply because of the rapid turnover of network addresses associated with dynamic addressing protocols. For instance, I may authenticate to a VPN server, drop my connection, reauthenticate, and end up with a completely new address. Or I may be walking from building to building, getting a new DHCP lease from each unique wireless access point I connect to on the way. The shift to hosted infrastructure, or "cloud," brings additional challenges. Like NAT, not only are you setting up and tearing down network connections, but also entire instances of an asset, including all running processes and memory on that asset. Getting ahead of these problems is crucially important when chasing down a host for investigation.

Many of these attributes are not as important or even relevant to some desktop, end-user, or lab systems. However, it's critically important to ensure that any and every host going into your datacenter, regardless of its purpose, has some details listed as to its owner and its function. Left to chance, there will be hosts that end up abandoned with no identifiable owner. Enforcing owner and other asset information tracking may seem like burdensome red tape, but it prevents things from slipping through the cracks and investigations reaching a dead end. Telling people they are accountable for a host will make them think twice about deploying it without the proper controls.

Minimum access policies for datacenters and other critical network areas need to include requirements for host attribution data. For example, we will not let a new host come up in the datacenter without being first entered into the correct systems of record. These requirements are particularly important in virtual environments where there is not a physical host for the "feet on the street" to examine, and a virtual server farm may contain thousands of hosts or instances. Virtual machine (VM) administrative software should contain VM attribution log data that can help identify a group or host owner, no matter the purpose of the VM.

A great example from an incident we worked on illustrates the importance of proper attribution, even in its most basic forms. Recently, Microsoft published a critical bug leading to remote exploitation, and we immediately set out to ensure that our enterprise was patched and prepared. We had a very quick patch deployment, including coverage for almost all impacted hosts in the company, except for about 10. Out of thousands of Windows hosts that successfully applied the critical patch, 10 remained vulnerable and on the network. Looking through the systems of record at the time, we knew the hosts were obviously running Windows, but there were no clues as to who owned them, what they were for, and why they were not yet patched. To add to the confusion, the hosts were geographically dispersed and had inconsistent host-names. Finally, after some major digging (ultimately a switchport trace to one of them), we discovered that they were audio/video control panels used in some of the conference and briefing rooms. These devices ran embedded versions of Windows that we were unable to patch through the normal mechanisms and required "high-touch" local support.

Eventually, we tracked down the vendor who had issued a patch to allow a new update, and even found the contractors responsible for their maintenance and required them to update the panels. Without a great deal of digital information, we used basic detective work to find the owners. Had a more solid metadata and contact requirement been in place, we would have been able to notify the proper support group immediately and have the hosts patched as soon as the vendor supported it, minimizing their potential downtime.

Network and security administrators have plenty of tools available for logically tracking down hosts like traceroute, Address Resolution Protocol (ARP) and address tables, Network Mapper (Nmap), Cisco Discovery protocol (CDP), and many others. However, as these anecdotes illustrate, it's very possible that hosts can simply be forgotten. How can you protect your network and business if you don't even know what systems there are to protect?

Identifying the Crown Jewels

When investigating the question for our organization of *What are we trying to protect?*, we discovered it was:

- Infrastructure
- Intellectual property
- Customer and employee data
- Brand reputation

The infrastructure equates to all the hosts and systems running on the corporate network, and the network itself. Protecting the infrastructure means ensuring that the confidentiality, integrity, and availability of the hosts, applications, and networks that underpin our organizational processes are protected. In our case, the intellectual property really refers to source code, current and future business and financial practices, hardware prototypes, and design and architecture documents. A data loss incident could result in losing credibility as a security solutions vendor. The same goes for brand reputation, which means a great deal in a competitive industry.

Many of these topics may be of concern to your organization as well. However, depending on the industry, there may be additional items to protect. Healthcare systems, for example, demand strict privacy protections and a solid audit trail of all patient information. Credit card payment systems may have additional monitoring requirements to ensure financial data isn't exposed. Financial and banking systems have additional controls in place to monitor for fraudulent transactions. Requirements can and will be dictated by industry standards, government regulations, and accepted best practices.

Regardless of industry, you can try to determine your own crown jewels by:

- Focusing on the applications and services that provide your critical infrastructure

- Deciding which data would be the most deleterious to lose externally and where it's stored

- Knowing which systems have the highest impact to ongoing operations if compromised

Make Your Own Sandwich

One of the very first assignments in an introductory computer science course is: write an algorithm to describe how to make a peanut butter and jelly sandwich. The idea being that you already know how to make one, but you have to *teach* the computer how to do it. Initial attempts to describe the algorithm verbally are usually horribly incomplete, and would never lead to an accurate sandwich designed by a software program. There are some basic assumptions, of course, like the computer knows how to access the necessary inputs (peanut butter, bread, jelly, knife), but how to actually make the sandwich is what separates the brain from the computer. It sounds like a simple task, but in reality it is far from it. Humans can quickly recognize relationships, inferences, or historical information, and take calculated risks based on reasonable assumptions. Even if you had never made a sandwich before, you would quickly figure out that the peanut butter and jelly are somehow applied to the bread. A computer will only do exactly what you tell it to do—nothing more, nothing less. In fact, describing the algorithm to make a sandwich to the computer is quite lengthy and complex.

In determining how to figure out what to protect on your network, we are giving you the algorithm, but it's up to you to provide the inputs. We can't possibly predict or infer what is worth protecting and what costs are justified in doing so for your environment. What we can do, however, is guide you to this understanding on your own. Answering the four questions posed earlier is the first step.

So how did you answer the *What are we trying to protect?* question posed at the beginning of the chapter? Hopefully, at this point, you've realized that your organization, along with most every other one, has something worth protecting, whether it's a physical product, a process, an idea, or something that no one else has. You, as the incident response or other security team, are tasked with protecting it. If someone stole the top-secret recipe for your famous soft drink, wouldn't the thief or anyone to whom they sold the secret be able to reproduce it at a potentially lower cost, thereby undermining your profits? Extend the recipe metaphor to things like software source code, ASIC and chip designs, pharmaceutical methods, automotive part designs, unique financial and actuarial formulae, or even just a giant list of customer data, and there are plenty of things to lose that could devastate a company.

Start with the obvious and move on to the more esoteric. If all your patient records are stored in a database, by all means you should log and audit all database transactions. If your software source code resides on multiple servers, be certain you have thorough access control and audit logs to prove precisely who accessed what data and when. If your proprietary formulas, recipes, or designs reside on a group of servers, you should have as much accounting as possible to make sure you can understand every transaction. If you're in retail, your datacenters and financial systems are critical, but don't forget the importance of points of sale (POS) at each location. Malware running on the POS systems skimming customer payment cards and personal information have proven disastrous for many organizations. For your most critical assets, you should be able to answer whether data left the company's boundary, either through a long-running encrypted session to a remote drop site, or if data was simply copied to a CD or a USB drive and carried off premises. It's easier said than done, and there are many challenges that can make nonrepudiation very difficult.

Enabling collaboration often comes at the cost of less access control, although the expectation of keeping private data private falls squarely on the shoulders of the security architects and the incident response team. Using the source code example, if there are various business units all working on a similar project that shares code libraries, it's possible that you'll have to permit broader access than you're comfortable with. The same goes for researchers from different universities or associations. Good security often comes as a double-edged sword. Placing onerous controls on a system can absolutely lock it down, but if it's unusable to its operator, what good is it? Striking a balance between business need and security is one of the more difficult problems to solve in the security world, and is an ever-present struggle.

We'll get into risk tolerance a bit more later, but understand that even though you may know what to protect and how to tighten controls to protect it, there will always be areas in which the security posture must be relaxed to enable progress, innovation, and usability. The most important thing to remember, despite any relaxed controls, is that you need to understand where the most valuable data lies, whether production, development, disaster recovery, or backup, and have a solid understanding of who accessed it, when, and from where.

More Crown Jewels

When considering the "crown jewels," don't restrict yourself to only data, hosts, or network segments. Consider an organization's executive employees, finance and business development leaders, engineering leaders, or system and network administrators.

These high-value targets have access to data interesting to hackers:

- Executives likely have access to financial or competitive information including mergers, acquisitions, or profit data that could be leveraged for trading fraud.

- Engineering leaders have schematics, diagrams, and access to numerous projects that could be stolen or modified by attackers.

- System administrators essentially have the "keys to the kingdom," and a successful attack on them could lead to catastrophic problems.

As such, it's important to focus specialized tool deployment and monitoring efforts on those groups of individuals. Beyond typical malware and policy monitoring, you may consider additional monitoring software on the high-value targets and more options for quick remediation. Different groups access different systems and types of data, so having an understanding of their roles and typical operations will augment this more focused monitoring. Forcing tighter controls at the system and network layer require attackers to become more creative to achieve their goals.

Despite the best security awareness efforts, social engineering rarely fails to work except against the most savvy (and sometimes lucky) personnel. Think phishing attacks against those who have the most to lose (or steal from). In one example, attackers successfully took out DNS services for the *New York Times*, part of Twitter, and other high-profile websites after phishing domain administrators at those organizations (*http://www.securityweek.com/how-syrian-electronic-army-pwned-some-internets-biggest-brands*). If attackers are really dedicated, and are either incapable of or have failed at good social engineering once all the old tricks are done, they might employ "watering hole" type attacks. This is where attackers compromise websites that are commonly visited by their targets in the hopes they will compromise at least one. Attackers are crafty and will find a way to exploit either software or human vulnerability. To combat the classic attacks, hopefully you have a layered endpoint protection plan for your entire organization, including host-based intrusion prevention, antivirus, and remote forensic capabilities. If you don't, these high-profile or high-value individuals and their devices would be a good place to start. From a monitoring perspective, you might analyze the plays more frequently, have a lower tolerance threshold for risky activity, or require an expedited escalation process.

Low-Hanging Fruit

After focusing attention on your crown jewels, don't forget about the rest of the organization. Despite the increased risk, your high-value assets account for only a small portion of your entire infrastructure. Mature organizations will have InfoSec policies specifically crafted to meet their business requirements. Culture, risk acceptance, past problems, legal requirements, any government regulation, and business relevance generally determine your organization's policies. Explicitly defining what is allowed or disallowed provides the policy backing required to justify proper security monitoring and incident response. When technological limitations prevent enforcement of the policies, you'll need some sort of monitoring to determine if and when that policy has been violated.

Common IT policies adopted by most organizations that affect security include:

- Acceptable Use Policy (AUP)
- Application Security
- Network Access
- Data Classification and Protection
- Account Access
- Lab Security
- Server Security
- Network Devices Configuration

Directives in these policies can seed your playbook with basic detection strategies to support your enforcement. For example, an AUP might prohibit port scanning or penetration testing. Lab policies may require encrypted authentication protocols, mandatory usage of web proxies, or basic system hardening practices. Network device policies may forbid certain protocols or require encrypted communications. Each of these specific types of network activity can be detected and reported against. Similar to security policies, organizations often maintain standards documents that specify additional requirements. Host hardening standards, system and application logging standards, and other technical guidelines all help define specific controls that can be audited or monitored.

Standard Standards

Once properly interpreted, regulatory compliance standards can be another source of detection ideas for your playbook. Too many organizations minimally adhere to the letter of the law to satisfy controls, while implementing incomplete and ineffective solutions that provide little value for detection. We like to refer to this as "checkbox security." Essentially, you are only checking a box in a list of requirements rather than truly securing your environment. This compliance-driven approach may satisfy the auditors, but it will not keep your data safe, and can ultimately backfire when a real incident occurs. Regardless of whether your organization is subject to regulatory overheard like the "Payment Card Industry Data Security Standard" (PCI DSS, or simply PCI) (*https://www.pcisecuritystandards.org/*), the Health Insurance Portability and Accountability Act (HIPAA) (*http://www.hhs.gov/ocr/privacy/*), or the Financial Services Modernization Act (FSMA, or the Gramm–Leach–Bliley Act, or GLBA) (*http://www.business.ftc.gov/privacy-and-security/gramm-leach-bliley-act*), like basic IT policies the intent, or spirit, of these standards can be turned into actionable objectives for your playbook. If passing an audit is your main (although misinformed) concern, then having a playbook (and handbook) in place that shows how incidents are handled if and when they occur will also go a long way toward showing due diligence despite any boxes you have checked.

Each high-profile standard has its own requirements and idiosyncrasies that go beyond the scope of this book. However, it's worth highlighting how the main ideas behind certain portions of the standards can be used to determine what you should protect, and in some cases, actually how to protect it. The Cloud Security Alliance's guidelines (*https://cloudsecurityalliance.org/*) are a good example of a measurable policy. Among other things, they describe various controls suggested when using cloud computing that are germane to most organizations, regardless of how they choose to host their systems and information. Additionally, they have mapped similar controls from many different regulatory compliance standards into a single Cloud Computing Matrix (CCM) (*https://cloudsecurityalliance.org/research/ccm/*).

Table 2-1 highlights a few example specifications from the CSA CCM that can serve as best practice ideas for security monitoring and play creation. For example, the controls suggest detecting some Layer 2 network-based attacks like MAC spoofing, ARP poisoning, DoS attacks, rogue wireless devices, and higher level mitigation capabilities.

Table 2-1. CSA Cloud Computing Matrix

Control domain	Control ID	CSA control spec
Infrastructure & Virtualization Security Network Security	IVS-06	...Technical measures shall be implemented to apply defense-in-depth techniques (e.g., deep packet analysis, traffic throttling, and packet black-holing) for *detection* and timely response *to network-based attacks associated with anomalous ingress or egress traffic patterns (e.g., MAC spoofing and ARP poisoning attacks) and/or distributed denial-of-service (DDoS) attacks.*
Infrastructure & Virtualization Security Network Security	IVS-12	... The capability to *detect the presence of unauthorized (rogue) wireless network devices* for a timely disconnect from the network.
Datacenter Security - Secure Area Authorization	DCS-07	... Ingress and egress to secure areas shall be constrained and *monitored* by physical access control mechanisms *to ensure that only authorized personnel are allowed access.*
Identity & Access Management Third-Party Access	IAM-07	The identification, assessment, and prioritization of risks posed by business processes requiring third-party access to the organization's information systems and data shall be followed by coordinated application of resources to minimize, *monitor*, and measure *likelihood and impact of unauthorized or inappropriate access.* Compensating controls derived from the risk analysis shall be implemented prior to provisioning access.

Risk Tolerance

Earlier, we touched on how risk awareness plays a big role in determining what to protect. An in-depth discussion of all the facets of risk management goes way beyond the scope of this book. Yet a brief discussion is unavoidable as risk management is directly tied to understanding your network and how to defend it. Fundamentally, the question to ask yourself is, *what do I have to lose?* Knowing what to protect and what you have to lose represent the first steps in dealing with risk management and building an effective security monitoring and incident response program.

Before you can get into all the risk handling methods like avoidance, transfer, mitigation, and acceptance, you have to know where the important systems and assets are located and what could happen if they were negatively impacted by an InfoSec breach. ISO 31000:2009 (*https://www.iso.org/obp/ui/#iso:std:iso:31000:ed-1:v1:en*) details how to manage risk and how to respond.

Risk treatment can involve:

- Avoiding the risk by deciding not to start or continue with the activity that gives rise to the risk
- Taking or increasing risk to pursue an opportunity
- Removing the risk source
- Changing the likelihood
- Changing the consequences
- Sharing the risk with another party or parties (including contracts and risk financing)
- Retaining the risk by informed decision

Connecting a computer to the Internet creates a risk. That is, if it's reachable by an attacker, it's likely to be attacked. Providing access to a computer system to more than one person increases the risk that something can go wrong, and the more people with accounts, the higher the risk becomes. Risk is proportional to the amount and level of access you provide. Really we're just talking about the principle of least privilege (*http://web.mit.edu/Saltzer/www/publications/protection/*), which refers to allowing a user access only to the data and tools required to fulfill their duties (rather than mass privileges per team or department).

Taking a cue from the ISO 31000:2009, you can "change the likelihood" of a problem by keeping tighter access control. Having tighter access control requires you to know who can log in (and who has logged in), when, from where, for how long, and why. If you don't know where your important systems are, and you don't know who is logging in, you've already increased your risk profile substantially. What we are saying goes a bit beyond ISO 31000, in that you must not only focus on the likelihood or prevention of a risk, but also on having an awareness of risk in your organization.

Can I Get a Copy of Your Playbook?

All this is to say that there is no exhaustive rubber-stamp approach to defining everything you need to protect. You should strive to make the best effort with the information you have, as it's the best way to inform your monitoring strategy. Again, you cannot begin to define your playbook strategy until you have a solid understanding of what is most important to protect. Our playbook is unique to our organization, as your playbook will be to yours. You will have different answers to the question of *What are we trying to protect?*, and while we wrote this book to help you develop your own playbook, only you can answer the four core questions. Like ours, the plays in your playbook help you protect the unique environment that you've been charged to monitor.

Chapter Summary

- You can't properly protect your network if you don't know what to protect.
- Define and understand your critical assets and what's most important to your organization.
- Ensure that you can attribute ownership or responsibility for all systems on your network.
- Understand and leverage the log data that can help you determine host ownership.
- A complex network is difficult to protect, unless you understand it well.

CHAPTER 3

What Are the Threats?

"By heaven, I'll make a ghost of him that lets me."
—*Hamlet*, William Shakespeare

It's 5 p.m. Friday, the last night of your on-call rotation as an incident investigator. You've just shut down for the weekend, and as you're about to leave the office, your mobile buzzes with a text message: "IT-OPS: Sev5 Possible production FTP server compromise. Ongoing conf call." You jump on the telephony bridge to learn that some sysadmins were troubleshooting a failed FTP server on one of their externally facing hosts. After remotely rebooting the server, they were unable to log into the host. A sysadmin in the datacenter connected to the local console of the host and encountered a large text box like the one shown in Figure 3-1.

The instructions detail how to wire the criminals the $5,000 ransom via Western Union, MoneyGram, or the now defunct Liberty Reserve, along with amateurish assurances that the cryptography could not be broken, and that they'll take no mercy on your data. Immediately, thoughts start running through your head as you jump into the incident lifecycle: How did the host get infected with ransomware? Is our customer data encrypted? Are there other infected or similarly vulnerable hosts? What customer-facing services are now offline with this host out of commission? Why didn't I leave work 10 minutes earlier?

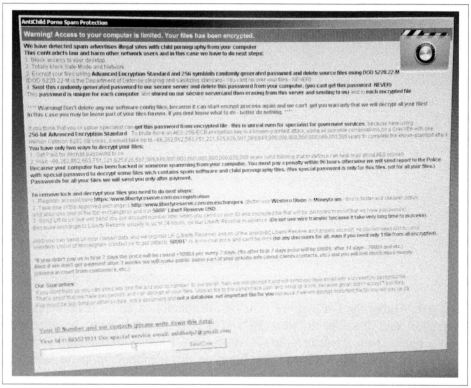

Figure 3-1. Ransomware screenshot

Before finally heading out for the weekend, you have the sysadmin shut down the host (it's already been rebooted anyway) and send you the hard disks for investigation. Later, when you receive the disks, forensics will reveal that the extortion attempt was the last in a long line of ways the attackers had abused the compromised host over the previous months. Their activities up to the ransomware installation included:

- Stealing the local password file
- Attacking other Internet hosts
- Selling proxy services through the machine
- Spamming (both email and SMS through a web service)
- Downloading every file on the server, including customer data
- Installing new software
- Obtaining online retail purchases, likely with stolen credit card information

- Applying for personal loans with stolen credentials
- Purchasing lodging for a vacation trip in Eastern Europe

Your investigation will find that the attackers initially guessed the host's weak FTP admin password, and incredibly, successfully reused it to authenticate and log in to the host as an administrator through the Remote Desktop Protocol (RDP).

This FTP server incident example highlights attackers acting opportunistically, exploiting a specific weakness and running wild. Defending against these threats (and others) to your organization requires understanding the attacker's motivation and intention to profit by compromising your network, systems, or data.

In this chapter, we'll focus on the need for understanding the nature of attacks and attackers, and why any computing resource or service is a target. We'll explain:

The method of attackers
Constantly shifting and adapting tactics to stay profitable and resilient.

The motivation of attackers
What you have to lose that criminals and dedicated attackers want.

After you understand how an attacker's modus operandi can cause your organization serious harm, whether financially, reputationally, or materially, you will be better prepared to develop methods to detect and prevent them. Beyond just understanding the technical details of an attack, you have to factor in situational awareness and nontechnical threats to your organization. Developing detection that's precise, comprehensive, and up-to-date will refine your monitoring and deliver better results.

"The Criminal Is the Creative Artist; the Detective Only the Critic"

Remember the "I Love You" worm from 2000? Hundreds of thousands of email messages went out around the globe with an attachment named *LOVE-LETTER-FOR-YOU.txt.*, most purporting to be from contacts in your address book. Who could turn down a love letter addressed directly to you from someone you know? Naturally, this was a hugely successful worm campaign, installed through a Visual Basic script (VBS) the victim executed when trying to read their "love letter." The attack was so successful that many organizations simply (temporarily) shut down their email services to prevent further spread. In subsequent years, system administrators and software vendors have addressed some of the major problems that led to this particular worm's success. Specifically, distrusting VBS as an email attachment type and adding additional checks in email clients to ensure that these types of files are not opened without a warning or prompt. It seemed like the attackers had been foiled—until they switched to other file formats and other effective social engineering methods.

Attackers loved Windows XP due to the operating systems' susceptibility to buffer overflow attacks. They could easily overwrite sections of memory on a target's system and execute code often with default administrator-level access. These problems (among other issues) led to a chain of damaging worms. In quick succession, there were SQL Slammer, Blaster, Nachi, Gaobot, and Sasser worms—all based on Microsoft vulnerabilities. This chain of worms prompted Microsoft (with Windows XP service pack 2) to reduce permissions on listening network services and turn on a firewall by default. Additionally, Microsoft hardened the OS by restricting access to system directories by normal users. Eventually, with Windows 7, Microsoft added memory overwrite protections such as Data Execution Prevention (DEP) or Address Space Layout Randomization (ASLR) to newer versions of Windows. It seemed like the attackers had been foiled—until they switched to different methods for memory overwriting, like return-oriented programming (ROP), and continued to search for loopholes in the default security configuration to abuse as quickly as possible before they were patched.

After Microsoft had raised the bar so that almost every easy avenue of attack was eliminated, infiltrators turned to accessory plug-in software like Acrobat, Flash, and Java, which hadn't received the same level of security development scrutiny as Windows. Oracle's Java Runtime Environment (JRE) plug-in allows Java applications to launch from the browser and run on the local system. This plug-in seems almost ubiquitous, with millions of installations. Understanding the widespread installation base of Java, as well as recognizing a seemingly unending supply of vulnerabilities, attackers targeted Java with numerous exploits. Every time Oracle released a new version of JRE, attackers would release previously unpublished vulnerabilities. The Java vulnerability/exploit cycle proved highly profitable for many criminal enterprises, and Java attacks were a staple in all the well-respected criminal exploit kits. According to a Cisco Global Threat Report, in just one month in 2013, 95% of exploits encountered on the Web targeted Java. Oracle finally responded to the rash of Java vulnerabilities by adding in additional sandbox and other security protections, while many operating system and browser vendors decoupled or disabled the in-browser Java plug-in unless explicitly enabled by the client. Java-borne infections dropped dramatically across the globe. It seemed like the attackers had been foiled—until they switched their focus again to attacking other browser plug-ins like Adobe Flash, Adobe Reader, and Microsoft Silverlight.

Saboteurs intent upon disrupting their enemies or causing general chaos have taken to DDoS attacks to shut down their victims. Volumetric DDoS (VDDoS) attacks—where an attacker exhausts his victim's network resources—are now the norm. User Datagram Protocol (UDP) amplification attacks are an efficient and effective method of VDDoS. The amplification occurs when a relatively small request to a particular service from a spoofed source address generates a disproportionately large response. In terms of amplification factor, a misconfigured NTP server is the most efficient. In terms of popularity, due to its prevalence and availability, attackers often abuse the domain name service (DNS) for VDDoS attacks. An attacker will masquerade as their victim (by IP address spoofing), send a relatively small request for something like a zone transfer, and generate a very large DNS response from many openly recursive DNS servers, thus flooding their victims with a deluge of UDP DNS traffic. Similar to the global call-to-action for email administrators in the 1990s shutting down spamming open-mail relays, the widespread use and effect of reflective DDoS attacks has forced a global call to action for DNS administrators to identify and fix misconfigured Internet accessible DNS servers. Administrators, in turn, strengthened their configurations, disabled recursion, and filtered access to their services. The point is that attackers will keep changing their strategy—while you are reacting to the latest campaign, they are creating their next.

Hanging Tough

Refreshingly, network defense has taken a higher priority in many organizations, and as an industry, we are getting better at stopping attacks as they happen. We have deployed network monitoring—intrusion detection, NetFlow, DNS query logs—that can tell us the hostnames and IP addresses of attackers. We can block IPs and hostnames easily—BGP Blackhole, Response Policy Zone (RPZ), ACL, and SDN. Yet a well-equipped and informed attacker maintains a resilient infrastructure to keep their services online despite blocking attempts.

As you can see, network security and defense is a never-ending arms race, with attackers exploiting anything available, and defenders attempt to head them off. As defenses evolve, so must attacks if they are to stay relevant. Incredibly, there are still plenty of relatively ancient worms probing networks worldwide, but the vulnerabilities that made the Microsoft RPC service and others such easy targets are no longer a viable option for a serious attacker. Defenses and controls have adapted, and attackers are forced to try alternative options to succeed in compromising systems. Attackers must not only avoid detection, but also keep their services up and running.

To evade mitigation, attackers have been known to use a popular and effective method called "fast flux DNS." Fast flux involves associating a single hostname with a multitude of unique IP addresses. Each DNS record then uses a short time to live (TTL) to allow for frequent rotation of attacker IP addresses. The IP addresses are often compromised hosts configured by attackers to proxy command-and-control (C2) traffic to the actual malicious infrastructure to ensure further resiliency. All this self-preservation on the attacker's part could be for naught if you are able to block traffic by DNS names.

In Figure 3-2, you can see the single hostname on the left has resolved for 15 unique IP addresses belonging to a total of 13 unique autonomous systems (ASN). Typically, even popular hostnames fronted by content delivery systems never have more than a few IP addresses. It's very unusual—and suspicious—to recognize this pattern.

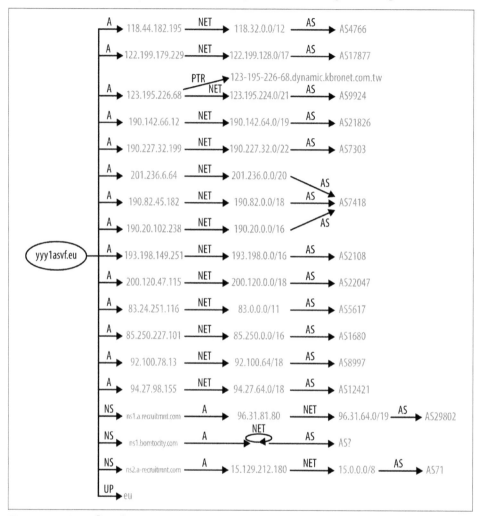

Figure 3-2. Fast flux diagram

As defenders got better at blocking the attackers, the attackers simply got better at staying online. Yet another method of DNS trickery involves domain generation algorithms (DGA), which create hundreds of thousands of unpredictable (to the victim) and incomprehensible hostname records:

d3d3aW4uY2lzY28uY29t.co.cc

r8jsf872hasklzY28sfa7.org

dfhdfihasascmfnd.com

rdfhnaiudyaspcm.ru

Attackers will register these domains, sometimes hours before they're to be used, and stand up their C2 infrastructure on only a subset of hosts. The next day, the domains are taken down, a new set generated, and the process repeated again. The victim would need to determine and block each of the generated domains every day to completely mitigate the malware C2 channel. This is a lofty goal considering malware like Conficker generated 50,000 domains each day! Because of the increased difficulty to defend against this attack method, an attacker can maintain a smaller but more agile infrastructure, changing C2 hosts daily to further avoid detection.

To remain resilient, attackers try to stay one step ahead of security researchers. If a researcher exposes all the details and components of a malware campaign, analysts and CSIRTs can directly apply any information about infection indicators into their monitoring systems. Therefore, creative malware authors make reverse engineering a slow process using various techniques in the malware itself. Malware authors often encrypt many parts of their code. Cryptographic keys also present challenges to researchers' attempts at reverse engineering. It's typical for malware to encrypt C2 communication, particularly the commands and instructions sent from the controller. Attackers don't want to expose their private keys, their application programming interface (API), or their commands and functions to researchers who can use them to thwart the malicious code, or publish details to those who can. Criminals also deploy encryption in other areas as well, like ransomware extortion where the attackers encrypt a victim's files with a strong public key, yet retain the private key in an attempt to extort a hefty sum.

In some cases, clever attackers have used online services (besides the venerable IRC) to run their C2 infrastructure. Several malware campaigns have attempted to use customized Twitter feeds to send instructions to their bots. Other attacks have leveraged email services like Gmail or Yahoo!, services that are not typically blocked by most organizations, to control compromised hosts. There are even cases of attackers encoding command strings in files hosted in commonly accessed public sites and code repositories such as *code.google.com*, blog XML feeds, or even cloud storage sites such as Dropbox. The bad guys try to hijack the popularity and good reputation of these services so that outright blocking is harder for defenders to do. You can't reasonably block all of Twitter just because one account happens to be a C2. Abusing well-known services and applications can help malware to hide in the deluge of legitimate traffic to those services.

Cash Rules Everything Around Me

There is no doubt the Internet is a noisy place. The noise is the result of automated processes (usually port or vulnerability scanning), systematically executing a set of predefined tasks. Just like with typical street crime, hosts and applications are "cased" to determine what valuables can be stolen or abused, and the best location to break in. In addition to providing a mechanism to download additional payloads, worms scan hosts for specific vulnerabilities to self-propagate to future victims. Spammers constantly scan TCP ports 25 and 587 for misconfigured or abandoned email servers that allow open mail relaying. Researchers, script kiddies, and pentesters probe networks and systems for weaknesses, looking for backdoors and vulnerabilities on any listening service. Minimal Internet searching or basic skills with a tool like NMAP and the NMAP Scripting Engine (NSE) can produce scripts to scan hosts for a myriad of vulnerabilities, including UDP amplification susceptibility, services with default credentials, or improperly configured web servers. DoS attacks have become brain-dead simple with tools like Low Orbit Ion Cannon (LOIC). The skill required to probe, compromise, and attack has reached a commoditized level. Widely focused threats should be considered the cost of accessing the Internet.

No matter what protections defenders put in place, attackers will shift to another vulnerable attack method. However, timing matters for the criminals, and the longer they maintain their infrastructure, the more likely they are to cash in when victims fall prey to their malware. Disrupting malware campaigns early limits the profit potential for the criminals, as it forces them to move to more unique approaches to avoid detection. Yet cybercrime does pay—criminals can make millions of dollars of laundered money and live lavish lifestyles in countries that turn a blind eye to prosecution or extradition. They often operate elaborate enterprises, complete with customer service, technical support, billing, and marketing departments to ensure they can compete with peers in their illicit industry. Like any successful enterprise, the criminal "business" has to adapt to the market conditions to stay profitable. While defenders have banded together to make it harder for these operations, the criminals simply shifted their emphasis to tricking the end user to run their software for them. Rather than waiting for virus-infected removable media to be passed around, attackers moved their malware to the network. Rather than spraying malware attachments in phishing email that will get dropped by corporate filters, attackers shifted to compromising Internet websites and advertising networks with malware downloaders.

The better the security protections, the more innovative and often brazen the attackers have to be. To avoid detection, rather than focus on developing complex malware, why not just steal code-signing certificates from trusted vendors and let your malicious code execute normally without inspection? Instead of cracking SSH password hashes, why not just steal the SSH private keys? Instead of malware downloading files to a system where an antivirus or host intrusion prevention system (HIPS) can inspect them, why not run it all within memory, controlled only by a registry key? If phishing attachments are getting deleted or scrubbed by mail gateways, why not send a link instead?

If attackers want to entice their victims to click a link, they simply need to make it relevant to their interests. Topics like current events, catastrophic storms, political or military conflict, celebrity gossip, easy money, ego stroking, and sex have been used in the past, and will always lure victims into clicking links.

 In general, humans are ridiculously easy to trick and manipulate. Regardless of the breadth of your technological controls, end users are often the weakest link in your security posture. This is why magic, pickpockets, and lotteries work—people are willing to believe what they want to believe, are susceptible to the power of suggestion, and are not always capable of measuring risk against their hopes and preconceptions. Combine the ease of manipulation with a highly diverse and vulnerable client software ecosystem (operating systems, client applications, web browsers, and browser plug-ins), and the casual attacker's job becomes easy.

Greed.isGood();

There are many different kinds of digital criminals. Spammers, bot masters, identity thieves, money mules, account harvesters, carders, and other miscreants constantly move data and money around the world in an effort to plunder the millions of vulnerable computers on the planet for their own purposes. Although motives and methods vary, each seeks to profit from your inadequate security (whether opportunistic or targeted), and each requires an infrastructure to ply their trade. To build a capable and scalable infrastructure, a digital criminal needs assets—*your* assets.

Independent journalist Brian Krebs has written extensively on the subject of cybercrime, criminals, and their targets. One of his most compelling pieces, "The Scrap Value of a Hacked PC," is a solid rebuttal to the often-heard statements "I don't have anything valuable on my computer, so I'm not worried about attacks" or "I have nothing to lose or hide." Most people don't realize just how profitable a compromised host can be to an attacker.

There are dozens of ways to monetize or otherwise abuse a hacked computer:

- Co-opting a PC with bot software to attack other organizations or make illicit purchases from your accounts/system.
- Turning your computer into a file/web server for hosting illicit or illegal content that will get traced back to you.

- Turning your computer into a proxy server that other attacks can bounce their attacks through.
- Stealing your credit card information and subsequently maxing the credit limit on stolen purchases.
- Running a Tor exit node on your computer, which can be used to implicate you in crimes such as child pornography.
- Stealing your email credentials, harvesting your address book, and spamming them with phishing attacks or other email-based fraud and scams.
- Using a PC to take part in a DDoS attack.
- Stealing resources to generate cryptocurrency, solve login CAPTCHAs, and take ad revenue through click fraud.
- Stealing other account credentials (e.g., Skype, Twitter, Gmail, Netflix, etc.) that can be sold online.
- Stealing account credentials to siphon money or gift cards from other accounts like iTunes, Amazon, or mobile services.
- Stealing bank account or other financial login information, and then subsequently transferring money.
- Identify theft with your information that can be used to open new credit accounts or apply for personal loans.
- Stealing product keys or serial numbers from software you have purchased.
- Extortion/coercion/blackmail using any data from your computer:
  — Webcam photos
  — Surreptitiously captured audio from your microphone
  — Saved photos
  — Email
  — Financial records
  — Legal records

Incredibly, this is just a sampling of the many ways your computer can be abused by attackers. There are, of course, other ways to profit from an attack, like stealing valuable information, trade, or military secrets. As attackers become more creative, the ways in which a computer can be used for nefarious (and profitable) purposes will continue to grow.

The resources and location of the compromised host also affect the potential value a specific attacker can extract. A personal PC on a residential network may not be as valuable to a "booter" (somebody who offers DoS attacks as a service) as a host with a fast network connection hosted on a large corporate or research network. However, from handling hundreds of incidents, it's quite interesting to see that many criminals have no idea of the value of the host they have just compromised.

 When you consider the attacker's narrow motivations, it's easier to understand how they might not realize what they could have had.

For example, we have witnessed servers hosting sensitive and valuable information compromised with routine click fraud malware simply to generate revenue for an attacker's advertising affiliate network. In most of these cases, the attackers set up a drive-by download attack whereby someone on the victim host (against policy) browses the Web and is inadvertently compromised. Perhaps not surprisingly, bot controllers have so many victims to manage, they don't realize the value of their victims. In one case, click fraud software was found on a lab domain controller. If the attacker had realized this, they could have stolen login credentials for everyone in the domain, including the administrators. While the value of the domain controller is extremely high, the attacker was exclusively motivated to generate click fraud revenue, and missed a potential opportunity for further pwnage.

Another example incident involved a different open FTP server connected directly to the Internet. In this case, after the server credentials were compromised, attackers abused the site by uploading gigabytes of high-resolution images of state, national, military, and international identification templates like passports, driver's licenses, military IDs, and other valuable documents. Anyone with these template files could simply add a photograph and adjust the content to match whatever personal information they liked. The attackers took advantage of a vulnerable server, its storage space, its fast Internet connection, and the organization's trusted IP address space.

I Don't Want Your Wallet, I Want Your Phone

You can put a password or PIN on your smartphone, but not everyone does that. It's faster to access data and applications on your phone when it's not locked, but it also leaves your data (including intimate, private details of your life) wide open to thieves. Before smartphones were pervasive and Internet use for mundane activities was commonplace, criminals had less convenient methods for stealing personal information. Dumpster diving for financial statements, fraudulent telemarketing, stealing documents from homes, offices, and mailboxes, and other low-tech methods proved to be successful, yet not trivial to accomplish. Identity theft is a huge problem for both industry and the consumer. Lives can easily be ruined, personal finances plummeted into bankruptcy, and reputations destroyed by losing private data to the wrong people. Today, a criminal needs only a reasonably effective phishing scheme or a stolen password to grab as many personal details as possible. More sophisticated criminals leverage mag stripe readers to siphon off credit and some debit card details that can be reused later. The laziest criminals can simply buy identities from carders on the black market who have already done the "hard" work of stealing, validating, and laundering the stolen info.

Beyond identity theft or impersonation, criminals can use stolen personal information for extortive purposes. One possibility would be a criminal threatening to release private conversations, documents, or images from your computer system(s) to the public or press unless they are paid a ransom. Malware sprayed to any vulnerable system might steal data or computing resources for profit. Numerous malware families have been known to use victim CPU cycles to generate bitcoins or send additional fraudulent emails.

Ultimate motivators for compromise range from crimeware, to financial attacks, to state-sponsored military or political attacks, to "hacktivist" campaigns that seek to disrupt the business of their ideological enemies. Even political sympathizers are motivated to participate in attacks against foreign governments and industries. State-sponsored groups are well funded, well trained, highly organized, and are compelled by a chain of command hierarchy. Criminal enterprises may also be well funded and trained, yet operate more like for-profit businesses. The execution of the attacks used by all groups stems from the same basic techniques, but crimeware groups often have little regard for the content of their victim's data, unlike a state-sponsored group. Crimeware groups opportunistically use extortion, fraud, and other methods to extract profit from their victims, whereas intelligence-focused, state-sponsored groups fall into the information harvesting or system disruption categories.

Some of these threat actors will be more relevant than others to your specific industry. If you work in the financial sector, you should know all about the various banking Trojans, but you won't necessarily be concerned with patient medical record privacy. If you work in facilities and power grid services, you may not care about click fraud and adware, but you are most certainly a desirable target for terrorists or state-sponsored groups looking to create havoc in their enemy's homeland. In any scenario, if you have computers connected to the Internet, or open to accepting removable media, an attacker can and will abuse them for their own purposes, bringing unwanted attention and potential devastation to your network and organization.

There's No Place Like 127.0.0.1

Risks arising from misconfiguration, operational errors, accidental data disclosures, or basic mistakes can be just as damaging and much more embarrassing than threats from the evildoers. Take, for example, an incident where a simple database patch, applied during a maintenance period, caused major problems with a billing system. This routine operation resulted in customers erroneously receiving confidential billing invoices intended for other customers. Naturally, this created massive confusion and frustration for everyone involved, not in the least because the invoices contained confidential internal data intended only for the actual customers. As a result, many days were spent performing customer notifications. However, the most significant impact to this incident was the financial reimbursement required for all affected customers. The company ended up losing money, not due to any external threat, but due to its failure to test all its processes after applying a software upgrade.

Even though this incident was not the result of external forces or threats, there was still a motivation at play here that, once understood and addressed, could prevent similar incidents in the future. In this case, and in most cases of misconfiguration or IT problems, the motivation is expediency. IT teams need to patch applications, bring up new services, and decommission old hosts all under tight timelines. Shortcuts such as not fully testing new deployments or applications can lead to problems like the billing mistakes previously mentioned that might be impossible to predict. Therefore, understanding the ramification of possible disclosure issues and having a plan ready for when it happens eases the burden for everyone involved and speeds up the response process.

Let's Play Global Thermonuclear War

Commoditized attacks differ from committed adversaries by the effort put forth to achieve their goals and the narrowly focused scope of their attack. Incentivized organizations like nation states, penetration testers, militaries, and groups or individuals with a keen interest will methodically reconnoiter your organization, identify and exploit your vulnerabilities, identify possible targets, and achieve a foothold to complete their objective. Detecting these adversaries is far more challenging than detecting malicious and typical Internet noise like port or vulnerability scanning. Committed adversaries have the funding, skills, and desire, and put forth effort to avoid detection.

In 2013, the Mandiant company released its "APT1 report" that detailed how Chinese military–sponsored groups of attackers were tasked with breaking into major U.S. and European companies to steal confidential information and maintain a presence on these networks. The APT1 group (comprised of a few teams with various skill levels) and others like "Comment Crew" operated under military command and launched numerous successful attacks. Notably, Google was compromised by a zero-day vulnerability in Internet Explorer opened by an internal victim. The ostensible purpose of the attack was to insert code into Google's Gmail services, which could help China keep track of purported dissidents and supposed threats to the Chinese government. Additionally, the attackers targeted Google's internal software configuration management (SCM) applications. In other words, the attackers wanted to compromise or bug Google's source code repositories with their own code.

The Google attack, also known as "Operation Aurora," was a high-profile incident. But there have been countless other state-sponsored attacks that rarely make the media, yet continue to present a threat. In many cases, attackers identify their targets by trolling the Web for contact information they can exploit for phishing schemes. Attackers have been known to search through LinkedIn with fake or stolen profiles looking for email addresses or other contact details, as well as attacking victims by stealing their personal, nonwork accounts. Even conference publications where a victim may have presented or even attended can be scraped for contact information and subsequently abused.

In the Aurora example, the attackers were motivated to spy on what they perceived as possible threats to their national security. Another high-profile case of state-sponsored attacks occurred several years ago at Iranian nuclear enrichment laboratories. The so-called "Stuxnet" malware ran rampant as a worm targeting Windows and mechanical control systems through Iranian facilities, causing severe hardware malfunctions resulting in a complete shutdown. Although the origins are still not completely clear, the United States and Israel have both been implicated as possible creators of the Stuxnet worm. The presumed motivation behind the successful attacks was to disrupt Iran's nuclear-refinement capabilities.

Another state-sponsored malware attack, likely also perpetrated by the Comment Crew under Chinese military orders, occurred between 2011 and 2012 in Israel. The Israeli Iron Dome missile defense system had been compromised by the attackers, and thousands of documents were exfiltrated out of Israeli networks. As with many of the most successful attacks, it all began with crafted phishing emails to get a foot in the door. Once inside, Comment Crew installed their own toolkits (ensuring a persistent presence), searched for the documents and research they were after, and exported everything out of the network.

Defense Against the Dark Arts

Criminals usually have a singular motive: profit. But state-sponsored attackers are following orders from their superiors and have radically different motives, typically of the political, military, or intelligence persuasion. During the Russia–Ukraine conflict in early 2013, both sides accused each other of participating in DDoS attacks against each other. As early as 2007, a large part of Estonia's Internet presence was under DDoS attack stemming from a different regional conflict. As more critical infrastructure and sensitive networks come online, information warfare attacks will only intensify and become another tool for any capable military power. Crimeware is a major problem, and every organization needs to consider their risk posture against these types of attacks. However, depending on the industry, organizations also need to consider that they may be targets for highly sophisticated attackers targeting their sensitive information, infrastructure, or relationships with other organizations.

Whether threats come from internal problems, crimeware, or highly motivated attackers, it's clear that you need to understand the reasons and motivations behind attacks to successfully defend against them. You don't want to spend all your resources on a fancy castle gate when your enemy can just walk through the back door. You also don't want to ignore basic system administration best practices to save on time or money when the outcome can be disastrous. Threat actors already know what they want when they launch attacks against your organization, and understanding this provides reasonable detail on where to invest in protections. Even though there have been diversionary incidents where attackers launch DDoS or other noisy attacks against an organization as a cover for more targeted and precise attacks, it's important to never lose focus on what's most valuable. Knowing what attacks are possible, along with knowing what you have to protect (and what you have to lose), builds a foundation for your incident response programs.

Without knowing how attacks work, and why they are happening, it's difficult to develop effective and efficient ways to detect them. Understanding attack types and methods enables you to develop your own methods of incident discovery that can be tracked in your playbook. The core idea of the playbook is to catalog and regularly repeat processes to discover incidents. If you stay cognizant of attackers' methods and motivations, your overall insight on good security improves and delivers the background details necessary to solve problems.

Chapter Summary

- To protect your organization, you must understand the threats it faces.
- If you don't think you have something to lose, you haven't thought about it enough.
- Crime evolves with culture and society. Online crime will increase as more things of value are digitally stored and globally accessible.
- Malicious activity can come from a number of sources, but the most common source is organized crime, followed by targeted attackers and trusted insiders.
- Different organizations face different threats; focus your efforts on protecting the high-value assets and make sure you monitor them closely.

CHAPTER 4

A Data-Centric Approach to Security Monitoring

"Quickest way to find the needle... burn the haystack."
—Kareem Said

Effective security alarms are only useful when introduced with efficient, precise, and where possible, automated data analysis. This chapter describes fundamental building blocks to develop and implement a tailored security monitoring and response methodology. To that end, we'll discuss:

- How to prepare and store your data
- How to give your operation authority and clarity with a solid logging policy
- What metadata is and why you should care about it
- How to develop and structure incident detection logic into your own playbook

Properly developing incident response methods and practices requires a solid plan and a foundational framework for every security incident response team. Finding security incidents and helpful clues to other nefarious behavior can be difficult. With no plans or framework in place, an incident response team can be immediately lost in a sea of data, or left with a dead end having no data (or no useful data) to analyze.

You could buy a bunch of expensive gear, point it all to a log management or a security incident and event management (SIEM) system, and let it automatically tell you what it knows. Some incident response teams may start this way, but unfortunately, many never evolve. Working only with what the SIEM tells you, versus what you have configured it to tell you based on your contextual data, will invariably fail. Truly demonstrating value from security monitoring and incident response requires a major effort. As with all projects, planning is the most important phase. Designing an approach that works best for you requires significant effort up front, but offers a great payout later in the form of meaningful incident response and overall improved security.

Learning from our early experience as a set-it-and-forget-it team, we distilled the basics for getting started with an effective data-centric incident response plan. Most importantly, you must consider the data: normalizing, field carving and extraction, metadata, context enrichment, data organization, all to set yourself up to create effective queries and reports within a sustainable incident detection architecture.

Get a Handle on Your Data

Data preparation requires as much forethought and execution as any other step in the data collection process. Failure to do so can have unanticipated and investigation-ending results. Those of us doing security work often fail to appreciate the importance of enforcing consistency during the preparation and organization of data sources. Simply aggregating logs into a single system may satisfy the letter of the law when it comes to regulatory compliance. And why not? Regulatory compliance may require central collection of data, but says nothing about preparing that data so that it can be effectively used for responsive monitoring or forensics. Data preparation, commonly an afterthought, satisfies the spirit of the law, and is a required process that supports any successful security monitoring infrastructure.

As you prepare your log data for analysis, think of the classic database model of extract, transform, and load (ETL). The concepts are largely the same for log preparation and analysis, but can be more or less structured depending on the type of data you intend to consume.

In 1999, the National Aeronautics and Space Administration's (NASA) Jet Propulsion Lab learned all too well the importance of consistency across data sources. NASA contracted Lockheed Martin to write an application to control thrusters in NASA's Mars Climate Orbiter. Lockheed's application returned thruster force calculated in imperial pounds. When NASA's navigation program consumed this data, it assumed the thruster force was specified in metric newtons. Because of the discrepancy between actual and perceived calculations, the Orbiter's navigation system was unable to correctly position itself for entry into Mars' orbit. NASA lost over $100 million when the craft disappeared in space. The costly accident resulted from failing to properly normalize data by converting measurement units before processing the data.

Data mining log events for incident response requires a similar type of preparation before analysis that NASA and Lockheed failed to perform. Rather than converting from imperial pounds to metric newtons, a security log repository may need to convert timestamps from one time zone to another, correlate hosts with IPs to NetBIOS names, index the true source IP address behind a web proxy, or rename a security device–supplied field to an organization's standardized field (for example, changing "dst IP" to "dest_IP"). Without ensuring proper data organization by including a standard (and consistent) nomenclature for event fields, you cannot compare or accurately link events between those disparate data sources.

When integrating a new data source, prepare for the possibility that the events may not only contain an entirely different type of data, but be formatted differently than any other data source you already have. To ease management and analysis of the data later on, you need to create an authoritative collection standard to organize event data. The standard should be applied to imported data as soon as possible. Mature organizations will apply the standard to originated data as well, influencing and enhancing data value across the organization.

Depending on the collection and search infrastructure, you may even be required to parse fields during data indexing time, as it's not possible at search time. Though events from different log sources may have unique structures, they often contain similar data, such as source IP address and destination IP address. All logs at a minimum should contain a timestamp. Identifying these common fields, parsing, and labeling the fields consistently for each data source is the foundation for correlating the disparate data during search time.

A great example of this concept is the Dublin Core (DC). Essentially the DC is a system of standard generic descriptors (metadata) that libraries can use for their archives (see Figure 4-1). Library systems that adhere to the DC can easily exchange information compatible with other library archiving systems.

Using a similar concept, security teams should ensure their digestible and queryable log data is also standardized with common field names for interoperability among queries and reports, as well as the various security monitoring technologies in place.

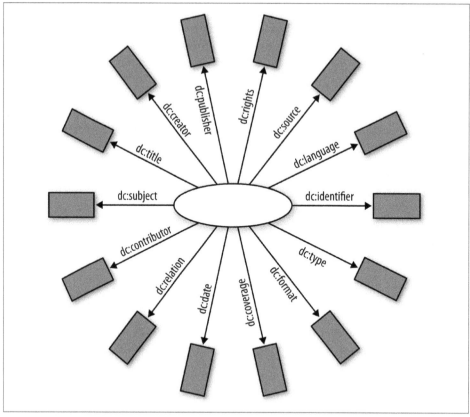

Figure 4-1. Dublin Core "hedgehog" graph (source: http://dublincore.org/documents/dcq-rdf-xml/images/hedgehog.gif)

Logging Requirements

Before taking on a log management project, it's important to understand and develop the proper deployment planning steps. Things like scope, business requirements, event volume, access considerations, retention strategy, diverse export platforms, and engineering specifications are all factors in determining long-term success. You must be able to answer the following:

- Will the detection be exclusively from network security devices, or will you gather host log/application data as well?

- Can you partner with other teams to share appropriate access to log data for troubleshooting, performance, and security purposes?

- By what process do you install an agent-based tool on a critical service, like a production email server, directory server, finance, or SCADA system? Is the risk of stability and availability worth the net gain in log data?

- What network changes (ACLs, additional routes, account permissions, etc.) are affected by a log collector or exporter, or what impact will traffic rate limiting have on log streaming and storage over the network if log data surges in volume?
- How much storage will you need and how many resources are required to maintain it?
- Beyond all the IT resourcing, how many analysts are required to actually review the alert data?
- Is there a comprehensive and enforceable logging policy? Have sysadmins enabled sufficient logging?
- What is the expected event volume and server load?
- What are the event/incident long-term retention requirements? How and when will data be purged from the system?
- How do you ensure no loss in availability of your data feeds, either because of problems with your own toolset or service delivery issues with your dependencies?

We expect that we'll get the proper logs with readable data from any host or service hosted by IT. Within your organization's IT infrastructure, a solid and unified (think: Windows, Network, Unix, mobile, etc.) logging standard is a must. Following the strict corporate security logging standard our team developed, we enforce the following additional aspects of log collection and management through a similar policy:

- Systems must log system events to satisfy requirements for user attribution, auditing, incident response, operational support, event monitoring, and regulatory compliance. Or more simply, who did what, from where, when, and for how long.
- Systems must forward logs in real time to an InfoSec-approved centralized log management system to satisfy log retention, integrity, accessibility, and availability requirements. When real-time transfer of log data is infeasible, it is acceptable for logs to be transferred from the source device to the log management system using an alternative method such as a scripted pull or push of log data. In such cases, your logging policy should state the frequency of the data sync. Ideally, no more than 15 minutes should elapse between the time the log is generated and the time it is received by the log management system.

 Organizational policies should specify a maximum delay between the time a log is created and when it is available in the log management system.

While this may be unattainable by some data owners or systems, the key is to have a stated policy from which exceptions can be granted if necessary.

- Systems that generate logs must be synchronized to a central time sourcing device (NTP) and configured for Coordinated Universal Time (UTC) (with offsets) and an ISO 8601 data expression format.

- Systems that generate logs must format and store logs in a manner that ensures the integrity of the logs and supports enterprise-level event correlation, analysis, and reporting.

- Systems must record and retain audit-logging information sufficient to answer the following:
  — What activity was performed?
  — Who or what performed the activity, including where or on what system?
  — When was the activity performed?
  — What tool(s) were used to perform the activity?
  — What was the status (e.g., success or failure), outcome, or result of the activity?

- System logs must be created whenever any of the following events are requested or performed:
  — Create, read, update, or delete documents classified with "highly confidential" or "restricted information" privileges.
  — Initiate or accept a network connection.
  — Grant, modify, or revoke access rights, including adding a new user or group, changing user privilege levels, changing file permissions, changing database object permissions, changing firewall rules, and user password changes.
  — Change system, network, application or service configuration, including installation of software patches and updates or other installed software changes.
  — Start up, shut down, or restart of an application or process.
  — Abort, failure, or abnormal end of an application or process.
  — Detection of suspicious or malicious activity, such as from an intrusion detection system, antivirus system, or antispyware system.

Just the Facts

Before you can prepare your data for analysis, you need data worth preparing. In the context of security monitoring, that means the data you collect needs to provide some investigative value, or can help identify malicious or anomalous behavior. The sheer number of potentially generated events, combined with the number of possible event sources, can leave you overwhelmed. Keeping all logs everywhere is the easiest strategy, but has some significant drawbacks. Too often, teams hoard logs because they think the logs might be useful by somebody someday. The paradox between logging and incident response is that you never know what log file(s) will be useful throughout the course of an investigation that could cover almost any aspect of a computer or network system.

Logs that have no security content or context waste storage space and index processing, and affect search times. An example of such a log might be a debug from a compiler or even from a network troubleshooting session that is archived into syslog. These superfluous events can make analysis daunting or be distracting to sort through when you're trying to find the gold. After you understand what type of events you need for security monitoring and incident response, you can proactively ensure that logs exist that contain the events you're after. How then, in this superfluity of messages, do you identify what events are of value?

A common mistake (one that we admittedly made) is to simply throw all alarms from all devices into the log solution, only to find that discovering incidents over the long term is difficult. Most likely, you would notice results immediately from the noisiest alarms for the most common, typical malware. However, after those issues have been tamped out, it can be difficult to find value in the rest of the alarms. If you have not tuned anything, there will be hundreds or thousands of alarms that may mean nothing, or are simply informational. Do you really care that a ping sweep occurred from one of your uptime monitors? Did a long-running flow alarm trip on a large database replication? You'll also need to consider the following:

- Sanctioned vulnerability scanners
- Normal backup traffic and replication
- System reboots or service changes during a typical change window
- Safe executables sent via email
- Legitimate SQL in a URL (that gives the impression of SQL injection)
- Encrypted traffic
- Health monitoring systems like Nagios

These are just a few of the many ways unnecessary alarms can clog up the analysts' incident detection capacity. It is true that some informational alarms can be useful, particularly if they are reviewed over a time range for trends and outliers. One example would be tracking downloads from an internal source code repository. If the standard deviation for the downloads rises dramatically, there could be unauthorized spidering or a potential data loss incident. A cluttered interface of alarm data is not only daunting to the analyst, but also a setup for failure as potentially valuable alarms may be lost or unnoticed in the sea of unimportant alarms, like in Figure 4-2.

Figure 4-2. Huge volume of web proxy events; over 1 million events in 24 hours with no reputation score (x_wbrs_score)

Some non-security–centric data sources generate only a portion of total log events that contain useful InfoSec content, such as a boot log or display/driver messages (dmesg). Knowing that a new and unexpected service is starting, or that a local USB rootkit driver is loading, is of security value, but knowing that a filesystem consistency check happened is likely less valuable. Other log events like common application errors, verbose troubleshooting logs, or service health checks may be useful to the system administrators, but provide little value to a security analyst looking at the broader landscape. Splitting off the useful security event log data from routine operational log data provides the most efficient option. Take, for instance, Cisco ASA Virtual Private Network (VPN) syslog data. The ASA produces approximately 2,000 different syslog messages. Buried in all that logging are three syslog messages that provide attribution information (713228, 722051, and 113019).

 To cut through useless log data, try to focus on how you will apply the data in investigations. Determining who did what, when, and where requires logs that can provide attribution, attack details, unusual system issues, or confirmations of activity.

If you're only trying to attribute remote VPN connections to IP addresses and users, failing to filter the almost 2,000 other message types will put undue overhead on your infrastructure and clutter your log analysis.

Useful security event log data can be found in non-security centric data sources by identifying activities such as the following:

- Access, authenticate to, or modify confidential info
- Initiate or accept a network connection
- Manipulate access rights

- System or network configuration changes
- Process state changes (start, terminated, HUP, failure, etc.)
- New services

Each of the events generated in the preceding list should contain the following information:

- Type of action performed
- Subsystem performing the action
- Identifiers for the object requesting the action
- Identifiers for the object providing the action
- Date and time
- Status, outcome, or result of the action

For established security event data sources, there's often less concern with identifying the activities just listed, and more concern with preparing the data. After all, an IDS or antivirus system's primary job is to provide you with information about the state of security for something, be it a network, operating system, or application. Despite the specificity of these types of events, additional filtering may still be required due to overwhelming volume, lack of relevancy to your environment, or for tuning to ensure accuracy. For instance, we know from experience that in most cases, TCP normalization IDS signatures fire loads of alarms because of network congestion and other expected behavior that the signature developers believe could be evidence of a potential attack or misuse.

Collecting only relevant data can have a direct impact on reducing costs as well.

In planning a log collection infrastructure, you might offset additional costs by having other teams share access to the log data, not for security monitoring, but for development, system administration, accounting, or troubleshooting issues.

The effect extends to more than a requirement for large hard drives and backup systems. Indexing licenses, system computer cycles, and analysis cycles to parse growing data sets are all affected by the amount of data you store. An organization's security and log management policies, preferably backed by the organization's legal counsel, will dictate mandatory data retention time. Resource-strapped organizations must think critically about precisely what to collect, where to store it, and for how long. Filtering unnecessary data can keep licensing costs down, save on computer cycles, and require less logical storage space. Working with system and application administrators on what they would consider suspicious, and working to understand the unique qualities of their log data saves time and effort in determining what data to keep or reject. Spending time and resources to make intelligent decisions regarding the data you need once at collection time will save time and resources every time the logs are searched. Only after you've identified the data to collect can you start to prepare the data for your collection and analysis systems.

Normalization

Once the logs have been filtered, you can begin to organize and compartmentalize the remaining security event data. Taking a tip from the NASA measurement SNAFU, it should be quite clear how important this next step becomes. Data normalization for the purposes of log mining is the process by which a portion, or field, of a log event is transformed into its canonical form. The organization consuming the data must develop and consistently use a standard format for log normalization. Sometimes, the same type of data can be represented in multiple formats. As a common example, consider timestamps. The C function `strftime()` (*http://en.cppreference.com/w/c/chrono/strftime*) and its approximately 40 format specifiers give an indication of the potential number of ways a date and time can be represented. ISO 8601 (*http://www.iso.org/iso/catalogue_detail?csnumber=40874*) attempts to set an internationally recognized standard timestamp format, though the standard is all too often ignored. That, combined with the fact that most programming libraries (*http://search.cpan.org/~drolsky/DateTime-Format-Strptime-1.54/lib/DateTime/Format/Strptime.pm*) have adopted `strftime()`'s conversion specifications (*http://docs.python.org/2/library/datetime.html#strftime-strptime-behavior*), means that application developers are free to define timestamps as they see fit. Having a diverse group of incoming timestamps from various logging systems can be troublesome when trying to match up dates and times in an investigative query. Consuming data that includes timestamps requires recognizing the different formats and normalizing them to the official, standard format.

Besides timestamps, other data elements requiring normalization are MAC addresses, phone numbers, user IDs, IP addresses, subnet masks, DNS names, and so on. IPv6 addresses in particular can be represented in multiple ways. As a rule, leading zeros can be omitted, consecutive zeros can be compressed and replaced by two colons, and hexadecimal digits can be either upper- or lowercase (though RFC 5952 (*http://tools.ietf.org/html/rfc5952*) recommends the exclusive use of lowercase). As an example, consider the following IPv6 address variations:

- 2001:420:1101:1::a
- 2001:420:1101:1::A
- 2001:420:1101:1:0:0:0:a
- 2001:0420:1101:0001:0000:0000:0000:000a

- 2607:f8b0:0000:0000:000d:0000:0000:005d
- 2607:f8b0::d:0:0:5d
- 2607:f8b0:0:0:d::5d
- ::ffff:132.239.1.114
- ::132.239.1.114
- 2002:84ef:172::

If web proxy logs identify requests from a host via a compressed AAAA record (no zeros), and DHCP logs attribute a host to AAAA address leases containing the zeros, for successful correlation, one of the AAAA records must be converted at some stage to link the results from both data sources. It's important to define the types of data requiring normalization *before* the logs are imported and indexed, rather than at analysis time to improve operational efficiency. Think of the regular expressions you might apply during some future search. For a regex to work properly on all the logs, the data needs to have regularity.

Playing Fields

Now that the log data is cleaned up after normalization and filtering, you can begin to consider how best to search it. Finding security events will be much easier if the logs are intuitive and human readable. The best way to carve up the logs is by creating fields. Fields are elements in a log file that represent a unique type of data. Every log file can have fields, and in fact some log files already have embedded fields like this DHCP log:

```
time="2014-01-09 16:25:01 UTC" hn="USER-PC" mac="60:67:40:dc:71:38"
    ip="10.1.56.107" exp="2014-01-09 18:54:52 UTC"
time="2014-01-09 16:25:01 UTC" hn="USER-PC" mac="60:67:40:dc:71:38"
    gw="10.1.56.1" action="DHCPREQUEST"
```

The DHCP server generated this log with descriptive, readable fields (time, hn, mac, ip, exp) nicely laid out in key-value pairs with spaces as field delimiters.

Consistent use of standard field names makes interacting with log data much easier. You might standardize on a field name of source_host for events from the monitoring infrastructure that include an originating, or source IP address. Authentication logs containing a username might label that particular attribute field user. Whatever the field is named, use the same label each time a newly acquired data source possesses the same field type. Most well-formed logs will have a timestamp. Networked event data sources will also include source or destination IP addresses. Additional common field types across the core security event data sources include:

- `timestamp` (date, or `_time`)
- `source IP` (host)
- `source port`
- `destination IP` (`s_ip`)
- `destination port`
- `hostname`
- `nbtname`
- `sourcetype`
- `eventsource`
- `alerttype`
- `event action`

This list represents our common minimum fields for any event source. These are the minimum mandatory fields we require before we decide whether to index an additional log source for searching. You want as much descriptive metadata as possible, without logging and subsequently indexing useless data or fields. Without an indication of who did what, when, and where, we can never attribute an event to any particular security incident. Not all fields in our list may be present from every event source, but when they are available, they provide the most basic information necessary to respond to an alert. `Alerttype` and `event action` broadly represent the type of security alarm and the details as described by an event source.

More information, at least in security event data, is often better than less. More fields can be extracted and leveraged with additional parsing to illustrate information unique to the event source itself. Beyond this basic metadata, some security event sources provide a wealth of information available as additional fields. For example, an IDS alarm may include more context about an alert than what is captured in either `alerttype` or `event action`. Take, for instance, an ASCII-decoded snippet of an IP packet payload. More fields allow for fine-tuned searching and provide more statistical sorting and comparison options when querying for incident data. A rule identifier is also common across data sources—such as an IDS signature—and should use the predefined label for that field.

Application documentation often contains information on the possible events and formats that an application might output to a log. This should be the primary reference for understanding what data a log source can provide. In the absence of such documentation, the CSIRT must coalesce the log data using context about the data source itself and type of messages being generated. For instance, attribution data sources like authentication servers are likely to associate an action with a host or user, while classic security event data sources like IDS contain some alert about an asset or observed action. If the CSIRT can't manage the log export options, or if it's not flexible enough to be tailored, post-filtering is the only option.

Fields in Practice

In our experiences dealing with mountains of log data, we've come to the conclusion that in any useful logs, there are always similar fields with different names that mean the same thing. We've also determined that you'll probably need to split out the fields exactly the way you want them, and it won't always be automatic. Knowing what fields help build queries and how to best extract the fields consistently across data sources goes a long way toward creating useful detection logic.

Comparable applications in different environments will likely produce similar log events with different formats. The following example is from one of our actual data sources. Our first event is raw data from a single host-based intrusion detection system (HIDS) log:

```
2015-09-21 14:40:02 -0700|mypc-WIN7|10.10.10.50|4437|The process
'C:\Users\mypc\Downloads\FontPack11000_XtdAlf_Lang.msi' (as user DOMAIN\mypc)
attempted to initiate a connection as a client on TCP port 80 to 199.7.54.72
using interface Virtual\Cisco Systems VPN Adapter for 64-bit Windows.
The operation was allowed by default (rule defaults).
```

Where to begin on how to split this singular log event into useful fields? An initial qualitative assessment of the message identifies | used as a field delimiter (with a very generous fifth field!). Other common delimiters include spaces, quotes, or tabs. Unfortunately, many events may lack a parseable delimiter entirely. Assuming the delimiter is unique to the message (i.e., it does not exist elsewhere within the event message), it can easily be parsed into fields with a Perl-like split() function.

There are a handful of other remarkable artifacts in the event. First and foremost is the highly recommended ISO 8601 standardized timestamp, with a date format of *year-month-day*, the use of a 24-hour clock specified to seconds, and an American Pacific Standard time zone defined as a numeric offset from UTC:

```
2015-09-21 14:40:02 -0700
```

Already there are questions to answer: How does this timestamp format align with other logs already in the log collection system? In this case, it appears to be using the desired ISO 8601 format, but how can you be sure what (or who) is generating this timestamp? Is this the client application, the collector's message received time, or something totally different?

Additionally, delimited fields include an IP address (10.10.10.50), a hostname (mypc-WIN7), a numeric rule identifier (4437), and a long event action field occupying the remainder of the event. As mentioned, source IP address and hostname should be fairly standard log attributes, so it's important to normalize these fields and match them up with other event sources. More queries around this one field and timestamp can yield much more information toward understanding an incident.

Lastly, the log message contains the event action. In this case, the log revealed that a Windows process successfully attempted to create a network connection over a VPN interface. At a minimum, this entire field can be labeled as Event Action. Bear in mind that the same log feed will likely contain various actions. There is so much information hidden in that single field that it's worth extracting additional fields to handle more flexible queries.

Consider what is necessary to properly extract fields from event data:

- Are the fields in a given log finite and enumerable?
- Do similar events generate a log message consistent with previous events of the same type? In the example, different operating systems or agent versions may generate similar but varying messages for the same action.
- Can the parser properly handle inconsistently formatted event actions?

Having consistency within event actions is crucial, because there may be additional attributes within the action itself worth parsing.

How does another log source compare to the HIDS data? The following is an event from a web proxy:

```
1381888686.410 - 10.10.10.50 63549 255.255.255.255 80 - -6.9
   http://servicemap.conduit-services.com/Toolbar/?ownerId=CT3311834
   - 0 309 0 "Mozilla/5.0 (compatible; MSIE 9.0; Windows NT 6.1;
   WOW64; Trident/5.0)" - 403 TCP_DENIED - "adware" "Domain reported
   and verified as serving malware. Identified malicious behavior on
   domain or URI." - - - - GET
```

In this example, we're missing the convenience of an obviously unique delimiter. Fields are delimited with spaces, but spaces also exist within field values themselves. In the preceding example, when there is a space in the field value, the entire field value is enclosed in double quotes as a means of escaping the spaces. Abstracted, the question becomes, how do you parse a field where the field delimiter is legitimately used in the field itself? A simple split() will no longer work to break the event into fields. This log event requires a parser with logic that knows not to split when the delimiter is escaped or quoted.

Beyond the difference between delimiters, the timestamp is in a different format from the HIDS data. In this instance, the web proxy uses Unix epoch time format. If, at a minimum, we have only the HIDS data and this web proxy data, at least one of the time values must be normalized so that the data can be easily understood and correlated during analysis. Log timestamp inconsistencies are rampant. CSIRTs should prepare to convert and format data in line with the organization's internal standard time format for each new type and instance of data source.

Similar to the HIDS data, the web proxy identifies with a client IP Address 10.10.10.50. The same standardized field name as used for source IP address should be used in the proxy logs. Because this is a web proxy log, we can expect basic HTTP information, all of which should be parsed into uniquely representative fields:

- URL
- Browser user-agent
- HTTP server response
- HTTP method
- Referer [sic]

As a final data source, let's compare DHCP logs to the HIDS and web proxy events. This example shows multiple events:

```
10/08/2013 20:10:29 hn="mypc-WS" mac="e4:cd:8f:05:2b:ac" gw="10.10.10.1"
    action="DHCPREQUEST"
10/08/2013 20:10:29 hn="mypc-WS" mac="e4:cd:8f:05:2b:ac" ip="10.10.10.50"
    exp="10/09/2013 22:11:34 UTC"
10/08/2013 22:11:34 hn="mypc-WS" mac="e4:cd:8f:05:2b:ac" gw="10.10.10.1"
    action="DHCPREQUEST"
10/08/2013 22:11:34 hn="mypc-WS" mac="e4:cd:8f:05:2b:ac" ip="10.10.10.50"
    exp="10/09/2013 02:11:33 UTC"
10/09/2013 02:11:37 hn="mypc-WS" mac="e4:cd:8f:05:2b:ac" ip="10.10.10.50"
    exp="10/09/2013 02:11:33 UTC"
10/09/2013 02:11:38 hn="mypc-WS" mac="e4:cd:8f:05:2b:ac" ip="10.10.10.50"
    action="EXPIRED"
```

Initial analysis again reveals fields delimited with spaces and clearly identifies fields in key-value pairs, with keys:

- hn (hostname)
- mac (MAC address)
- ip (source IP Address)
- gw (gateway)
- action (DHCP server action)
- exp (DHCP lease expiration timestamp)

Notice that each value in the tuple is also double quoted. This is important, because the data source may identify additional key fields. Even if documentation identifying each field is lacking, an analysis should manually enumerate each field with a large enough sample set of log data.

Proper analysis requires a very strict parser that only matches what's already been identified. With this parsing, do any messages fail to match? Is the parser overly greedy or too specific? An iterative approach to parsing allows for finding rare exceptions. For example, if the mac field looks to be lowercase a–f, 0–9, and colons (:), then start by writing a regular expression that will *only* match those characters. Run the parser and identify any missed events that should have been caught, perhaps from events containing MAC addresses with uppercase A–F. The same process applies to any fields that require parsing.

Similar to the VPN and web proxy logs, the DHCP data is using yet another time-stamp format. It's using the *month/day/year* format and a 24-hour clock. But what about time zone? Did the DHCP administrators neglect to configure an export of time zone information in the log message, or does the DHCP server not even support exporting the time zone? Either way, determination and normalization of the event time zone is a responsibility of the custodian—as opposed to the log analyst—and must be performed prior to writing the event data to the collector. Incorrect or disputed timestamps can quickly jeopardize an investigation.

Whereas earlier we looked at individual HIDS and web proxy log messages, a number of DHCP log messages are presented in this example. While each event has meaning and value individually, the combined events show a single DHCP session over the course of approximately six hours for a single host. We label multiple log entries that all describe different phases of a single event as a transaction. Continuing to use DHCP as an example, the different common phases of a DHCP session include:

- DISCOVER
- OFFER
- REQUEST
- ACKNOWLEDGEMENT
- RENEW
- RELEASE

The first four phases—DISCOVER, OFFER, REQUEST, ACK—are all individual events (log messages) that comprise a DHCP lease. Identifying a successful DHCP lease transaction provides attribution for hosts in the DHCP pool. Therefore, grouping the phases of a DHCP lease together and being able to search on the completed transaction itself rather than individual messages eases an analyst's ability to confirm an IP was assigned to an asset at a given time:

```
10/08/2013 20:10:29 hn="mypc-WS" mac="e4:cd:8f:05:2b:ac" gw="10.10.10.1"
     action="DHCPREQUEST"
```

```
10/08/2013 20:10:29 hn="mypc-WS" mac="e4:cd:8f:05:2b:ac" ip="10.10.10.50"
    exp="10/09/2013 22:11:34 UTC"
```

There are additional instances where it's ideal to identify transactions in log data that have the potential to span multiple events, such as VPN session data, authentication attempts, or web sessions. Once combined, the transaction can be used for holistic timelines or to identify anomalous behavior. Consider a transaction identifying normal VPN usage. If the same user initiates a new VPN connection before an older connection has been terminated, it may be indicative of a policy violation or shared VPN credentials—both the responsibility of a CSIRT to identify.

Fields Within Fields

As stated previously, additional attributes may exist within individual fields that are worth parsing themselves. Consider the action from the HIDS alert, and the Requested URL from the web proxy log:

```
HIDs 'Event Action' field:

The process 'C:\Users\mypc\Downloads\FontPack11000_XtdAlf_Lang.msi'
    (as user DOMAIN\mypc) attempted to initiate a connection as a client
    on TCP port 80 to 199.7.54.72 using interface Virtual\Cisco Systems
    VPN Adapter for 64-bit Windows. The operation was allowed by default
    (rule defaults).

Web Proxy 'Requested URL' field:

http://servicemap.conduit-services.com/Toolbar/?ownerId=CT33118
```

Both fields contain data that very well could be a field in and of itself, and may possibly be a field in another data source. The HIDS log identifies the following additional fields:

- Path (`C:\Users\mypc\Downloads`)
- Filename (`FontPack11000_XtdAlf_Lang.msi`)
- Active Directory domain (`DOMAIN\mypc`)
- Destination IP address (`199.7.54.72`)
- Port (`80`)
- Protocol (`TCP`)
- Verdict (`operation was allowed`)

The URL from the web proxy contains the following additional fields:

- Domain (`conduit-services.com`)
- Subdomain (`servicemap`)

- URL path (`Toolbar/`)
- URL parameter (`?ownerId=CT331183`)

Though lacking in this example, the web proxy URL could have just as easily contained a filename. Each of these fields is a potential metadata attribute that can be used to correlate, or link, the HIDS or web proxy event with another data source. From the HIDS event, an analyst may want to determine what other hosts also contacted the IP address on port 80 by searching NetFlow data. Or the analyst may want to correlate the filename identified in the web proxy log with HIDS data to see if the same filename attempted execution on the same or other hosts.

Had NASA at least done some data normalization, they would have differentiated between units of measurement and potentially controlled their spacecraft as intended. A calculated value, much like a timestamp, can and will be represented in multiple different ways. An organization can choose to use any representation of the data they want, as long as the usage is consistent, the data representation has meaning to the organization, and any deviations from the standard format are adjusted and documented prior to analysis time. However, understanding data's significance requires context, which can be garnered using metadata.

Metadata: Data About Data About Data

Metadata is a loaded term. It's an imprecise word that broadly attempts to describe both data structures and data components. In other words, it is both a category and a value. Figuratively, metadata is the envelope, and the letter inside is the data, but the fact that you received a letter at all is also data. Metadata is, in fact, itself data. This tautology manifests itself when applied to the concepts of incident response and security monitoring. Metadata could be a single component, like the field descriptor in a log file (e.g., source IP address), or it could also be the log file itself depending on how it's applied to a security incident or investigation. To determine whether something is metadata, simply apply these two age-old maxims: "it depends," and "you know it when you see it."

Metadata for Security

In the context of security monitoring, we consider metadata as it applies to log and event data. Metadata is a collection of attributes that describes behavior indicative of an incident. It is more than the sum of all of its parts. As an example, NetFlow logs are both wholly metadata and comprised of metadata elements that contain values. Looking at a typical NetFlow log (version 5), you have a standard list of fields including:

- Source and destination IP addresses and ports

- IP protocol

- Network interface data

- Flow size

- Flow duration

- Timestamps

These elements provide basic context for every network event. This contextual information is metadata that describes the event in generic terms. However, consider the following information derived from a NetFlow record: a two-day flow from an internal host transmitting 15 gigabytes of data to an external host from source port 30928 to destination TCP port 22.

Because of the nature of this traffic (unusually large and encrypted outbound file transfers), we could make a circumstantial judgement based on the context that data exfiltration has occurred. However, it could have just as easily been a really big (and benign) SCP/SFTP file transfer, or a complete dead end. Knowing when our assumptions are being tested, or that we may have imperfect log data, always factors into achieving conclusive closure for an investigation.

Log data alone means very little. The context built from log data matters the most. Metadata brings us a step closer to understanding what the events in a log represent. We derive context by organizing and sorting raw data into metadata, or groups of metadata, and applying knowledge and analysis to that context. When the log data is massive, reducing to, and searching with metadata elements yields understandable and digestible information, cutting through to the most valuable information and providing the capability to search efficiently.

Blinded Me with [Data] Science!

In 2013, the *New York Times* published details on the United States National Security Agency (NSA) and its metadata gathering and analysis program exposed by NSA insider, Edward Snowden. According to the leaked secret documents, the NSA performed "large-scale graph analysis on very large sets of communications metadata without having to check foreignness of every e-mail address, phone number or other identifier" (*http://www.nytimes.com/2013/09/29/us/nsa-examines-social-networks-of-us-citizens.html?smid=pl-share*). Despite the constitutional ramifications for American citizens, on the surface, the operation was colored as a benign exercise. According to the NSA, they were only looking at connections and patterns between various phone numbers and email addresses to help identify terrorist cells or plots. The data they mined included phone call and email records. From those records, they extracted metadata like source phone number, destination phone number, call date, and call duration. With this metadata alone, the NSA had enough information to build statistical models around their log data to make assumptions. An agent could confirm that unknown person A made phone calls to suspicious persons B, C, and D. By association, the Agent would assume suspicion for person A as well, making them a target of a larger investigation. However, the real power, as well as a big part of the controversy, stems from how the NSA "enriched" their surveillance with additional components (and how they obtained those components).

As we've described already, context around data and metadata makes all the difference. If we yell "fire" in an empty building, it means nothing. If an officer yells it to their soldiers, it means something completely different. If we yell it in a crowded public place, we've potentially committed a crime. The piece of data (the word *fire*) is identical. However, the context in which it's used is totally different, and as such, it has a dramatically different impact. The NSA used both publicly and privately available data to enhance its analysis. According to the *New York Times*, sources of public information could include property tax records, insurance details, and airline passenger manifests. Phone numbers could be associated with a Facebook profile, which could infer a human owner of the phone number, along with a wealth of other data that the person was willing to share on Facebook. With these additional data sources, the NSA could develop a profile with more than just a basic list of call records. Seemingly benign phone record data when combined and correlated with other attribution data could generate context. This context could help the agency with its profiling and investigations, and provide more intelligence on a suspect than they would have had with just statistical graph modeling.

Putting the contentious ethical and legal concerns aside and getting back to the playbook, a similar approach could be used in security incident response. We describe data and classify its log file containers by extracting metadata, and then apply logical conditions and calculations to yield information. That new information is then analyzed to create knowledge that drives the incident response process.

Metadata in Practice

In one incident, we detected an internal client attempting to resolve an unusual external hostname. The domain looked suspicious because of its random nature (i.e., lots of ASCII characters arranged in a nonlinguistic pattern). We remembered from a previous case that a dynamic DNS provider who has hosted many malicious sites in the past hosted this particular domain as well. On the surface, so far all we knew was that an internal client was trying to resolve a suspicious external hostname. We did not know if it successfully connected to the Internet host or *why* it attempted to resolve the hostname. We did not know if the resolution was intentional on behalf of the client, if it was a result of remotely loaded web content, or if it was unexpected and potentially malicious. However, we had already realized a bit of metadata. We knew:

Metadata	Metacategory: Data
The remote hostname appeared randomly generated.	Hostname: dgf7adfnkjhh.com
The external host was hosted by a dynamic DNS provider.	Network: Shady DDnS Provider Inc.

With this metadata alone, we could not have made an accurate judgement about the incident. However, combining these elements with other metadata began an illustration of what happened and why we should have cared. This information, along with our experience and encounters with these types of connections in the past, led us to presume that the activity was suspicious and warranted additional investigation. This is an important concept—having responded to incidents in the past with similar characteristics (e.g., this particular combination of metadata), we deduced that this was most likely another security incident. More precisely, we applied our knowledge derived from experience to these metadata components.

Building on the initial metadata we now had:

Metadata	Metacategory: Data
The DNS lookup occurred at a certain time.	Timestamp: 278621182
The internal host sent a DNS PTR request.	Network protocol: DNS PTR
The internal host had a hostname.	Location: Desktop subnet
	Source IP Address: 1.1.1.2
	Hostname: windowspc22.company.com
The internal host resolved an external host.	Location: External
	Destination IP Address: 255.123.215.3
	Hostname: dgf7adfnkjhh.com
The external host was hosted by a dynamic DNS provider.	Network: Shady DDnS Provider Inc.
	ASN: SHADY232
	Reputation: Historically risky network
The remote hostname appeared randomly generated.	Hostname: dgf7adfnkjhh.com
	Category: Unusual, nonlinguistic

However, we were stuck with very little context. Similar to only knowing that a phone number reached out to some suspicious phone numbers, we were left with statistical models, some bias based on previous investigations, and a hunch to figure out if the connection was indeed unexpected.

Context Is King

To determine whether this was a malicious event indicative of malware or some other type of attack demands, we include more context. Looking at NetFlow data from the client host before, during, and after the DNS lookup, we assessed other connections and assumptions based on metadata yielded from the flow records. From the flow data, we could see numerous HTTP connections to Internet hosts in the moments leading up to the suspicious DNS request. After the DNS request, we saw additional HTTP connections on nonstandard ports to other remote hosts. Up to this point, we still had very little confirmed evidence to go on. NetFlow could not provide enough useful context for this event to take us further. However, when NetFlow is associated with other metadata from the event, it can provide additional details. It is great to confirm that connections occurred, but with no additional context or packet contents, we had not moved closer to confirming an infection or security incident. We knew nothing more than that an internal client made some suspicious connections. Because of our prior knowledge on those types of connections (i.e., the context we've developed experientially and applied to our play), the only reason this host was highlighted for investigation was because of the suspicious destination.

At this point, we have realized enough metadata to get us speculating about what actually happened with this host. Was it a malicious connection, or was it just an oddball DNS request? We had lots of data, some metadata, but no real actionable information yet. As already mentioned, we flagged this event as suspicious because of our prior experience looking at similar threats. This experience resulted in the development of knowledge, which we could apply to the information we've collected.

> The evolution of knowledge is: data→information→knowledge.

We applied our knowledge that connections to random-looking hostnames are generally bad (domain-generation algorithm) to data (the passive DNS logs) and extracted information: that an internal client may be at risk of a malware infection. This last piece is what will inform the security incident if one is necessary. Without more context, though, we still don't know that it's truly "bad." An algorithm can predict or discover a domain-generation algorithm, but it will not be capable of understanding its context within the transaction.

Context enrichment provides more context by enhancing our current data sets. We can pivot on various pieces of metadata to narrow down our focus to a digestible window and continue to build the case for an incident. We can take the metadata values of timestamp and source IP and add those to an additional query. Our web proxy log data is often a wealth of contextual information. Looking at web-browsing activity in a linear fashion can help to uncover unusual activity. In this case, we pivoted on the source IP field at the same timeframe the suspicious DNS lookup was performed. The proxy log data showed typical browsing to a regional news site. However, mixed in with the browsing, we noted a few HTTP connections to domains apparently not part of the news website.

The power of the web is its ability to link together various organizations and networks. However, this also allows many, many remote objects to be pulled in by the client browser just from the action of reading the news online. The domains referenced matched up with the domains from the passive DNS collection system. Right after those objects were fetched from the suspicious domains, we saw a different browser user-agent, namely `Java/1.7.0_25`, attempting to pull down a Java Archive (JAR) file from yet another odd-looking domain:

```
278621192.022 - 1.1.1.2 62461 255.123.215.3 80 -
  http://dgf7adfnkjhh.com/wp-content/9zncn.jar -
  http://www.newsofeastsouthwest.com/ 344 215 295
  "Java/1.7.0_25" - 200 TCP_MISS
```

After this happened, the host intrusion prevention (HIPS) logs indicated the same Java JAR file trying to unpack and make additional HTTP requests to another remote domain for a DOS executable. The executable was fetched by the Java client, and the host intrusion prevention logs showed system-level modification attempts from the newly download executable. Fortunately, the HIPS blocked the executable from causing any damage, but at this point, based on all the context provided by metadata, we can clearly call this an exploit attempt, followed by a multistage malware dropper:

Metadata	Metacategory: Facts
A known vulnerable Java plug-in attempted to download additional JAR files from other odd domains.	User-Agent: Java1.7.0_25
	Hostname: dgf7adfnkjhh.com
	Category: Unusual, nonlinguistic
	Vulnerability: Java1.7.0_25 Plugin
	Filetype: JAR
HIPS blocked execution after JAR unpack	Filetypes: JAR, EXE, INI
	Filenames: 9zncn.jar, svchost.exe, winini.ini
	Path: \Users\temp\33973950835-1353\.tmp
	HIPS action: Block

So to get from raw data in the form of passive DNS logging to responding to a security incident, we had to take multiple transformative and additive steps. We reshaped the raw data with contextual information synthesized from additional data sources, with the help of metadata, into usable information. We applied our existing knowledge of suspicious indicators to the information we developed from our log queries to ferret out details of an actual security incident. However, this whole exercise took no more than five minutes to investigate.

Going forward, we can take streamlined queries to find the same or similar behavior in the future, and roll those into regular, high-fidelity reports. Illustrating by way of key-value pairs with fictitious field names:

```
external_hostname=DDNS, AND
http_action=GET, AND
remote_filetype=JAR, AND
local_filetype=REG, AND
local_path="\windows\sysWOW64" OR "\windows\system32", AND
HIPS_action=block
```

A query that can yield results based on this context will provide plenty of detail for investigation, and could potentially roll into a regular report. Metadata and context provide seed material for new reports based on investigating singular events with an experienced eye for finding odd behavior.

Metadata is the catalyst that allows you to transform raw data into information. You cannot organize your data further without metacategories, and you cannot query efficiently without it. One of the best parts of relying on metadata is that it is reusable. Many fields were common for all the data sources mentioned in the preceding investigation. Basic details like timestamps, IP addresses, hostnames, and the like are typically available in all event sources. It's a matter of how to correlate those event sources around the metadata fields available. At the end, once you have a good method for regularly distilling raw data into security incidents, you have a report. When you have a collection of repeatable reports, you have an incident response playbook.

Chapter Summary

- There are many ways to provide security monitoring and incident response, but the best approach will leverage an understanding of an organization's culture, risk tolerance, business practices, and IT capabilities.

- Log data can record critical information that can be used in security investigation, as well as providing foundational data for an entire security monitoring program.

- Well-prepared and normalized log data is essential for efficient operations.

- Metadata is a powerful concept to help simplify log data and analysis.

- Context around data and assets is an indispensable component in a successful monitoring strategy.

CHAPTER 5

Enter the Playbook

"Computers are useless. They can only give you answers."
—Pablo Picasso

Most large entities are faced with a crazy level of network and organizational complexity. Overlapping IP address space, acquisitions, extranet partners, and other interconnections among organizational and political issues breed complex IT requirements. Network security is inherently complicated with a large number of disparate data sources and types of security logs and events. At the same time, you're collecting security event data like IDS alarms, antivirus logs, NetFlow records and alarms, client HTTP requests, server syslog, authentication logs, and many other valuable data sources. Beyond just those, you also have threat intelligence sources from the broader security community, as well as in-house-developed security knowledge and other indicators of hacking and compromise. With such a broad landscape of security data sources and knowledge, the natural tendency is toward complex monitoring systems.

Because complexity is the enemy of reliability and maintainability, something must be done to combat the inexorable drift. The playbook is an answer to this complexity. At its heart are a collection of "plays," which are effectively custom reports generated from a set of data sources. What makes plays so useful is that they are not only complex queries or code to find "bad stuff," but also *self-contained, fully documented, prescriptive procedures for finding and responding to undesired activity.*

By building the documentation and instructions into the play, we have directly coupled the motivation for the play, how to analyze it, the specific machine query for it, and any additional information needed to both run the play and act upon the report results. Keep in mind, however, that the playbook isn't just a collection of reports, but a series of repeatable and predictable methods intended to elicit a specific response to an event or incident.

For our framework design, every play contains a basic set of mandatory high-level sections:

- Report identification
- Objective statement
- Result analysis
- Data query/code
- Analyst comments/notes

The following sections detail our requirements and definitions for analysts to create additional playbook reports. It's certainly possible to have additional sections depending on your end goal; however, for our purposes of incident response we've determined that the sections just outlined are the most precise and effective, without collecting superfluous information.

Report Identification

Our reports are identified in short form by a unique ID, and in long form by a set of indicators that give context about what the report should accomplish. The long form is formulaic and amounts to the following:

```
{$UNIQUE_ID}-{HF,INV}-{$EVENTSOURCE}-{$REPORT_CATEGORY}: $DESCRIPTION
```

{$UNIQUE_ID}

Our report identification (ID) numbers use a Dewey Decimal-like numbering system where the leading digit indicates the data source (Table 5-1).

Table 5-1. Playbook report identification numbers

Unique ID range	Event source	Abbreviation
0–99999	Reserved	N/A
100,000–199,999	IPS	IPS
200,000–299,999	NetFlow	FLOW
300,000–399,999	Web proxy	HTTP
400,000–499,999	Antivirus	AV
500,000–599,999	Host IPS	HIPS
600,000–699,999	DNS sinkhole and RPZ	RPZ
700,000–799,999	Syslog	SYSLOG
800,000–899,999	Multiple event sources	MULTI

We include an event source tag and event source number in each play for easier grouping, sorting, and human readability. It also allows us to run easier queries for metrics against a particular event source to include the numeric ID. We've padded several digits after the leading digits with 0s for room for expansion and subcategories for future data sources and feeds. The remaining portion of the report ID is a unique, mostly incrementing report number. Providing a number to each report, and assigning it to a class organizes the results. Well-organized reports make it easier to understand visually and enable better analysis. The reports can be easily sorted and the numbers provide for additional operations later in the incident response process, like reporting and metrics. If we were to add an additional host-based product to our detection arsenal, we can easily fold it under the 500,000 range—perhaps in a 501,000 series. It's not likely we would have 1,000 reports for one event source, so the padding is adequate.

{HF,INV}

The next portion of the report identification is the report *type*, which is currently either "investigative" or "high fidelity."

High fidelity means that *all* events from a report:

- Can be automatically processed
- Can't be triggered by normal or benign activity
- Indicate an infection that requires remediation, not necessarily a policy violation

Investigative means that *any* event from a report might:

- Detail a host infection
- Detail a policy violation
- Trigger on normal activity (which may require tuning)
- Require additional queries across other event sources to confirm the activity
- Lead to development of a more high-fidelity report

Our level of analysis depends on a very simple rule: a report is either high fidelity or it isn't.

High fidelity means that all the events from a report or query are unequivocal indicators—that is to say a "smoking gun" for a security incident. It's proof beyond a reasonable doubt versus a preponderance of evidence (including circumstantial evidence). In our system, high-fidelity incidents automatically move on to the remediation step of the incident-handling process. Hardcoded strings, known hostnames or IPs, or regular expressions that match a particular exploit are good examples of things that can be included in a high-fidelity report. However, the reports that make up the vast majority of the playbook are not high fidelity. Only about 15% of our reports are high fidelity, yet those reports make up the bulk (90%) of the typical malware infections we detect.

Reports that cannot indicate with 100% certainty that an event is malicious are deemed "investigative." More investigation is required against the events to determine if there's truly a security incident or a potentially tunable false positive. The investigation may result in a true positive, a false positive, an inconclusive dead end, or it may lead to the creation of additional investigative reports to further refine the investigation. Investigative reports that mature through tuning and analysis could eventually become high fidelity if we can confidently remove all nonevents.

{$EVENTSOURCE}

The *event source* identifies which source, or sources, that the report queries. The leading digit of the report ID will always correlate with the event source, which can be seen in Table 5-1.

{$REPORT_CATEGORY}

We've developed report categories that apply to the types of reporting we've achieved (Table 5-2). Keep in mind that you might consider choosing similar categories that align with or are exactly those prescribed by other organizations. The Verizon Vocabulary for Event Recording and Incident Sharing (VERIS), as well as the United States Computer Emergency Readiness Team (US-CERT) and others, have standard categories of incident you can use to compare metrics.

Table 5-2. Playbook report categories

Category	Description
TREND	Indicators of malicious or suspicious activity over time and outliers to normal alerting patterns and flows
TARGET	Directed toward logically separate groups of networks and/or employees (e.g., extranet partners, VIP, business units)
MALWARE	Malicious activity or indicators of malicious activity on a system or network
SUSPECT_EVENT	Indicators of malicious or suspicious activity that require additional investigation and analysis
HOT_THREAT	Temporary report run with higher regularity and priority to detect new, widespread, or potentially damaging activity
POLICY	Detection of policy violations that require CSIRT response (IP, PII, etc.)
APT	Advanced attacks requiring special incident response
SPECIAL_EVENT	Temporary report run with higher regularity and priority for CSIRT special event monitoring (i.e., conferences, symposia)

{$DESCRIPTION}

The free-text *description* component to the report title provides a brief summary of what the report attempts to detect. For example:

```
500002-INV-HIPS-MALWARE: Detect surreptitious / malicious use of
    machines for Bitcoin mining
```

This report name tells the analysts its unique ID is 500002. The leading 5 in the ID indicates the report searches HIPS data. It's an investigative report, which will require analyst resources to confirm that the implicated host has unauthorized Bitcoin mining software installed.

Objective Statement

The *objective statement* describes the "what" and "why" of a play. Experience has taught us that as queries are updated, they can drift from the original intention into an unintelligible mess without a good objective statement. The target audience for the objective statement is not a security engineer. The objective statements are intended to provide background information and good reasoning for why the play exists. Ultimately, the goal of the objective statement is to describe to a layperson what a play is looking for on the network and leave them with a basic understanding of why the play is worthwhile to run. It should be obvious to the analyst why this report is necessary, and it should meet at least one of the following criteria:

- Tells us about infected systems (bots, Trojans, worms, etc.)
- Tells us about suspicious network activity (scanning, odd network traffic)
- Finds unexpected/unauthorized authentication attempts to machines
- Provides summary information, including trends, statistics, counts
- Gives us custom views into certain environments (targeted reports, critical assets, hot-threat, special event, etc.)

The important thing to keep in mind for an objective statement boils down to *Is this the best way to find the information, and if so, how can it best be presented?*

The following example objective shares a high-level overview of the issue that requires the report to be scheduled and analyzed:

Sample Objective

Today, malware is a business. Infecting machines is usually just a means to financial ends. Some malware sends spam, some steals credit card information, some just displays advertisements. Ultimately, the malware authors need a way of making money by compromising systems.

With the advent of Bitcoin, there is now an easy way for malware authors to directly and anonymously make use of the computing power of infected machines for profit.

Our HIPS logs contain suspicious network connections, which allow for the detection of Bitcoin P2P activity on hosts. This report looks for processes that appear to be participating in the Bitcoin network that don't obviously announce that they are Bitcoin miners.

Result Analysis

The result analysis section is written for a junior-level security engineer and provides the bulk of the documentation and training material needed to understand how the data query works, why it's written the way it is, and most importantly, how to interpret and act upon the results of the query. This section discusses the fidelity of the query, what expected true positive results look like, the likely sources of false positives, and how to prioritize the analysis and skip over the false positives. The analysis section can vary a lot from play to play because it's very specific to the data source, how the query works, and what the report is looking for.

The main goal of the analysis section is to help the security engineer running the play and looking at report results to act on the data. To facilitate smooth handling of escalations when actionable results are found, the analysis section must be as prescriptive and insightful as possible. It must describe what to do, all of the related/interested parties involved in an escalation, and any other special-handling procedure.

For high-fidelity plays, every result is guaranteed to be a true positive so the analysis section focuses more on what to do with the results rather than the analysis of them. As we mentioned, the vast majority of reports are investigative, and therefore require significant effort to ensure they are analyzed properly. The following sidebar shows what a thorough analysis section might look like.

Sample Analysis

This report is fairly accurate. Bitcoin operators use port 3333, which is rather unique. The report simply looks for running processes talking outbound on port 3333/TCP. A few IPs known to host services on 3333 have been excluded from the query, as have the names of some processes like "uTorrent" that are somewhat likely to generate false positives.

Most of the results produced by this query are obviously malicious. For example:

```
2013-08-09 11:30:01 -0700|mypc-WS|10.10.10.50|
    The process 'C:\AMD\lsass\WmiPrvCv.exe' (as user DOMAIN\mypc) attempted
    to initiate a connection as a client on TCP port 3333 to 144.76.52.43
    using interface Wifi. The operation was allowed by default (rule defaults).
```

And:

```
2013-08-07 22:10:01 -0700|yourpc-WS|10.10.10.59|
  The process 'C:\Users\yourpc\AppData\Local\Temp\iswizard\dwm.exe' (as user
  DOMAIN\yourpc) attempted to initiate a connection as a client on TCP port
  3333 to 50.31.189.46 using interface Wifi. The operation was allowed by
  default (rule defaults).
```

There are also programs that use Bitcoin as a way to pay for the service:

```
2013-08-08 01:10:01 -0700|theirpc-WS|10.10.10.53|
  The process 'C:\Program Files (x86)\Smart Compute\Researcher\scbc.exe'
  (as user DOMAIN\theirpc) attempted to initiate a connection as a client
  on TCP port 3333 to 54.225.74.16 using interface Wifi. The operation was
  allowed by default (rule defaults).
```

For analysis:

- If you want to confirm the IP being communicated with is actually involved in Bitcoin transactions, simply Google the IP along with the word "bitcoin." There are many services that list all bitcoin nodes and bitcoin transactions.

- For internal <-> internal traffic on port 3333/tcp, the alert is almost always a false positive triggered by someone internally picking port 3333 to run a service. Real Bitcoin activity should always involve internal <-> external traffic on port 3333/tcp.

- For processes that look malicious, send the host for remediation (re-imaging).

- For processes that are semi-legitimate, like "Smart Compute\Researcher\scbc.exe", contact the user and inform them they must uninstall the software. See the internal Acceptable Use Policy for more information.

- See *http://www.smartcompute.com/about-us/* for details on the software.

- For the few cases where the 3333 traffic isn't Bitcoin related, or where it isn't easy to tell if the mining is malicious, simply ignore the results.

Data Query/Code

The query portion of the play is not designed to be stand-alone or portable. The query is what implements the objective and produces the report results, but the specifics of how it does that just don't matter. All of the details of the query needed to understand the results are documented in the analysis section. Any remaining under-the-hood details are inconsequential to the play and the analyst processing the report results. Queries can sometimes be rather complex due in part to being specific to whatever system the data lives in.

We'll cover query development in depth in Chapters 8 and 9. The primary reason we include the query in the report, aside from the obvious need to use it, is that we want to ensure our play tracking and development system is in sync with our log management and query system, and to help educate each other with creative methods for developing queries. Analysts can often reuse logic and techniques from queries of already approved plays.

Analyst Comments/Notes

We manage our playbook using Bugzilla. Using a bug/ticket tracking system like Bugzilla allows us to track changes and document the motivation for those changes. Any additional useful details of a play that don't belong in the aforementioned sections end up in the comments section. For a given objective, there are often a number of ways to tackle the idea in the form of a data query. The comments allow for discussion among the security engineers about various query options and the best way to approach the play objective. The comments also provide a place for clarifications and remarks about issues with the query or various gotchas.

Most plays need occasional maintenance and tuning to better handle edge cases and tune out noise or false positives. The comments allow the analysts processing reports to discuss tweaks and describe what is and isn't working about a report. By keeping all of the notes about a play as addendums, it's possible to read the evolution of the play. This enables us to keep the playbook relevant long term. It also provides for additional management options like retiring reports and reopening reports.

The Framework Is Complete—Now What?

We have talked with plenty of security teams from different industries all around the world. Many of them have figured out mature approaches that work to secure their networks. Many more just want us to give them the playbook as though it's a drop-in solution. The framework as we've just defined it *is the playbook*. We've put together a straightforward framework based on our experiences with incident detection, our current tools and capabilities, our team structure and expertise, and our management directive.

The framework stands well on its own, but at some point, plans must be put to action. After you've fine-tuned your plan to clean up data so it can be searched, and developed a democratic way of detecting current and future threats, it's time to put your methods into practice. Security operations depend heavily on solid process, but good security operations also depend on effective and sustained threat detection. The playbook requires regular maintenance once you add in the operational moving parts like analysis, play review, threat research, and the like.

Chapter Summary

- Developing a playbook framework makes future analysis modular and extensible.
- A thorough playbook will contain the following at minimum:
  — Report identification
  — Objective statement
  — Result analysis
  — Data query/code
  — Analyst comments/notes
- An organized playbook offers significant long-term advantages for staying relevant and effective—focus on organization and clarity within your own framework.

CHAPTER 6

Operationalize!

"Everybody has a plan until they get punched in the face."
—Mike Tyson

Everything up to this point, the ideas and questions in the first five chapters, has served to prepare you to create a playbook you can deploy. Your playbook should reflect that you've asked relevant questions and built a plan and plays that are as unique as your organization and its assets. Your playbook should reflect that you identified what threats to look for, what assets and information you intend to protect, how to lay out the architecture, how to prepare the data, and how to get the logs flowing. That plan is now ready for operationalization! This chapter will explain, by way of example, how to put your plan into action, how to avoid operational problems, and how to keep it running smoothly.

To really make it work, we'll discuss some key questions throughout the chapter to ready your playbook for real-world security operations. These questions are core to keeping the playbook a living thing:

- How can I determine the amount of resources needed to analyze the entire playbook?
- What systems will I need in place to make my plan work?
- How can I manage a living playbook?
- How can I avoid operational problems?
- How can I make reporting and alerting more efficient?

Simply having a playbook and detection logic is not enough. Your plays must actually run to generate results, those results must be analyzed, and remedial actions must be taken for malicious events. Operationalizing your security monitoring requires solid planning to transition from a set of ideas and requirements into a reliable, measurable, and sustainable functional system.

As *South Park* has so aptly dramatized, commercial organizations are infamous for skipping the critical, central step of understanding how to execute business plans. The "Gnomes" episode (*http://www.southparkstudios.se/full-episodes/s02e17-gnomes*) of the animated sitcom illustrates the problem of an incomplete business plan, with their version:

- Phase 1: Collect underpants
- Phase 2: ?
- Phase 3: Profit

In your business plan, the playbook is phase 1. However, unlike the underpants gnomes, you will develop a strategy for your incident response team to achieve success in your monitoring program in phase 2. Regular review and analysis of security event reports from your log management systems will lead to incident detection. The whole point of the playbook is to create a framework that can be applied to real data. The execution, phase 2, is to accurately detect and respond to security incidents leveraging the intelligence and analysis described in your plays. We can convert ideas about detection into actionable items for a team of analysts like opening a tracking case, contacting a sysadmin, or notifying an escalation team. In phase 3, you'll finally enjoy the profits in the form of well-documented, well-measured, and well-vetted incident detection data that proves your incident response team is capable, effective, and worth the investment to protect your organization.

We want to continue to open the black box that is productized one-size-fits-all security monitoring. Be wary of claims by security product vendors that their tools can do it all. You cannot rely exclusively on canned and opaque logic developed by a third party. When a report returns event data, you should be able to understand *why* and *what to do with it*. The types of threats you face, the trends you see in your own environment, and the pressures applied by your management chain determine how you interpret success with the playbook. Your priorities should be to improve the successful detection rate, build reports and queries that are more efficient, justify technology expenditures, and ensure your analysts have adequate resources to analyze results.

Playbooks Can't Respond to Incidents on Their Own

The playbook is only a plan. It doesn't find incidents on its own, nor can it predict what issues may arise once deployed into action. There are real-world challenges to consider.

The following are questions we ask of our plays time and again; keep these topics in mind while considering how to operationalize your playbook:

- Scheduling (Is real time necessary? Are there enough analysts to keep up with the event flow?)
- What detection metrics are you required to show?
- Do you have a sufficient process to guide you from detection idea to problem remediation?
- How do you avoid duplicate cases from repeated alarms?
- What will you do about changing escalation paths, staff turnover, and analyst responsibilities that require adjustments to your playbook processes?
- What mitigating capabilities and supporting policies exist to allow you to take action on confirmed malicious events?

We'll explore some answers to these questions in the following sections, but it's important to thoroughly understand your business requirements and try to anticipate future requirements before actually building new systems and processes.

You Are Smarter Than a Computer

Even in a utopian world where you have a fully automatic detection and response system, at some point a human must take an action. Whether that's validating the detections, working on an incident case, contacting a client, or dealing with remediation, there will always be a place for the human security analyst. Automation speeds up the response process and removes additional work required by analysts. However, haphazardly querying log data for unusual events does not always lend well to automation. The path to high fidelity (and thereby more efficiency) is paved by developing, investigating, and tweaking reports until their logic is a guaranteed detector of malicious behavior, and each result can be confirmed a true positive.

Developing reports to detect malicious behavior is only the beginning of a play's lifecycle and doesn't cover the full breadth of operationalizing the playbook. Those same reports must be maintained as part of the responsibilities of a security monitoring team. As threats evolve, old reports will fade from relevancy, while newer, more appropriate reports will be created and deployed. Trends in threats help analysts identify areas of the organization that need additional protection, architecture review, or alternative detection tactics, including developing new reports. Even if you were somehow able to defend all your systems and detect all of the threats you face today, the pace of technology ensures we will face something new tomorrow. By including regular maintenance of plays as an integral part of your group's operations, you'll keep the playbook fresh with new threat detection techniques and plays that will prepare you for the current threats as they unfold.

People, Process, and Technology

People are the integral part of these processes you're developing as part of your security monitoring service. No computer or program can replace context-informed human analysis. Unlike flowchart-style decision making like computer software, humans can effectively reason, consult (and develop) contextual indicators, and analyze motivation or other human idiosyncrasies.

Bruce Schneier has said, "Security is a process, not a product" (*https://www.schneier.com/essays/archives/2000/04/the_process_of_secur.html*). Supporting your monitoring process requires analysts, data managers, and infrastructure support personnel. You'll have to determine either how many of those different resources you need, or how best to use the resources you already have. Figuring out how many people are necessary to operationalize your playbook requires taking measurements at various stages in the system. For example:

- How many alarms are collected every day?
- How long does it take on average to analyze an alarm or an entire report?
- Is each report always analyzed in its entirety?
- Are we spending enough time revisiting the validity of our older reports?
- What is the projected volume of security alarms in the future, and what would we do in the event of a major outbreak?
- Is the staff skilled enough to understand our report results?
- What role do analysts play in remediation efforts, and what about incident recidivism?
- Can plays be run automatically, or do they require human interaction to retrieve results?

All of these are factors to consider when attempting to put the plan into action, and can help you predict how much analysis work will be necessary. For our own playbook, we regularly revisit these questions to ensure we're resourcing our program correctly and have appropriate and accurate coverage. We posed these questions because they have had significant resonance with our own playbook deployment.

Outbreaks must be handled differently from typical infections to triage properly and ensure the right groups are engaged. Insufficient communication with the IT teams has led us to remediation expediency issues. Some of our early reports created so many results requiring investigation that it was impossible for some analysts to complete their review in a workday.

 Automate your playbook systems to ensure results are delivered to the analysts. More complex analysis may not lend itself well to automation if the investigation process involves disparate data sources or data across incompatible tools. However, the majority of your saved queries should stand on their own. Ad-hoc approaches to reports can work well for a quick look or query development, but an automatic schedule of report delivery ensures consistent handling and saves the analysts' time by avoiding any operations. An analyst can simply review the results that have been prepared based on logic from the play and with data from various event sources.

For most reports in your playbook, eventually a human (team) has to review the result data output from the playbook. This is no different from any other security monitoring approach. SIEM, log management, or managed security solutions all require eyes on a screen and cases to document. To keep up with security threats, maintain situational awareness, and ensure proper response, it's unreasonable to have a network engineer or system administrator work "on security" part-time, as is common practice.

 Operationalizing your playbook demands additional work processes to go from ideas to security alarms to incident response.

You will need at least one dedicated and full-time human to analyze your security event data.

There are some important considerations to review when (re)establishing your incident response process and working with an analysis team. It's important to understand how many people and what skills you require for an analysis team. Look for some set of skills that spans topics like threat-centric or security knowledge, computer networking, application layer protocols, databases and query languages, Unix, Windows, basic parsing and command-line familiarity (bash, grep), security monitoring tools (IDS), and basic troubleshooting. Depending on the volume and complexity of data, the network, policies, and the incident response expectations, a small organization may be able to retain only two or three analysts, while a larger corporation could staff dozens.

For organizations with too few dedicated security analysts, the actual available headcount may define with what frequency and what volume alerts can be handled per day or week. Ideally, organizations are staffed to run and process all defined reports, with enough flexibility for new reports to be created and analyzed. Even so, a full staff does not guarantee a complete lack of resource saturation. Resources may be less available during incidents, outbreaks, holidays, or because of sick or personal time off. During these time periods, it is important to provide remaining staff with a prioritization for each report. Priority may be defined because of service-level agreements (SLAs) or regulatory controls, to detect a recent threat, or by event severity. Priorities must be identified so that less critical reports can be temporarily ignored until staffing levels return to normal.

At Cisco, we process millions of log events each day from various event sources, although not all of them require a follow-up investigation. With an insufficient number of analysts, we wouldn't be able to keep the playbook running sustainably. That is to say, our staff could analyze the reports we already have, but there would be no time for tuning, adjustment, or creating new plays. A playbook can be created and executed, but making some of these considerations regarding staff before enacting anything official improves the potential success. It's difficult to know precisely how many analysts are required because many of the previous questions cannot be fully answered until the playbook is already in action and measurements taken. A phased approach allows for an ease into the playbook process and routine, and provides early metrics that can help adjust to anything, like the workload, before it's a completely baked-in process.

Proper IT operations are also critical to support the tools and processes on which your monitoring depends. If analysts depend on running queries and daily reports, the query and reporting system had better be available every day! Given that log analysis is a full-time job, it's not wise to expect the analysts to be exclusively responsible for monitoring and detecting system health and uptime. An incident response team requires some division of labor to ensure that the complex system runs efficiently and doesn't overburden the analysts with system administration and housekeeping tasks. Analysts should understand those systems and how they yield the log and event data, but log analysis and incident handling demand significant attention and should be their primary focus.

With regard to analysts and staffing, your options essentially boil down to:

- Paying a managed security service a regular subscription fee to "do your security," with little to no context about your network; the service might, however, handle a broad spectrum of security beyond incident response (e.g., vulnerability scanning)

- Tasking a part-time "security person" to work on a best-effort security monitoring system (e.g., a SIEM) when they have time
- Hiring a sufficient number of security analysts and tailoring your security operations to your business requirements
- Calling in an emergency response team after your organization has been compromised

The first two are best effort and may work for very small networks and homogenous environments. However, the third option gives everyone else the most flexibility, the most options (i.e., in-house, relevant metrics) for describing the return on investment, and most importantly, maximum efficacy and overall security. Calling a professional, but temporary, incident response team after the fact will stop the bleeding and may offer helpful consultation, but in the end, the organization is left with the specter of a future compromise whether or not newly recommended controls are deployed. Having the ability to respond to your own incidents, and having as much detail available before it happens, provides total control to an organization when a security incident occurs.

Organizations turn to managed or contracted security services for many reasons, not the least of which are cost and the practicality of running a well-staffed internal security organization. What you save in cost, however, you lose in accuracy and precision when it comes to incident response. Almost anyone can read the output of a SIEM report, but what matters is what happens after the results are delivered. Only with solid context and an understanding of the network can an analyst truly understand the impact of an incident, or even whether to escalate it at all. Beyond the context, a good analyst understands the holistic structure of the organization, its mission, its tolerance for risk, and its culture.

Trusted Insiders

In most incident response teams, the more experienced members naturally serve as the top tier of the escalation chain, while the more junior members are still learning the work. At Cisco, we chose to split the team into two groups—investigators and analysts. Both roles support security monitoring and incident response services; however, the job responsibilities differ.

Investigators handle the long-term investigations, cases involving sensitive or high-profile systems or victims, and escalations from the analysts. This senior team also shapes the incident response strategy and detection methodologies. The analysts are responsible for analyzing and detecting security events in monitoring reports generated from various data sources. Their role involves extensive interaction with the investigators, along with other InfoSec and IT teams to help improve network security and monitoring fidelity.

Playing good defense requires an understanding of the offense's potential moves. Analysts must understand:

- Your organization's environment
- Software and system vulnerabilities
- Which threats matter and why
- How attacks work
- How to interpret data from playbook reports
- How to detect new threats

If the primary job is to respond to results from playbook reports, analysts are expected to understand the alarm and why it fired and respond accordingly. Event investigations, often with little context, require critical thinking and connecting the dots between bits of data to make a case, and call upon the analysts' ability to grasp the situation in its entirety.

For our analyst staff, we look for individuals who display an ability and desire to learn. Security is a mindset, not a skill set.

 Problem solving, troubleshooting, and critical thinking are more important than knowing a lot of technical minutiae.

Their breadth of experience along with help from others within the team provides a solid foundation for playbook development. The analysts are responsible for *owning* the playbook: keeping it updated by creating new plays, analyzing results from existing plays, and tuning reports and techniques as necessary. Analysts that are more senior advise and help develop and edit new plays, while assisting in providing context from institutional knowledge.

Don't Quit the Day Job

Creating new plays is arguably the most important aspect of the analyst's role. We expect analysts to understand not only how to find suspicious events, but also to understand why it's important to do so. Fundamental knowledge of security principles coupled with real IT experience is the first step in understanding the need for security monitoring and incident response. To develop additional plays, analysts need to be in tune with what's happening in the security community. Knowing how to detect the most current or significant threats requires reading about and understanding the latest attack methods, subscribing to security research blogs, Twitter/RSS feeds, and other sources of security information, and then regularly running sample checks against internal log data. Analysts don't have to understand every component, mutex, registry change, and process launched by a particular malware object, but they must be able to answer the following questions:

- What's our risk to the new threat?
- How does it arrive on a victim host?
- What signatures does it exhibit that can be used to detect again?
- How do we confirm a compromise?
- What's the best course of action to take for remediation?
- How can we detect and stop it in the future?

These elements make up the bulk of a new play, and clearly expounding on them in the play objective, analysis, and notes will make it easier for the other analysts to understand the original researcher's logic.

When it comes to log analysis, the staff must understand the alerts described in log data, or be able to determine when an event is irrelevant. Of course, they could rely on the more senior staff to guide their understanding of tools and analysis techniques, but they are empowered as our first line of defense for detecting malicious behavior. As long as data keeps flowing, the first-tier analysts can review all the predefined security reports and respond appropriately. Having worked hundreds of incidents, it's clear to us that there are countless examples to learn from. For every security event, we want analysts to have a broad set of experiences to draw from. If something looks bad, they try to come up with hypotheses for how it could be legitimate and then test them against the event and surrounding context. If an event looks normal or benign, we do the opposite. We encourage the analysts to always try to understand both ends of the possible explanation spectrum. This helps to guide the level of response and investigation necessary for each report.

For example, what if you created a report (using a regular expression) that detects suspicious HTTP posts, yet some of the results are clearly not malicious? First-tier analysts don't necessarily have to fully understand or translate the regular expression in English to realize the event may not be a true positive after reviewing additional attributes of the log (e.g., hostname, URL, source IP, etc.). Thinking about the alarm and what is already defined in the play's objective, analysts might consider the regular expression imprecise, or perhaps a client coincidentally retrieved a URL that matched the expression perfectly, yet was hosted at a benign domain.

This is where the tuning and updating portion of the analyst's role comes into play. After analyzing the results, the analysts must be able to incorporate their findings into the playbook notes. We expect that confirmed false positives and notes on how to improve a query will be added to the play as it goes through its regular and ongoing review. The analysts can make their future tasks easier and more efficient by suggesting and implementing tuning of their reports, based on evidential findings in the result data. Tuning ideas and report enhancements are best discussed in regular analyst meetings, so the whole team understands not only what might be changing, but also to understand how they can help optimize other reports. In our experience, group collaboration for event tuning benefits everyone, and makes the detection methods more precise.

Critical Thinking

Besides understanding which events to ignore, analysts must understand when a questionable event is indicative of something more significant. Putting a host on the Internet guarantees it will be probed. Actual web application attacks often look like common web vulnerability scanners; however, common application scanners are often a prelude to many actual, customized attacks. From data logs, skilled analysts should be able to differentiate web application attacks that match the pattern or technique of a commonly available vulnerability scanner or commercial penetration test suite, from attacks that are more directed, might have been successful, or could have a negative impact on a web service. A seasoned sysadmin or webmaster could likely determine the fidelity of the alarm, but we also expect that a good analyst could deduce the propriety of most log messages based on their skills and research.

For our first-tier analysts, we look for these types of analytical skills to ensure quality monitoring and less time wasted on unnecessary process. Analysts must understand why it matters if a host sends repeated failed login requests to a domain controller, or if a client resolves domains on a blacklist. We can prescribe tasks and workflows as explicitly as possible in the analysis section of the play, but there will always be a need for critical thinking, articulation, and a deeper understanding than pattern matching and machine learning.

We can teach security concepts, but understanding how all the moving pieces fit together in a complicated system requires hands-on experience. To mentor junior staff, support your monitoring design, architect new monitoring solutions, and set the threat detection strategy, you need experience. An ideal candidate for a higher-tier team will have a practical, if not operational, background in InfoSec and skill sets rooted in system and network administration, security research, or secure application development. Security events happen on hosts and over networks, against applications running on those hosts, and can involve the entire stack supporting a product infrastructure. Highly skilled system and network engineers understand how to properly build and maintain enterprise systems and networks. Presumably then, they also know how to recognize when the same systems are built or operating improperly or insecurely.

All this assumes you have super-talented, critical-thinking, and well-seasoned analysts. It also assumes that you have the capacity and budget to have such a staff. A staff of one analyst will rely on automation much more than a larger team, and will spend most of their time investigating events that cannot be automated. More often than not, we're asked to "do more with less." Because the cost of labor is expensive, hiring a large team of skilled analysts may be out of reach. Although there's no avoiding the requirement of having at least one full-time analyst for anything but a tiny network, there are steps you can take (depending on the maturity and capability of IT services) with automation that will lessen the impact of insufficient staff. Specifically, focusing on automating high-fidelity events and leveraging some feed-based plays (e.g., sinkhole services, bad domain lists, and filename indicators) will free up time for more investigatory work.

Systematic Approach

We've got the plan, we've got the right people, and now it's time to start analysis. To get to analysis and step 3 (profit) of the *South Park* "Gnomes" example, we need a few more components of the framework in place. Although there are a myriad of methods for achieving a successful data-centric monitoring approach, fundamentally our playbook strategy requires:

- A playbook management system
- A log and event query system
- A result display or presentation system
- A case tracking system
- A remediation process system

As you define and design these systems, consider where you might consolidate some of these functions to simplify operational overhead. Although the playbook management system or repository is largely independent, the query and presentation systems may be combined naturally as report results are presented from the log query system after a search. We'll get into more detail on these systems in the following sections. The key requirement is coherent, repeatable, and explicit report presentation and analysis.

 We cannot stress enough the importance of building in your core metrics from the beginning of development, rather than attempting to bolt it on at the end.

Figure 6-1 details the various processes and provides example metrics that can, and likely should be, collected at each step.

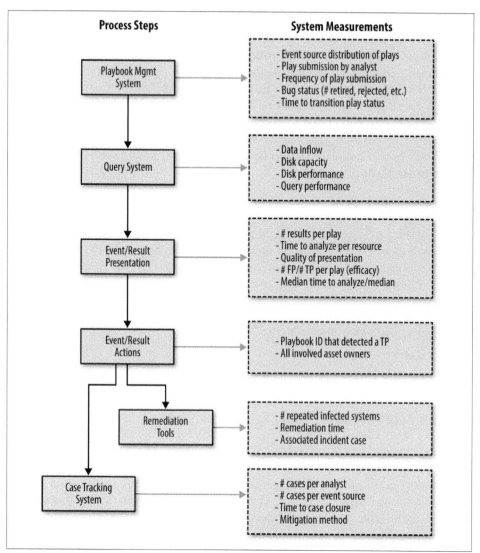

Process Steps

Playbook Mgmt System

Query System

Event/Result Presentation

Event/Result Actions

Remediation Tools

Case Tracking System

System Measurements

- Event source distribution of plays
- Play submission by analyst
- Frequency of play submission
- Bug status (# retired, rejected, etc.)
- Time to transition play status

- Data inflow
- Disk capacity
- Disk performance
- Query performance

- # results per play
- Time to analyze per resource
- Quality of presentation
- # FP/# TP per play (efficacy)
- Median time to analyze/median

- Playbook ID that detected a TP
- All involved asset owners

- # repeated infected systems
- Remediation time
- Associated incident case

- # cases per analyst
- # cases per event source
- Time to case closure
- Mitigation method

Figure 6-1. Security monitoring process and example metrics

Playbook Management System

As mentioned in Chapter 5, Cisco's CSIRT uses Bugzilla as its playbook management software. Before moving to a more formalized playbook management process, the analysts were already using and familiar with Bugzilla for IPS tuning and process/ report adjustment requests. We didn't need anything fancy, and we didn't need an expensive commercial tool with tons of features. We needed a quick ramp up and a tracking system that was easy to use. Bugzilla is not necessarily designed for our purpose (it's meant for tracking bugs in software development projects), but it works well (Figure 6-2). It is capable of meeting our requirements for maintaining and managing the playbook. Namely, it has the ability to:

- Create custom fields
- Track play progress and lifecycle
- Provide basic notification (email, RSS, etc.)
- Run queueing and assignment functions
- Automate reports and metrics
- Document and log changes

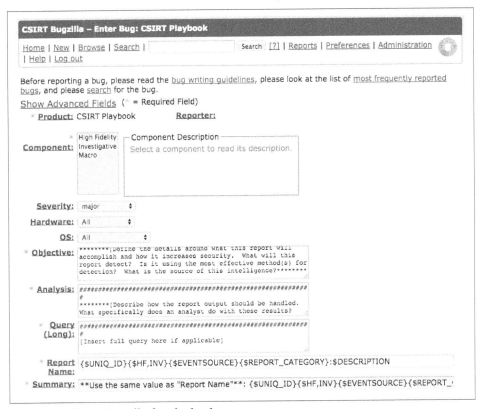

Figure 6-2. Using Bugzilla for playbook management

We can create free text fields to track different attributes (report name, objective, analysis, query). We can track which analysts submitted which reports. The status of each report can be toggled from "submitted" all the way to "retired" or even "reopened." Bugzilla's comment section allows our team to collectively track feedback, event samples, tactical changes, and tuning for each report. Over time, the evolution and history of the report can be clearly observed by reading the comment section.

Each of these fields allows us to measure various components of the playbook. At this point in the process, we have no indication of how many results each report generates, how long it takes the reports to run, or which analyst is analyzing which report. However, there are some metrics worth capturing:

- Frequency of new report submission
- Distribution of reports over data sources
- Progress of discussion and preparation for new plays
- Time to deployment

You don't want to leave any cards on the table, so any event source that can be used for detection should have plays in the playbook. The report naming structure described in Chapter 4, with specific numerical ranges identifying each event source, demonstrates the distribution of reports across your event sources. However, the goal should not necessarily be to strive for an even distribution of plays across event sources. If one event source excels at detecting the majority of events or the most common threats in your environment, then by all means build as much logic as you can based on that event source. The same advice applies for targeted attack methods. You should invest in the most effective tools first.

To maximize efficiency, ideally you want the most results with the least amount of cost and effort. To achieve that, you need to focus on the right data sources and measure efficacy on a continual basis. In addition to ensuring a layered approach to monitoring by incorporating as many tools into your plays as reasonable, identifying which tools are being used in which plays can help to justify a return on investment (ROI) for new or particularly expensive tools. Still, if you're asked to prove a new security technology was worth the investment, it's handy to have quick access to any and all reports based on the event source through a quick Bugzilla search.

Security event monitoring is a constantly changing practice, and to ensure that you're protected from tomorrow's threats, you must continually develop new and relevant plays. Measuring the rate of report submission is one way to identify how successfully you're addressing new or different threats. Haven't had a new report submitted in over 30 days? Maybe it's because the analysts are overextended and have had no time for new play creation, or it could be that your team has fallen behind the times.

Measure Twice, Cut Once, Then Measure Again

Plays should go through a QA process before they are fully integrated into production. When first submitted, the plays are open for feedback, restructuring, improvement, and tuning. When deemed production worthy by informal consensus, the plays are moved to a deployed state. Over time, a play may become obsolete for a variety of reasons, including an expired threat, a policy change rendering the detection logic unnecessary, or too little efficacy for the resources required to analyze the play. When obsolete, you should transition the report to a retired state.

Measuring the time to transition between submitted and deployed states can highlight whether reports have received adequate quality assurance (QA). Reports requiring extensive QA may be indicative of other problems—an ill-defined report, a lack of QA effort, or difficulty resolving the play's objective. It's also possible that an objective is too complex, or has too many variables that cannot be addressed in a single report. Measuring the time to deploy can also help determine if there are any issues slowing the process of converting detection methods to actions. If play approvals are stuck for weeks in the same state (e.g., "In Progress"), there may be a problem in getting play approval completed properly. Further analysis of the report and initial comments can help spot weaknesses in the process, which can be further addressed by better education or more staffing.

Our playbook contains the collection of statuses shown in Table 6-1, used throughout the lifecycle of a play (Bugzilla bug).

Table 6-1. Report status

Status	Meaning
NEW	Submitted for review
IN-PROGRESS	The QA team is reviewing the bug
DEPLOYED	The QA team has accepted the bug and the associated query has been moved to the production event query system
REJECTED	The QA team concluded that the particular bug is not a valid or an acceptable entry to the playbook
RETIRED	The bug and associated playbook item have been decommissioned
ASSIGNED-TO	The bug is assigned to a higher-tier analyst for review and long-term ownership

Report Guidelines

We have explicitly defined how the playbook review process works and communicated that information to the incident response team. Everyone has an expectation of what makes a good play, and how to turn a good play into a great one.

During the QA process, the team will often reference the checklists presented in Tables 6-2 through 6-4 to ensure that the fundamental questions about a play's efficacy and reliability have been addressed.

Table 6-2. Checklist for report accuracy

Technical accuracy and effectiveness	• Does the threat still exist or is the objective still worthwhile? • Does the existing report accurately address the report objective?
Goal and query rot	• Is the report criteria (domains, IP addresses, URLs, etc.) still an indicator of malicious activity? • Has the threat evolved enough that criteria should be changed / added / removed?
Current accuracy	• Do we have reason to believe the report is missing malicious activity due to a bug, gap in logs, or other technical issue? • Does mitigating an issue affect our ability to detect malicious behavior via the current data source? • Does the analysis section of the report contain sufficient detail that it's clear how to analyze the bulk of the report's results?
Future efficacy and goal coverage	• Could the report ever produce future results, or has the criteria decayed to the point that it's useless? • Can any derivative reports be created based off similar, but updated, new, or related threat information?

Table 6-3. Checklist for report cost and quality

Report quality and cost	• Do the report results require expertise or experience to analyze, which limit the number of people capable of analyzing the report effectively?
Documentation and result quality	• Is it possible to distinguish between false and true positives, or are there results where there's no simple way to tell? Can the analysis section be improved to address this?
Cost-benefit trade-offs	• Can reasonable tweaks be made to the report that will reduce false positives without affecting true positives? • Are there false negatives that could be converted to true positives without significantly increasing false positives?

Table 6-4. Checklist for report presentation

Efficient and complete result presentation	• Are all of the fields useful for analysis? If not, do they provide vital event context? Are there any useful fields that could be added?
	• Can context be added from other data sources that would significantly aid the result analysis?
Fields and context	• If the report uses a formatting macro, is it the best one to use? If not, is there a good one to use?
Data summarization and aggregation	• Are there redundant events that could be collapsed into a single event, or are there ways to aggregate events by a field such that related events could be analyzed together?

Reviewing High-Fidelity Reports in Theory

High-fidelity reports, by definition, don't produce any false positives. Without false positives, there is very little downside or resource expenditure for running the report. As long as a high-fidelity report is technically accurate and the targeted threat still exists, there is no reason to retire a high-fidelity report. Often, as high-fidelity reports age, it is common not to receive any results for weeks or months at a time. When a report hasn't returned results in a long time, it can be difficult to tell if that's because the report or the data source is broken, or if the specific threat the report looks for simply hasn't shown up in a while. Determining the reason requires more research into the threat. Any information about the threat that can help reviewers should be referenced in the bug. While researching the current state of the threat, be on the lookout for new variants or similar threats that could be targeted by new reports.

Reviewing Investigative Reports in Theory

Unlike high-fidelity reports, investigative reports are often quite complicated, and the variety of results that could show up can be staggering. In addition to all of the technical report criteria, investigative reports must be evaluated on a subjective cost-benefit basis.

The cost of an investigative report primarily comes in the form of time spent by analysts reviewing the results to find the actionable, true positive events. The more results in a report, especially false positives, the higher the cost. There is no objective way to compare costs to benefits, so any effort to compare them must be based on a subjective estimation of the threat to the company and the value of the time spent by the report. Even though the cost-benefit ratio of an investigative report is subjective, any measures that can reduce the number of false positives without affecting usable results are clearly beneficial. The same goes for any measure that can increase true positives without affecting false positives.

For reports where the number of false positives is low compared to true positives, the report is worth keeping. It's only when false positives significantly outnumber true positives or when false positives significantly increase the report analysis time that there is a chance the report is too costly to run and should be retired. The report should be considered for retirement in cases where the report is costly to run, and there are no technical measures available to improve it.

In any case, where there is a question about the efficacy of a report, it should be scheduled for discussion in regular analyst review meetings.

Reviewing Reports in Practice

The first step to reviewing a report is to fully understand the report objective. If the objective isn't clear, it must be revised. When everyone understands the objective, you should run the report and use the analysis section to help guide you through processing results. If the report doesn't return any results, you can query a longer period or search case tracking tools for examples from previous reports.

Keep all of the technical report evaluation criteria in mind while analyzing results. Tweaks and improvements to the report query are common and can often save a lot of analysis time in the future. Always consider making additional reports whenever possible if the detection criteria overwhelm a single report. Be on the lookout for ways to relax the query, by making it less specific without adding too many false positives. Relaxing the query can give you a glimpse of legitimate activity the query is currently ignoring but is similar to the report objective.

After reviewing a report using the technical criteria, if the report is investigative, move on to the subjective quality-cost estimation. Based on your time running the report, if you think the evaluation time is significant or if the number of false positives is overly burdensome, do your best to summarize the issue(s) in the comments for the report bug. The more comments you make about the pros and cons of a report, the easier it will be for others to understand and review the report in the future. A regular playbook tuning meeting is also a good place to discuss with your team your experience and concerns with evaluating the report and its overall cost and efficacy.

Event Query System

In Chapter 5, we introduced the data query/code section of the playbook. This is where the play objective changes from an English sentence to a machine-readable event query. The query is the exact question and syntax that will return results based on the objective from the query system. Whereas a play's objective identifies to a human what the play attempts to accomplish, the query executes within the query system to retrieve the results. Think of the event query system like an Internet search engine. You type in what you want to find, perhaps sprinkling in a few commands to tailor your results, and then you either get what you want or you don't.

Query systems will vary from organization to organization. They may consist of an open source logging solution, a relational database, a SIEM, a large-scale data warehouse, or a commercial application. Whatever system is used, they all provide a similar function—trigger events based on detection logic.

Security and other event log sources export their alarms to a remote collection system like a SIEM, or display them locally for direct access and processing. It's up to the SIEM to collect, sort, process, prioritize, store, and report the alarms to the analyst. Whether you choose a SIEM or a log management and query solution, the important part is ensuring you can get regular, concise, actionable, and descriptive alarms from your detection methods.

A Note on SIEM

A SIEM purports to solve the problem of "correlating" event data across disparate log sources to produce valuable incident data. However, it takes a gargantuan effort to ensure that this investment works, as well as a heavy reliance on system performance and proper configuration. Although system and performance issues affect every type of incident detection system, the static logic and limited custom searching are the primary downfalls of the SIEM. A security log management system, however, enables highly flexible and precision searching.

When properly architected, deployed, and manicured, a security log management system can be the most effective and precise tool in the incident detection toolkit, if only because of its searching and indexing capabilities. There's another bright spot for security log management versus putting everything into the SIEM and analyzing its reports. For incident detection, there are essentially two methods for finding malicious activity: ad-hoc "hunting" or reporting. Log management is the best way to provide these capabilities out of the box.

When measuring query systems, the focus should be more about collecting and analyzing system performance analytics, as opposed to playbook efficiency metrics. After all, the quicker you can process your data, the quicker you can detect threats.

Result Presentation System

You've built logic to detect a specific threat, and you have the query running at regular intervals in your query system. Now what? How do you get the results of that query to your resources so they can investigate whether the results indicate malicious behavior? If you have results from high-fidelity reports, is there a process to automatically do something with those results? The possibilities for presenting results are numerous. SIEMs and most products have the ubiquitous "dashboard," often of questionable value. Emails, email attachments, comma-separated values (CSV) files, custom-built dashboards, custom web pages, and event queues are other options to get result data to your analysts. Keep in mind that investigative reports are just that—they require further investigation to separate the wheat (malicious events) from the chaff (false positives, benign, or indeterminable events). Because employees are your most expensive and valuable asset, you must ensure their time is being used as effectively as possible. The more consistently a report can reliably highlight malicious events, the higher fidelity the report will become and the less investigation your analysts will have to perform.

One of the best ways for your analyst to view investigative results is by looking at the identical data set in different ways. As an example, consider a simple play that identifies the most frequent events over a certain period from a particular sensor. The data has already been sorted by a count of the events. But is that count ascending or descending (meaning, are you viewing the highest or lowest volume events)? Both views warrant equal inspection, but for different reasons. Whereas high-volume alarms can indicate widespread abuse of a vulnerability such as an open mail relay or UDP amplification attack, low-volume events may identify more furtive attacks. In Chapter 9, we'll discuss ways of actually implementing these different data views. For now, you should be aware of them in the context of how changing the view can affect your understanding of a true positive event.

In our playbook management and event query systems, we are interested in collecting quantitative measurements to determine how well those systems are performing. While keeping your result presentation system in mind, begin thinking about how you might qualitatively measure your system's effectiveness. Here, the question you strive to answer should be, "Am I viewing this data in the most ideal way to achieve my play objective and identifying a particular threat?" When looking at individual event results, you should consider the following method of manipulating the presentation of the same result set to achieve a potentially better view:

- Deduplicate events containing identical field values
- Add necessary or remove superfluous event fields
- Change result grouping or sorting (e.g., most frequent events, as described earlier)

Let's assume that you've modified the presentation of your results by one of the preceding methods. How do you know if the new view of your results is better than the previous presentation? There are some additional data points that can help you understand the best way to display information to your analysts:

- Number of total events per result set
- Time to analyze each result
- Result efficacy (true positive, false positive, benign, indeterminable)

Capturing the total analysis time per result enables the ability to calculate the average time to analyze the entire play. The summation of this value for every report will give you a total mean time to process the entire playbook. Based on the time required to analyze all reports, you can determine how many resources to allocate to report processing. Ideally, the number of events will be low and the time to analyze those events will be short. Pay attention to how adjusting different result views produce a different number of results.

After being investigated, results should be categorized by their ability to produce a desired or intended result, or *efficacy*. This efficacy measurement will help you identify the value of a play's logic. There are four possible categories for a given result that identify the play's effectiveness:

True Positive
    The system correctly detected a valid threat against an extant risk as per the intended detection logic.

False Positive
    The system incorrectly detected a threat, or there is no extant risk.

Benign
    The system correctly detected a valid threat, but there is no apparent risk due to the condition being expected.

Indeterminable
    Not enough evidence to make a decision, or inconclusive.

True positive results are the underpants the *South Park* gnomes are constantly trying to procure. These confirmed malicious events are the reason you built your monitoring program and the goal of the entire playbook. This is the "bad stuff" we're attempting to find. Higher ratios of true positives indicate higher fidelity plays. Alternatively, false positives indicate a flaw in the play's detection logic, which requires review and improvement if possible. It's a good thing you have a playbook management system to track the progression of a play as the play is constantly being tweaked. Of course, it may be impossible to remove all false positives from some report results, but the more you filter out, the higher the report efficacy and analyst performance. Benign events exist when the event is neither a false positive nor a true positive, even though it matches a subset of attributes from both cases.

Take, for instance, an event that an analyst attributed to an authorized vulnerability scanner. The detection logic achieved its objective—identifying behavior indicative of an attack. However, the "attack" was not malicious in intent. Instead, the vulnerability scanner should be tuned from the report so that it doesn't appear in subsequent results. It's considered benign because labeling it as anything else will wrongfully affect the efficacy measurements. An event that cannot be confirmed as true positive, false positive, or benign is considered indeterminable. Indeterminable events occur when there is a lack of information available. An inability to attribute an asset, failure to confirm the detected activity, or nebulous black-box vendor detection logic can all contribute to problems confirming or denying the efficacy of a play's result. Labeling the event a true positive will positively skew the number of successfully detected threats over time, giving a false impression that the play is more effective at detecting events than in reality. Conversely, labeling the event a false positive will negatively skew the detection system's efficacy, portraying a poorer play performance than in reality.

One of our goals is to ensure that the playbook is a well-oiled machine. Again, it's a living document that must be manicured over time. To get an indication of how well your detection logic is working per any given report, you can calculate the median time to analyze a play's results divided by the median true positives per play execution. Assuming for a minute that a true positive from one report is equivalent in value to a true positive in another report, the more true positives identified per amount of time will indicate a higher value report. However, not all plays are created equal. Your organization will likely have higher value reports than others. Reports that identify exploits against known vulnerabilities in the environment or attacks against high-value assets are likely more valuable than a report identifying policy violations of peer-to-peer traffic. Still, you will find it useful to know how effective your plays are compared to the time it takes to analyze the plays' results.

Playbook Reminders

Here are some playbook reminders to keep in mind:

Start small

It is important not to get overwhelmed with events. Start with a specific report or network segment, tuning that as much as possible before moving on to the next item. Tuning is an ongoing process, and it is the means by which the monitoring system is made useful. By trying to tune events from all reports, progress on any one particular report will be much slower. Each data source should be tuned as much as possible before adding more sources. Understand thoroughly how "normal" traffic appears before moving on to the next report. By following the tuning process, false positive alerts will be reduced, thus making those events that do fire higher fidelity. Without tuning, alerts will inevitably overwhelm the monitoring staff by producing events irrelevant to the environment being monitored. This ultimately causes the monitoring system to be ignored or disabled.

Timestamps

As we discussed in Chapter 4, you must ensure timestamps on all data sources are in sync. Ideally, they would be standardized on UTC in ISO 8601 format, but at a minimum, all data sources need to be of the same time zone and format throughout your organization. Any discrepancies from different time zones must be accounted for manually, which can slow the correlation process considerably.

Escalation procedures

Use defined, approved, and easily accessible playbooks and escalation procedures. For any actions that require involvement from or are dependent on business units outside of the monitoring team, procedures must be created in partnership with those teams. The resulting processes must also be easily accessible by those teams and regularly tested and documented in your incident response handbook.

Allies in support teams

The larger the network being monitored, the more distributed knowledge becomes about events on the network. Establishing relationships with members of IT teams will help reduce incident resolution time when you know who to go to, and they have your trust to help solve the issue. If a security team becomes known as the "no" team or the group who gets in everyone's way, then no one will help them. It's impossible to accomplish anything without the help of system owners.

Ultimately, you should eliminate the results that don't have context to the objective of the play. Those superfluous results should either be tuned and removed from the report, or if malicious in and of themselves, added to a separate and new report. Each cycle of filtering and tuning the report makes the play more effective at achieving its objective, and therefore of becoming a higher fidelity play.

Incident Handling and Remediation Systems

While not necessarily application based like Bugzilla or a log indexing and management system, there are still additional processes and systems required to complete the overall incident handling process.

As described in previous chapters, the classic incident response lifecycle consists of:

- Preparation (research, applying lessons learned)
- Identification (detection)
- Containment (mitigation)
- Eradication (remediation)

- Recovery (restoration of service)
- Lessons learned

As a short-term fix, each play in the playbook identifies a threat that must be immediately contained. This "stop the bleeding" phase prevents further disruption, and allows for time to investigate and take swift action to eliminate a threat. Ultimately, we eradicate the threat and learn from the incident to improve our detection and response time for future incidents. Measuring when and how quickly a threat was dispatched is just as important as how quickly it was detected. Eradication, or remediation, at some point in the process, will most likely require intervention with the affected asset owner and an agreeable, policy-backed plan to return the asset back to its properly secured state. In other words, depending on policy, how do you get an infected system back online with as little disruption as possible?

To maintain proper separation of duties—that is to say, preventing CSIRT from being judge, jury, and executioner—later phases like remediation are best left to IT and support teams. How then do you ensure timely and thorough completion of all requirements if someone other than you or your team is responsible for remediation tasks? For example, local IT support might be handled by a different group than the incident response team. Or in some cases, the end user may be responsible for restoring their personally owned device back to normalcy and compliance. It's important to measure time to remediation in order to prevent duplicate detection (i.e., you detect the same host twice for the same malicious activity), as well as to confirm your playbook efficacy. In other words, you can clearly show what risks threatened your organization (and for how long) if you have an accurate timeline of events from start to finish.

You must ensure that the remediation processes are not only effective to prevent recurring infections, but also that the remediation processes are actually followed properly. Many times in the past, we have sent hosts for remediation to the various teams responsible, only to have detected the same compromised host a second and even third time. Further investigation uncovered that the agreed-upon remediation process was not followed. For certain Trojan infections, we require a mandatory operating system reinstallation (also known as a *reimage*), yet the IT analysts responsible for remediation simply ran a virus scan and then closed the case when it came up empty. This is obviously a big problem, and while it cannot necessarily be solved with a better playbook, it is good to have the relationships we discussed earlier, as well as buy-in from senior leadership to support your efforts. For larger enterprises, it's also paramount that your remediation expectations extend to wholly owned subsidiaries and extranet partners as well.

Case Tracking Systems

At some point in the incident response process, whether it's a fully customized data-centric model like ours or a SIEM-based one-size-fits-all model, you'll have to track and document work in some form of case or incident diary. Case tracking and incident management systems maintain a record of what happened during the incident, the affected assets, and the current state of the incident. When an analyst determines that an investigative play successfully identified a malicious event, they must exercise the subsequent steps in the incident response lifecycle and begin by documenting all relevant details into a case. The case tracking system should track any relevant information necessary to satisfy the lifecycle:

- The Playbook ID or number that generated the confirmed true positive event
- Assets/asset owners involved in the incident
- Initial detection times
- Source and/or destination host information (i.e., attackers or victims)
- Theater, region, or business unit(s) affected
- Remediation state
- Mitigation method
- Time to mitigate the threat
- Escalations and the resources required for short- and long-term fixes

Over time, these data points can be used to identify trends in your monitored environment. Do you repeatedly see issues with assets from the same segment, owner, or type of system? Which reports have been successful in detecting that malicious behavior? Is your average time to remediate within expectations? If containment routinely takes longer than expected, is it due to a broken escalation procedure, ineffective dependent resource, or lack of follow-through by your own analyst? By identifying these problem areas, you now have justifiable audit trails that you can use to improve the entire process. Making this data transparent to everybody involved in the process provides indisputable evidence to hold them accountable and ensure your mitigation and remediation requirements are satisfied.

No one loves working cases, but it's an indispensable part of the job, and the more detail and accuracy you put into your own case data, the better your chances are for surviving an audit and improving your own understanding of the incident. It's also your chance to highlight any issues, architectural or otherwise. For example, could this incident have occurred if we had already implemented a better authentication solution or other components that fellow analysts may find helpful? Any decent case tracking system will provide the option to assign cases to various queues or individuals. This makes escalation much simpler, in that an analyst can simply reassign a case to an escalation engineer when they need more help. Our team uses a custom case tracking system, but it has to integrate with the various commercial incident management systems so we can shift case data between them. We chose not to use an already deployed commercial system because the information contained in our case management system is highly confidential and unavailable to the rest of the company. We need to maintain tight control over the data in our system, and our incident response team handles the complete administration of these tools.

Keep It Running

Your playbook is full of plays that produce events for your analysts to investigate. You have systems to record data points to measure your processes. You're cognizant of how data is presented to your analysts. How do you ensure that your operation continues to run smoothly and that you don't lose sight of why you collected underpants in the first place? To keep it all running, you must do or have:

- Research and threat discovery
- A feedback loop between the operational running of and objective/analysis sections of the playbook
- A tested QA process for submitted plays
- Metrics to refine and improve detection

Your monitoring system depends on continued availability of input data to be processed. If attackers stop the logging service on their victim's host machine, how will you investigate further? Service monitoring and health checks rarely monitor a log process status. Any potential failure point in the system—attackers, hard drive space, processor resources, data feeds, and connectivity—can affect the availability of the data and therefore the entire system. Two fundamental methods of ensuring availability involve building redundancy into your system and monitoring the status of each potential failure point. Redundancy and service monitoring are IT functions not specific to security monitoring. Your senior technical staff with backgrounds in system or network administration should understand the various underlying components that might break, how to detect when they break, and how to build resiliency into the system.

You should perform quality control tests regularly to ensure that your systems are functioning normally. Even with service monitoring of the infrastructure, environment changes can cause unexpected or missing results in reports. Periodic review of tools and processes should include testing detection, analysis, escalation, and mitigation of events. A failure at any of these points may be indicative of a larger problem with the infrastructure. Regulatory compliance or customer/client requirements may also require quality control checks for certain monitored segments. These checks are especially important to ensure reliability when offering monitoring and analysis as a service to clients. As a simple test, we will set up a random DNS lookup or IRC channel join from a host in a sensitive environment, and then wait to see how long it takes the analyst team to discover and escalate it. These types of tests along with coordinated tabletop exercises will keep the team on their toes, and will help ensure that people are always watching the network and ready to pounce on any prescribed or unusual event.

Keep It Fresh

Your organization faces a threat landscape that is ever changing and evolving. Adapting to these changes is the only way to keep your security monitoring program relevant. Ultimately, you are responsible for identifying which threats your organization faces. However, the security community is a collaborative community, sharing intelligence, research, and ideas. If you're at a loss for where to begin, don't fret. News articles, blog posts, conferences, and special interest groups are all excellent sources of information identifying trends in the industry that may be relevant to your organization. You can further supplement the community effort with in-house research by combing through the mountains of data you've collected. Research and threat discovery are the cornerstone by which any good detection logic is built.

Locally sourced intelligence is highly effective, doesn't have any of the disadvantages of a giant statistical cloud offering (*http://www.cisco.com/web/solutions/cloud/index.html*), and can be more precise and effective for your organization. This is particularly true when responding to a targeted attack. If you have gathered evidence from a prior attack, you can leverage that information to detect additional attacks in the future. If they are targeted and unique, there may be no security feed available to tell you about the threat. Another advantage to internal intelligence is that it is much more context aware than a third-party feed. You and the rest of your IT organization —hopefully—know the function and location of your systems. With proper context (that can only be developed internally), external feed data could be extremely helpful, or worthless, depending on your response process and capabilities.

Like the threat landscape, organizations themselves evolve. Staff turnover, reorganizations, new tools, new hires, and promotions all threaten to interrupt the smooth operations of your security monitoring program. Like the aforementioned IT controls, these interruptions are not specific to security monitoring, but also must still be heeded. As discussed in Chapter 5, the playbook itself is structured to include all necessary information relevant to each play. New staff should easily understand what each play is attempting to accomplish, as well as how to analyze results from the play.

In this chapter, we've discussed different metrics to identify workload discrepancies and potential knowledge gaps. It is up to you to interpret these measurements to determine adequate training for your staff, or to adjust analyst responsibilities so that detected events can be investigated. Use the guidance we've provided, and where possible, predict what metrics will be the most important and include them at the beginning. Proper metrics will provide measurement of human performance, as well as report and operational efficiency. This rings particularly true when you are completely replacing an older system, or attempting to measure the return on investment for your efforts related to your playbook.

Creating a playbook is one thing, but (re)designing your incident response team and capabilities around it is something completely different. Not only do you have to have a talented staff and a solid playbook, but you have to think strategically about how to provide the most efficacious security monitoring for your organization. Writing this all down, it makes a lot more sense than the backwards approach we have taken in the past. We started with the tools and technology, and tried to make it fit our idea of what incident response should be. Perfect hindsight shows that we needed a good plan, a better approach, and a battle-worthy process. Taking a structured approach to data preparation and play construction is foundational to our continuous monitoring process. Grooming data unique to our organization, putting smart people in front of it, keeping it updated and relevant, and developing novel ways to detect bad behavior give us the edge that no product or suite of products could ever match.

Chapter Summary

- A playbook is just a plan and a list of actions to take, but it's nothing but an academic exercise without putting it into operation.
- Proper staffing and training are necessary for an effective incident response team.
- Nothing can replace human intelligence and institutional knowledge (context).
- A playbook requires constant tuning and adjustment to stay relevant.
- Several systems and processes are necessary to keep a playbook running:
  — A playbook management system
  — A log and event query system
  — A result display or presentation system
  — A case tracking system
  — A remediation process system

CHAPTER 7

Tools of the Trade

"...a vision without the ability to execute it is probably an hallucination."
—Stephen Case

In the early days of the security industry boom back in the late 1990s, there were only a handful of dedicated security product vendors. Most commercial security tools were offshoots or acquisitions by larger companies, and when the topic of network security tools was discussed, *firewall* or *antivirus* were the first words to come to mind. Today, there are literally hundreds of companies with security products and services that cover just about every aspect of information and network security. From password managers and social media leak detection to content-aware firewalls and breach detection systems, there is an abundance of security technology available. Many vendors offer expensive all-in-one tools or managed security services that purport to take all your data and abstract it into actionable security monitoring. The security industry has grown so huge that it has become a commoditized niche industry. You can spend millions on security solutions under the guise of protecting your network.

However, we reject the concept of the security "black box," or the one vendor that claims to do it all without providing sufficient detail about how detection actually happens or even if it's working properly. Proprietary detection methods and indicators are not helpful when attempting to investigate a possible breach. We know that we can never detect nor prevent 100% of the security incidents 100% of the time. Data matters most, and architectural inadequacies—highlighted by your security tools—help drive precautionary changes. Any solution must provide a rich body of evidence for incident investigation and confirmation. Lacking thorough evidence puts you at risk of failing to detect attacks and unnecessarily disrupting host or user access. Crafting your own playbook is an individualized process that's unique to your organization, regardless of what tools and event sources you already have or plan to acquire. It demands you peel back the cover on your technologies to understand specifically what to look for, what details are available, and more importantly, *how* to detect incidents.

The right tools for your environment depend on a myriad of factors, including budget, scale, familiarity with the products, and detection strategy. With a reliable set of fundamental tools, adherence to security best practices, and a data-centric playbook approach, you can extract and utilize all the information you need. In this chapter, we'll discuss limitations and benefits of core security monitoring and response tools, deployment considerations affecting efficacy and accuracy, examples of successful incident detection, and how to use threat intelligence to enhance your detection capabilities.

Defense in Depth

Just as you need more than a hammer to build a house, you need a variety of tools to properly build out a decent incident detection infrastructure. Defense in depth requires that you have detection, prevention, and logging technology at multiple layers so that you don't miss important event data and evidence for investigations. Remember that you will *never* discover every incident as it happens—there will always be a place for post-hoc investigation. Determined attackers will find a way to flank your defenses no matter how deep, or exploit the weakest link in your systems (usually human trust). However, when it comes time to investigate and trace every step of the attack, you will need as much specific and relevant data as possible to support the investigation. Defense in depth also helps with additional redundancy in security monitoring operations. If a sensor or group of sensors fails, or is under routine maintenance, other tools can fill in at different layers so that complete visibility isn't lost.

Successful Incident Detection

To help shape your thinking about how to build out sufficient defense in depth, let's consider some classic models and compare their layered approaches to network and information defense.

Table 7-1 illustrates the seven layers of the Open Systems Interconnection (OSI) reference model and their corresponding defense-in-depth layers:

Table 7-1. OSI layers mapped to detection layers

OSI model layer	Defense-in-depth layer
Application layer	Log files from servers or applications
Presentation layer	System logging, web proxy logs
Session layer	System logging, web proxy logs

OSI model layer	Defense-in-depth layer
Transport layer	Intrusion detection
Network layer	Wireless intrusion detection and switch port filtering
Data link layer	Switch port controls and filters
Physical layer	Switch port controls and filters

Just like Ethernet frames, datagrams, and packets, good incident detection will build upon layers. Detection logic for application-level security might come from indexed and searchable logs that show what happened before, during, and after a process or application has launched (or crashed). For the application layer, you should be logging all authentication failures and successes on critical systems. At the transport and network layers, you can monitor for unexpected or anomalous connections to Internet hosts, fake IPv6 router advertisements, or unexpected internal host traffic. At the data link layer, you can monitor switch CAM tables for ARP spoofing or (de)authentication attacks on your wireless infrastructure.

Another model to help you think about defense in depth is the "intrusion kill chain," a framework developed in part by U.S. company Lockheed Martin to describe the steps required in a successful attack (Figure 7-1). Advanced attacks by determined adversaries occur in organized, multistage processes, chaining together various methods and exploits to achieve their goal. Just like in an advanced attack, however, defenders can use their own chain to detect or block the attackers' techniques.

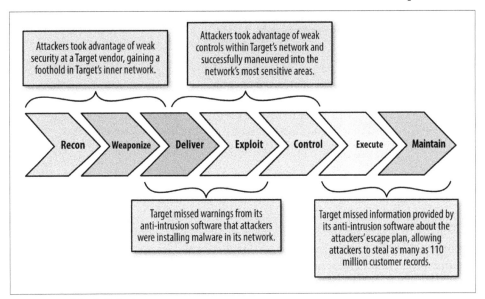

Figure 7-1. The kill chain

Detection capabilities exist for almost every step of the kill chain, whether before or after successful exploitation (Table 7-2).

Table 7-2. Kill chain phases mapped to detection layers

Kill chain phases	Defense-in-depth response
Recon	Recon can be detected by monitoring unusual connections and probes to external web applications, phishing campaigns, or externally facing services with your security sensors. Good results from indicators may get lost in a sea of Internet scanning, but it's worth watching for anomalies from outside and inside the network.
Weaponize	Weaponized exploits can enter your network through numerous methods, but due to high rates of success, the most likely compromise is via email phishing, company website/credentials compromise, or drive-by/watering hole attacks on external services known to be used by the target. Direct attacks on external applications after some probing can be seen in IDS or web/application firewall logs.
Deliver	Network IDS and host-based security like intrusion prevention systems or antivirus can send out an alarm at every stage except the weaponized phase.
Exploit	Antivirus and host intrusion prevention logs can indicate exploit and malware installation attempts.
Control	The control, execute, and maintain stages offer the best chance of successful detection, given that data eventually has to leave your network to return to the attackers or an affiliate.
Execute	System log files, behavior anomaly analysis, or other traps and controls might help to stop the attackers from getting what they came for. Unusual system activity might not be detected. However, better readiness and minding the valuable assets improves your chances of foiling the attackers' plans.
Maintain	Once inside, attackers will persist in retaining control of any successfully compromised system, either to retain a platform from which to launch additional attacks or to continue exfiltrating sensitive and confidential data. Proper password hygiene and top-notch OpSec frustrate or invalidate additional lateral movement, and system authentication logs offer invaluable details.

 What happens if your organization undergoes an unscheduled security audit? If penetration testers start probing your network from the outside, even if it gets lost in the sea of other probes, you can at least point to logs at the end of the audit to indicate you "detected" them. Logs of this type can also be used later when creating a timeline or investigating later.

The big takeaway from both models is the need to have detection at every layer possible. If you only invest in breach detection, intrusion detection, or antivirus, you'll be missing data from a whole class of attacks and techniques. You will still detect event data, but you will never have the complete picture, and reconstructing a timeline will be impossible. Understanding how an incident unfolds enhances an organization's security protections, and it helps avoid compromise a subsequent time by influencing improved architecture and policy standards.

Hack me once, shame on you; hack me twice, shame on me.

Web Attacks

A watering hole attack occurs when an attacker compromises a website known to be accessed by the victim or members of the victim's organization. Like a crocodile waiting for prey to inevitably drink water from the hole, so does the attack wait for their victim to access or log in to the compromised website.

A drive-by attack (or drive-by download) happens when an attacker compromises a victim web application (the patsy), or hosts their own malicious site, and then injects exploits or redirection to other victim sites. In the end, more victims pile up as the attacker's tools (commonly commercial exploit kits) silently execute from the web browsers of unsuspecting victims. Unlike a direct attack on a known site like the watering hole example, attackers leveraging the drive-by method often inject their scripts into syndicated advertising networks to improve victim exposure to their attack.

The Security Monitoring Toolkit

To investigate any security incident, you need evidence. Any worthwhile security monitoring tool will generate event data that investigators can analyze. To build a corpus of information for monitoring the security of your network, you need tools, their data, and somewhere to store and process it. Putting together the right toolkit demands you understand your network topology and scale, your business practices, and where protection is the most critical. It's also important to understand the pros and cons of the various security monitoring tools available. You need to know how to use tools properly to get useful information from them, as well as how the tools actually work. Some abstraction in your toolkit is fine, but the more familiar you are with how the tools operate, the more effective they become. All tools require some level of configuration to ensure they are relevant to your network, and many tools require ongoing tuning to ensure you are not overloaded with useless data. System health monitoring and event validation are paramount if you intend to keep the service running. Remember that, in the end, the tools are what feed data into your playbook. Choose wisely and understand your requirements well before investing in a commitment to any technology.

Log Management: The Security Event Data Warehouse

To execute a playbook efficiently, you need to aggregate all security logs and events into a searchable nexus of data and metadata. Classically, incident response teams pointed their event data to SIEMs for this purpose. However, with modern toolkits and log collection architectures, it's possible to shed the burden of expensive, inflexible commercial SIEMs for a flexible and highly customizable log management system (*http://blogs.cisco.com/security/to-siem-or-not-to-siem-part-i/*). The playbook is about much more than just a tool, like a SIEM, that returns report results. The objectives in the plays help communicate what the team is doing and help prioritize areas to focus on based on "what we're trying to protect." The analysis sections are the documentation and prescription for the analysts; the play comments and feedback are a place for analysts to discuss issues, tweaks, and so on.

Ultimately, having only a SIEM delivering report results without the other support infrastructure around it is less valuable to your organization than the comprehensive playbook. No automation or algorithm can make accurate, situationally aware decisions based on security alerts like a human can. Pairing readable log information with proper understanding of your metadata will yield excellent results. Log management and analysis systems render your information in a variety of configurable ways, opening an enhanced search and reporting engine for logs.

Developing an organization-wide log collection system, containing network, system, and application logs, offers ample benefits to your IT department, as well as InfoSec and application developers. IT and developers need accessible log data for debugging or troubleshooting operational or software issues. For security, we want all syslogs and system logging we can get, along with our multitude of security monitoring technology logs.

Deployment considerations

A log management solution has to be large enough to store all security event logs and speedy enough to allow for event retrieval and querying, but how do you accomplish this? Will you need a 50,000-node Hadoop cluster or a single syslog server? We've described what makes logs useful ("who did what, when, where, for how long, and how did they do it"), meaning that anything that doesn't provide this level of information generally can be discarded. We've also discussed how logs hold the metadata truth necessary for creating repeatable searches and reports for your playbook. A good log management system will return data that looks a lot like the original log data as generated by the system, versus a digested alert produced by a SIEM. Getting closer to the real event gives you much more flexibility in understanding why it happened, and helps to research additional attributes without the prejudice of an automated alert.

The trick to a successful deployment with real log data is to collect and tag what you can, and filter out what you don't need or can't interpret. Adding context inline to raw event data will also help tremendously. For example, if you can flag an IP address in a log event as matching a list of known bad actors, you might look at an alert with more suspicion. It can also be helpful to include internal context as well, such as tagging address ranges by their function (datacenter, domain controllers, finance servers, etc.)

or tagging user IDs with job titles to help recognize targeted attacks against vulnerable and/or valuable targets like executives.

Like with most tools, there are many log management systems available, from commercial to open source with a wide variety of architectures and options. When deciding which tool to choose, consider that a proper log management system needs to:

Be flexible and modular
> It would be naive to think that you'll never add more security event sources to your detection arsenal. The log management system must be able to support future event sources, support various log formats from free to highly structured text, and support log transport methods like syslog over UDP/TCP to Secure FTP (SFTP) and others.

Parse and index log event data
> You must be able to extract usable fields from your log sources. IP addresses, timestamps, event context, and other details are important to break out from the raw log message. This means you will have to employ some type of regular expression against the raw log data to parse and extract fields. After extraction, the fields must be loaded into an index, cluster, table, graph, or database so they can be searched later.

Provide a robust and simple query interface
> Providing an expressive and functional query interface allows your analysts to develop readable and effective queries that lead to playbook plays. Having mathematical and statistical operators available also makes developing queries easier. Often it's helpful to identify trends or outliers in event data. Determining quantity (i.e., number of events, hosts, events by host, etc.) and other statistical relationships will help with both development and report presentation. Supporting a basic syntax or language for query development also enables anyone to share ideas and work on refining their queries or adding more advanced query features as necessary. If the query interface isn't easy to use, it's likely some analysts will use it improperly or not at all. In the event of a security emergency, you also need the ability to retrieve search results quickly rather than spending time developing an overly complex query or graph analysis.

Retrieve log data with ad-hoc and saved searches
> Having all the supported log data in your management system is one thing; knowing how to get useful information from it is another. To create a playbook, you'll need the functionality of saved searches to recall data for later analysis. SIEMs generally deliver canned queries and reports that purport to inform you of security incidents. A log management system should provide a concise method for saving and scheduling searches and reporting event details. Unless you have analysts looking at screens all the time, you'll need a way to queue up event data for future review. Result presentation is also a big factor in deciding which

solution to adopt. If you can develop reports that are readable and understandable, you can move alerts through the team and the standard processes with a common understanding of their significance. Presentation delivery mechanisms like graphs, dashboards, and HTTP or email feeds can give your team and case handling tools plenty of alert data. Exporting event data in any format (JSON, XML, CSV, etc.) is a nice capability that can be leveraged to feed other applications, such as remediation tools, case tracking, or metric and statistical collection systems. Tying your detection systems with other systems improves response time and removes the possibility of human error.

Ensure availability of your log management system and the data feeds contained within
System, network, and database administrators measure their availability in terms of 9s. A 99.999% uptime equates to less than five minutes of downtime total per year. What level of service availability can you expect or are you able to offer to your analysts for the security feeds? Most security monitoring data feeds are dependent on external teams, whether it's a span from a network administrator or event logs from an Active Directory administrator. As a consumer of their data, system maintenance, configuration changes, and hardware or software crashes on systems can cause outages within your own service offering beyond your control. You should set up service availability checks specific to your requirements, and establish escalation procedures with external groups when you detect service interruption.

In a nutshell, the essential pros and cons of log management tools come down to this:

- A SIEM ties you to views and alerts defined by the vendor, or to formats they support, whereas log management gives you flexibility to detect and respond in the method you define.

- Log management systems can provide the flexibility and modularity necessary to discover and respond to threats potentially unknown to canned commercial systems.

- Log management systems require a lot of time investment to ensure they are optimal and expedient, but the return for that time investment is unparalleled visibility.

- Storing and indexing lots of data in a log management system can be expensive, but looking back at a prior event is critical to any incident response operation.

Intrusion Detection Isn't Dead

Having just finished the final touches on a massive intrusion detection deployment for my organization at the time, I was a little disappointed (and incredulous) after reading the widely respected Gartner research group's prediction (*http://www.informa tionweek.com/gartner-intrusion-detection-on-the-way-out/d/d-id/1019463?*) that "IDS as a security technology is going to disappear." The argument back in 2003 was that IDS would become irrelevant as securing systems and network architecture along with additional security controls and risk management would become more ubiquitous. Intrusion detection it turns out was, and remains to be, far from dead. The additional security controls described were easier said than done, and the complexity of datacenters and networks has only increased over the years, making them more difficult to secure. Not to mention the additional risks assumed by partner network interconnects, acquisitions, and cloud-hosted services. Network detection of data exfiltration, external attacks, internal attacks, or any cleartext network traffic that can be matched against a pattern can (and in most cases, should) be monitored by an intrusion detection system. Why? Because an IDS provides a customizable view of a network session, from buildup to teardown, and as such, other than a full packet capture, provides the most possible level of detail. There are countless ways to detect incidents using an IDS, from esoteric TCP sequence number manipulation to simple pattern matching using regular expressions against HTTP. The strength and utility of the IDS boils down to both where you deploy the sensors, and how well you manage and tune their alarms.

The one salient point from the Gartner research article was that an IDS often produces a significant amount of false positives, or alarms that represent only benign activity. This is completely true. However, also consider that if you bring home a new cat and you never feed or vaccinate it, it's not going to be an effective pet either. An IDS is not a plug-and-play technology. It requires proper deployment, tuning, and event management to be a useful tool in your defense-in-depth strategy. Running an IDS network means routine work on the system, so plan to review monitoring techniques and policies regularly. This is so important to our team that members meet weekly to discuss the IDS findings and any tuning issues that need resolution.

Deployment considerations

With most things in the computer world, there is always more than one way to accomplish a task. The same goes for security technologies. There are numerous ways to deploy most of the tools listed in this chapter and IDS presents a classic InfoSec dilemma right out of the gate: Do we block traffic inline, or do we log attacks offline for analysis?

Inline blocking or passive detection. In its most simplistic form, you can send a copy of network traffic to an intrusion detection sensor, or you can deploy it (now called an intrusion *prevention* system, or IPS) inline with network traffic. Inline deployments offer the obvious benefit of transparent traffic blocking or redirection capabilities, similar to that of a network firewall. What sets the IPS apart from a firewall are the signature matching and upper-level protocol inspection capabilities of the sensors. In general, a firewall blocks based on a preconfigured policy. The IPS will block based on a policy, but has much finer controls on when and what to block. Many vendors offer numerous ways to actually block the traffic, including commanding the IPS to generate a firewall rule or ACL to deploy on another device. Most commonly, however, an inline IPS will simply drop the traffic on its incoming network interface.

Inline deployments offer the benefit of both preventing some attacks, as well as generating log data that can be mined and searched later. A new play might look at IPS blocked traffic from internal hosts that might indicate a worm infection or perhaps a malware callback to an external host. Another report might also look for exploit attempts blocked by the IPS from internal hosts attempting to gain unauthorized access (or possibly just penetration testing). Even if a connection is blocked, it's worth noting and investigating, because the source host generating the alarm may either be compromised or up to nefarious activity, potentially including other techniques that may go unblocked or even undetected.

Although inline deployments sound attractive, they are not without their flaws. Of primary concern is the most fundamental component in the system: the network interface. The ubiquitous, cheap pieces of circuit board and copper you are forcing your whole organization's network connectivity through. If it experiences impaired capacity, insufficient throughput, or crashes, what impact will that have on the rest of your network? Redundant sensors all have to inspect the same traffic to ensure continuity. If adequate (and timely) failover or expensive high availability options are not present, a network outage resulting from device unavailability can cause SLA breaches, production roadblocks, wasted resources, and possibly missed attacks.

Hardware failover issues aside, there are other considerations to factor in when planning an inline deployment. It's important to understand that even with the most conservative timer configurations possible, the spanning tree protocol (or rapid spanning tree protocol, RSTP) can fail to reconverge during an inline sensor outage. When an inline sensor goes down in an environment running RSTP, if the switch's configured "hello" time interval expires before the sensor's interface returns to operation, the switch will send traffic down a different path. This means when the sensor returns to service, it may no longer be receiving traffic. Similar problems can occur with routing protocols such as Open Shortest Path First (OSPF) if the timers expire before the IPS comes back online. This type of scenario can occur when a sensor is rebooting or even if a new policy or signature update is applied, forcing a software restart.

The other main issue with inline deployments is signature fidelity. Losing all connectivity due to a hardware or software problem is catastrophic, but there are more sinister problems that are harder to troubleshoot. Network latency and any application or protocol that is sensitive to the additional delay created by IPS inspection can create difficult-to-solve problems. If a TCP or link error occurs on the remote end of a connection, it's possible that an inline sensor may reject the retransmission because the sequence numbers are unexpected, or some other network or transport layer error occurs, resulting in dropped traffic.

More concerning with an inline deployment is the fact that legitimate traffic might be blocked, or that false positive alarms will also result in erroneous blocks. As mentioned previously, constant tuning is required to keep IDS relevant. To stay viable and accepted by users, network security must be as transparent as possible while remaining effective. Blocking or dropping traffic improperly will result in application problems and user-experience degradation. Further, in the event of a targeted attack, you may not want to block the outbound traffic as part of the investigation. For example, if an attacker is attempting lateral movement or data exfiltration within your organization, rather than simply blocking their traffic outright (assuming it's even possible), you may want to gather as much detail as possible (e.g., packet captures, files, etc.) that show the precise attack methods involved. You don't want to tip your hand to any advanced adversary that you are on to them until you have what you need. Once understood and analyzed, it's then acceptable to resume blocking their traffic. Now that you've captured additional data, you have more details to justify even stricter controls to further secure your attacker's targets and watch for new attack indicators.

Additionally, because your sensor is inline with production traffic, expect repeated scapegoating of the device when something goes wrong with the network. Anyone who has completed a successful inline deployment of a security tool has experienced this phenomenon. It's the ugly side of Occam's razor that if something goes wrong, it must be the new technology the security team deployed. This puts the security team in a troubleshooting role anytime something happens that could be blamed on the IPS.

The best approach when going inline is to start with a passive deployment that has no impact to network operations. This gives you time to tune your sensors and get comfortable with their operation while researching failover capabilities and the other foibles of inline technology.

However, if you have made the decision *not* to go inline, the only alternative is passive detection. This means the IDS will not block any traffic and will only send notifications when traffic might have been blocked (were it in inline mode). Remember, in both modes, you still get event log data that can be queried and turned into plays. Passive mode, however, affords you greater confidence in network operations and uptime, and is a desirable approach in environments with higher throughput and uptime sensitivities (ecommerce, trading systems, etc.). Attack traffic will still need to be mitigated, but you will now have log data to further investigate and utilize in your defense-in-depth strategy to stop attacks at other layers.

Location, location, location. Where you put the sensors in your network traffic flow is just as important as deciding whether or where to go inline. When you think about the intended goal of an intrusion detection sensor, you realize in order to provide any value, it needs to be monitoring the most relevant network traffic between systems you are trying to secure.

The most sensitive, and often critical, parts of an organization's IT infrastructure typically occupy the DMZ or the datacenter. DMZ networks are the front face of your organization, whether they are web servers, application services, development labs, or even your Internet connections. With an appropriately restrictive security architecture and adequate network segmentation, only hosts in the DMZ networks should be able to connect to the Internet directly.

Naturally, it makes sense to deploy intrusion detection between the DMZ and the Internet, as well as between the DMZ and the internal network (Figure 7-2). Monitoring these two choke points ensures that you inspect all traffic into and out of your organization's network (unless, of course, wise guys are using a mobile wireless connection like 3G/LTE).

Comprehensive detection coverage demands inspecting at gateways to various classes of traffic, but it also demands data segmentation, or deduplication (e.g., datacenter to Internet traffic may be inspected and logged twice).

In general, the most important business critical systems operate in an organization's internal datacenter. While many applications and services are increasingly hosted externally through third-party extranet or cloud-based vendors, it's rare that an organization won't at least have some critical services operating in their datacenters—local Windows domains and controllers, authentication services, financial systems, sensitive databases, source code, development servers, and many other important pieces of an organization's IT infrastructure. The datacenter boundary is a great place to deploy additional intrusion detection. Anything into or out of the datacenter should be monitored. The same goes for any network segment hosting critical services or data. Choosing the most appropriate network intersections to monitor will greatly improve your deployment experience. Ideally, it would be wise to collect at all possible choke points, like desktop or lab uplinks, or intra-datacenter traffic. For larger organizations, in most cases, the traffic volume for this inline approach is overwhelming and not likely to yield as many actionable results, if only because of the additional volume of data inspected. In smaller environments, monitoring most network interconnects makes sense as long as you can accurately deduplicate alarm data that might have triggered twice for the same connection.

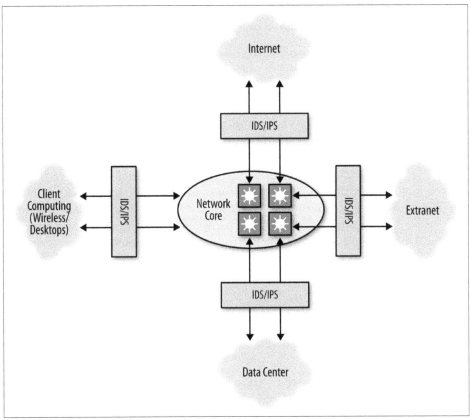

Figure 7-2. An example of an effective IDS or IPS architecture

Let's look at real-world examples

We have already hinted at a few possible reports leveraging the power of IDS. In one specific report, we employed IDS to detect Structured Query Language (SQL) injections. Using the built-in generic SQL injection signatures (looking for classic signs like the SQL commands UNION followed by SELECT, substring((select, Drop Table, or validations like 1=1) combined with a basic string match for some known attacks against content management systems, we developed a report that produces great results when someone is attempting to attack web infrastructure. The following is example data yielded as a result:

```
GET
    /postnuke/index.php?module=My_eGallery&do=showpic&p=id=-
    1/**/AND/**/1=2/**/UNION/**/ALL/**/SELECT/**/0,0,0,0,0,0,0,0,0,0,0,0,0,0,0,0,0,
    concat(0x3C7230783E,pn_uname,0x3a,pn_pass,0x3C7230783E),
    0,0,0/**/FROM/**/md_users/**/WHERE/**/pn_uid=$id/*
    HTTP/1.1
Connection: keep-alive
```

```
User-Agent: Mozilla/5.00 (Nikto/2.1.5) (Evasions:None) (Test:000690)
Host: us-indiana-3.local.company.com
X-IMForwards: 20
Via: 1.1 proxy12.remote.othercompany.com:80
X-Forwarded-For: 10.87.102.42"
```

Notice the User-Agent Nikto (a common web application vulnerability scanner) looking for SQL injection success against the Postnuke content management system running on host *us-indiana-3.local.company.com*. The Via and X-Forwarded-For headers indicate the host's attack was proxied through an external web proxy. Here the IDS digs deep enough into the packet to not only parse the HTTP URI header, but also the HTTP transaction log that gives us the true source IP behind the web proxy. A slight addition to the default generic signatures yields specific data about this attack. We identified the host owners of *10.87.102.42*, and through interviewing, discovered they were performing an authorized penetration test against our host, *us-indiana-3.local.company.com*, without notifying our team beforehand.

IDS can find and report malware infections as well. If host-based protections are absent or have failed, IDS may be able to capture data as it leaves the network. In this example, the IDS detected an HTTP connection that contained no cookie information, no HTTP referrer, and matched a particular URL regular expression—the combination of which are known confirmed indicators of the Zeus banking Trojan:

Signature:

```
alert tcp $HOME_NET any -> $EXTERNAL_NET $HTTP_PORTS (msg:"MALWARE-CNC
   Win.Trojan.Zeus variant outbound
connection - MSIE7 No Referer No Cookie"; flow:to_server,established;
   urilen:1; content:"|2F|"; http_uri;
pcre:"/\r\nHost\x3A\s+[^\r\n]*?[bcdfghjklmnpqrstvwxyz]{5,}[^\r\n]*?\x2Einfo\
   r\n/Hi";
content:!"|0A|Referer|3A|"; http_header; content:!"|0A|Cookie|3A|"; http_header;
   content:"|3B
20|MSIE|20|7.0|3B 20|"; http_header; content:"|2E|info|0D 0A|"; fast_pattern;
   nocase; http_header;
metadata:impact_flag red, policy security-ips drop, ruleset community,
   service http;
reference:url,en.wikipedia.org/wiki/Zeus_(Trojan_horse);
   classtype:trojan-activity; sid:25854; rev:5;)
```

Result:

```
sensor=sensor22-delhi.company.com event_id=154659
msg="MALWARE-CNC Win.Trojan.Zeus variant outbound connection -
   MSIE7 No Referer No Cookie"
sid=25854 gid=1 rev=5
class_desc="A Network Trojan was Detected" class=trojan-activity priority=
   high src_ip=10.20.124.108
dest_ip=[bad.guy.webserver]
src_port=3116 dest_port=80 ip_proto=TCP
blocked=No
```

```
client_app="Internet Explorer" app_proto=HTTP
src_ip_country="india"
dest_ip_country="united states"
```

You can see the source host (`src_ip`) that's making an HTTP callback to a Zeus C2 server (`dest_ip`). Also note the `blocked=No`, which indicates we simply detected this connection and did not block it. Subsequently, after confirming this event with other data sources, we blocked all access to the `dest_ip` from anyone in the organization.

Limitations

IDS is a powerful post-hoc investigation tool only if it correctly captures alarms when something has happened. Unfortunately, you have to know what you want to detect before you detect it, and unless there is already a signature written and available, you will miss out on some attacks. By its nature, a signature-based system will never be fully up to date. A typical IDS signature cannot be developed until an exploit or attack is already identified. The time between exploit release and signature development appears to be shrinking; however, there's also the delaying issues of quality control checking signature updates. Having to make sure a poorly written signature in an automatic signature update doesn't break anything is a lesson learned from years of managing global IDS deployments. This additional testing time subsequently delays both production deployment and rolling the new signature into new or existing reports in the playbook.

Many IDS vendors offer additional inspection capabilities that go beyond simple pattern matching with regular expression in a signature-based format. Anomaly-based detection and automatic threat research from cloud connected services can expand the capabilities of our favorite glorified packet capture and matching device. That said, an IDS has its limitations:

- It must be able to inspect every port and protocol to remain relevant.
- It's dependent on quality and accurate signatures.
- There are multiple, successful IDS evasion techniques available.
- Its output is only as good as its tuning.
- Throughput and performance can become issues on high-traffic networks.
- In general, it has only static (passive) detection methods through a signature-based approach.
- You don't necessarily know if an attack was successful.

Because an IDS alarm fires, it does not mean there's a security incident. Hosts on the Internet with no filtering *will* get port scanned. Because of this simple fact, there's not a lot of value reacting to basic scanning alarms from the Internet toward your systems, although it is worth watching trends and outliers in scanning activity. IDS signatures typically alarm for exploit attempts (via either exploit kits or application vulnerability attacks), known malware signatures, or network or system anomalies observed on the network. If you see a client host connecting to an exploit kit, do you know whether the host was infected? All the IDS really tells us here is that they may have been exposed to malware, but not that it executed. Tying the IDS log data with host-based data or other data sources becomes important to accurately identify an incident worth a response.

The essential pros and cons of network intrusion detection come down to:

- IDS gives you a platform to selectively inspect network traffic and attacks.
- Deployment location is critical for efficacy and impact.
- Tuning is mandatory, and although it can be a lot of initial work, it will eventually pay off in efficiency.
- Inline or passive deployment depends on your appetite for risk versus your tolerance for outage.
- IDS and IPS are both reactive technologies, given their dependence on known signatures. The gap between threat release and signature release is rapidly closing, although they will never be synchronized.

HIP Shot

Network IDS is clearly designed to capture malicious activity when it's headed out the network or into a sensitive area. The chokepoint/outbound detection strategy we use finds plenty of activity, and it's nearly impossible to escape to the Internet without our team noticing. However, one of the main weaknesses of network intrusion detection is that you do not have an accurate depiction of what's occurring in traffic (or system processes) that never crosses a chokepoint. Naturally, if you are watching all the outbound traffic, you will most likely identify call-home traffic; however, if you don't detect it for whatever reason (e.g., infrequent or unpredictable patterns), the attack will still succeed. What's worse is that other internal systems could have been adversely affected and gone undetected. In advanced attack scenarios, lateral movement after compromising a single host (aka patient zero) is a common next technique to maintain a foothold. As aforementioned, you cannot have IDS at every gateway because of performance and scaling issues; therefore, you need an alternative solution for detecting what's happening on intra-subnet and intra-segment traffic. This is where intrusion detection forks into the host-based world.

Deployment considerations

Remember with network IDS (and every other security tool), we are after event logs that we can index and search. With a host-based intrusion detection or prevention system (HIDS/HIPS), we not only block basic attacks and some malware, but we also get log data, rich with metadata specific to the host that can point to malicious activity, as well as attribution and identification data we might not otherwise see on the network.

It's worth differentiating between the commonplace antivirus and the more sophisticated HIPS software. While both technologies can leverage signature-based detection, not unlike a network IDS, HIPS goes a step further allowing application profiling and anomaly detection/prevention with custom rules. A HIPS typically uses kernel drivers to intercept system calls and other information to compare to its policy. Although not a traditional HIPS product due to its focus on different low-level operations, Microsoft's (free) Enhanced Mitigation Experience Toolkit (EMET) has some illustrative capabilities that perform similar to a HIPS. Protecting memory addressing through randomization, preventing data from executing on nonexecutable portions of a stack (Data Execution Prevention), and other memory-based protections give EMET an advantage when it comes to some advanced malware not yet detected by a signature- or file-based system. Remember that a signature-based system, no matter how good, will always be reactive and cannot prevent an attack until it's known. Behavioral or anomaly-based security systems can protect against attacks that have *never been seen*, even if they are never written to a file.

However, a traditional HIPS focuses on file rather than memory-based attacks. The file approach makes techniques like whitelisting work well, particularly for smaller or controlled environments where you can always allow known files and their proper locations, registry keys, etc., without warning or blocking. Another useful HIPS strategy is rather than whitelisting everything, simply raise alarms when certain unusual conditions exist, like Windows registry key permanence changes. A HIPS is also perfect for detecting the download or execution of malware droppers. Some techniques include:

- Watching for writes to protected system directories or even common user directories, including:
  - *%Temp% = C:\Users\<user>\AppData\Local\Temp*
  - *%Appdata% = C:\Users\<user>\AppData\Roaming*
  - *C:\Program Files(x86)*
  - *C:\Windows\System32\drivers*
- User database or registry changes

- Modification of running processes, particularly common services, including *explorer.exe, iexplore.exe, java.exe, svchost.exe, rundll32.exe, winlogon.exe*
- Blocking and/or logging network connection attempts from other hosts

Let's look at real-world examples

This last point is key for developing a strong layer of detection internal to the network. This is where you could find lateral movement—something other network-based tools cannot provide. For example, if a host is compromised (regardless of its HIPS status) and begins scanning or attacking other hosts that are not behind a monitoring network chokepoint, you could rely on other HIPS agents on the network to record a log message that attacks or scans have occurred.

The following example was logged from a HIPS infrastructure:

```
2014-10-30 19:02:08 -0400|desktop-nyc.us.partner|10.50.225.116|
    2014-10-30 19:07:08.000|The process 'C:\WINDOWS\system32\svchost -k
    DcomLaunch' (as user NT AUTHORITY\SYSTEM) attempted to accept a connection
    as a server on TCP port 3389 from 10.50.225.242 using interface PPP\modem\
    HUAWEI Mobile
    Connect - 3G Modem\airtel. The operation was denied.
```

In this alarm example, we see plenty of interesting data. We know that *10.50.225.242* tried to connect to and launch a protected Windows service (svchost) on the HIPS protected host *10.50.225.116 (desktop-nyc.us.partner)* on TCP port 3389. The connection was denied, but we can also see this host was not on our corporate network or wireless infrastructure. The network interface as reported by the HIPS is 3G wireless network. This alarm indicates that a remote host attempted to launch the Windows remote desktop service against one of our internal hosts when they were using their 3G modem. It would be a major concern if the client was using their modem while on the corporate network, as it creates an unprotected bridge to the outside and potentially hostile networks. Remember that you can only have network-based detections at the natural gateways and chokepoints. An out-of-band network connection will go unmonitored, and it presents a significant risk to the organization. The HIPS in this case tells us exactly what happened, to whom, how, and when. It's also possible that this alarm fired when the client had their laptop at a remote location using their 3G modem and was attacked. The alarm may have been subsequently reported when the client reconnected to the corporate network and HIPS head-end log services.

Beyond the attack data in this log message, we also have a wealth of client attribution data. Let's say we don't have a solid system that has a record of who or what asset had a particular IP address at a particular time. Most authentication servers will provide this information when a client authenticates to the network, but what if they were on a network segment that didn't require authentication? From this alarm alone, we know that the system *desktop-nyc.us.partner* had the IP address *10.50.225.116* at least for a few minutes on October 30, 2014, around 11 p.m. UTC. We can apply this information to other event data, which can be helpful if we have other logs that implicate *10.50.225.116* in some other security alert or investigation. What would be even better in this case would be a standard hostname that included a username. Something like *username-win7* could help us immediately find an owner, or at least a human we can question as part of an investigation. We can cross-check bits of metadata here with other security log indexes that may not have any user information. For example, if we are looking at a network IDS log from around the same time that has less information, we can simply refer to this event to find a hostname or username.

The following is another example that provides attribution data, as well as some collateral log data that doesn't necessarily indicate an attack or malware, but can be revealing in the context of an investigation:

```
2014-10-20 07:45:52 -0800|judy32-windows7|172.20.140.227|
  2014-10-20 07:52:22.227|
```

The process 'C:\Program Files\RealVNC\VNC Server\vncserver.exe' (as user NT AUTHORITY\SYSTEM) attempted to accept a connection as a server on TCP port 5900 from 10.1.24.101 using interface Wired\Broadcom NetXtreme Gigabit Ethernet. The operation was allowed.

In this case, we can see the client *10.1.24.101* logged in to user judy32's Windows 7 system using VNC (a common remote desktop sharing application). The HIPS indicated that the connection was allowed. There's nothing here that demonstrates anything nefarious, if the VNC session was expected. If it was not expected, then it would reveal unauthorized access to judy32's PC. If the login was authorized, and then some other malicious event occurred on the PC, we cannot say for certain whether it was judy32 or someone else causing the issue.

Limitations

HIPS has plenty of caveats like any other tool. Primarily, it's another piece of client software that has to be installed. If your organization doesn't have tight control over every endpoint, then a HIPS deployment will never reach full coverage, leaving you exposed on unprotected hosts. If you already have security software running like antivirus or other security software, there may be client or support fatigue in keeping them all running at the expense of system performance. The HIPS software, like any other, will have system requirements that may not be possible, depending on your environment, standard software images, and hardware profiles. Where hosts are not fully managed by a central IT authority, the endpoint client environment software and configuration diversity will require a significant investment in tuning the HIPS detection profiles. This is not that different from network IDS, but it's an often overlooked fact about a HIPS deployment. In an opt-in-style system, imagine the possible variations of client applications that may require filtering or tuning after the HIPS is loaded onto the system.

Another consideration is the host type itself. Adding any additional software, particularly agents with potential kernel shims, introduces a bit more risk to stability and availability. A system administrator or system policy may not allow installation of any uncertified software on critical services like a domain controller, directory, or email server.

All intrusion detection requires tuning, and the HIPS is not exempt. Tuning a HIPS can be a very complex and ongoing process, depending on the complexity of the software profiles on the client PCs. The more you can safely whitelist up front, the easier the tuning will be. Categorizing log data into application exploits, network events, and known blocked malware can make developing playbook reports easier because basic detection categories of HIPS alarms are already set. Proper filtering will help reduce the HIPS server database footprint, while providing only usable security log information. Logging all *.exe downloads seems like a great idea to detect malware; however, if users are allowed to download and install anything, searching through the large resultant data set will require plenty of tuning to ignore false events. However, logging when new *.exes are launched from a protected system directory (particularly if the source process is in a user temporary directory) offers a narrow view into possible malicious activity.

As with all security event sources, if the logs are never reviewed, then the tool is dramatically less effective. HIPS can generate enormous amount of log data, filled mostly with benign or useless information. Monitoring fatigue will be common until precise reports are developed. Tuning the HIPS alarms to ensure you receive the most useful data (i.e., operations monitoring the most sensitive parts of a system), as well as removing information about legitimate software, requires significant effort, but will produce an extremely helpful corpus of log data that fills the intra-network detection gap. HIPS plays an integral part in the host-based defense layer and can inform on areas that network monitoring may miss.

The essential pros and cons of host intrusion detection come down to:

- Client-side security offers unparalleled visibility to what's happening with a host. Network-based detection is mandatory, but good host controls provide something that the network cannot.

- HIPS can offer additional, useful information that can help with user/host attribution.

- Not every system can run a HIPS, and like all IDS technologies, investment in tuning the alarms is mandatory.

- HIPS logs can be chatty (even after tuning), although they can leave invaluable clues after an incident.

- Host-based controls are difficult to maintain and implement in areas where there is little control over the end-user computing environment (mobile devices, personally owned devices, etc.)

Hustle and NetFlow

The concept has many names: NetFlow, Jflow, Netstream, Cflowd, sflow, and IPFIX. Vendor implementations and standards definitions vary slightly, but the essence is the same. Each technology creates a record of connections—a flow—between at least two hosts, including metadata like source, destination, packet/byte counts, timestamps, Type of Service (ToS), application ports, input/output interfaces, and more. Cisco NetFlow v9, as defined in RFC 3954 (*http://www.ietf.org/rfc/rfc3954.txt*), is considered the industry standard, and is the basis for the IETF standard IP Flow Information Export (IPFIX) (*http://tools.ietf.org/html/rfc7011*). As the IPFIX RFC points out, there are multiple definitions for a "flow." Simply put (and per the IPFIX RFC definition), a flow is "... a set of IP packets passing an Observation Point [a location in the network where IP packets can be observed] in the network during a certain time interval." Functions applied to each flow determine the aforementioned metadata.

Unlike other data sources such as packet captures, IDS, or application logs, NetFlow is content-free metadata—simply put, this means that the details of what transpired *in* the connection are not reflected in the flow data itself. Historically, this has meant NetFlow was primarily suited for things like network troubleshooting or accounting, where it was more important to know that a connection happened than to know what transpired during the connection. However, though NetFlow lacks payload data, it is still useful as a security monitoring and incident response tool. From our experiences, NetFlow is used in almost every investigation, whether it's to create a timeline of compromise, identify potential lateral movement of an attacker, provide context for an otherwise encrypted data stream, or simply to understand the behavior of a host on the network during a suspected time window.

Deployment considerations

Like the other network-based detection methods, the placement of your NetFlow collection infrastructure has a huge impact on your results. Just like there are numerous versions and takes on the NetFlow/IPFIX concept, there are also a number of ways and configurations to consider when deploying flow collection.

1:1 versus sampled

Often, network administrators configure NetFlow to export only a sample set of flows. Sampling is fine for understanding the performance and state of network connections, and helps reduce the overhead for flow storage space and traffic between a flow exporter and collection. But in the context of security monitoring or incident response, sampled NetFlow introduces gaps in the timeline analysis of a host's behavior. Without a 1:1 flow export ratio, it's impossible for you to understand exactly what happened before, during, and after a compromise.

We've heard it many times before—the fear that exporting 1:1 flows will cause performance hits on routing devices. However, 1:1 NetFlow should not cause a degradation in performance. On most platforms (dependent upon hardware), NetFlow is hardware switched, meaning that the processing happens on application-specific integrated circuits (ASICs). In effect, this offloads processing resources from the processor to hardware, so the impact on performance of the router is minimal. You must work with your network administrators to understand the need for and to configure non-sampled NetFlow data at all your export locations.

NetFlow on steroids

NetFlow has historically been a content-less data source that describes which hosts connected to whom, at what times, and over what ports, protocols, and interfaces. If you only look at flow data, information about the content of those connections or the data being transferred between hosts can only be inferred via context. Host naming standards, DNS hostnames, common port assignments—they all reveal some bit of possible information about a connection. For the purposes of this book, the authors generated a NetFlow record for what looks like a typical web connection:

Start time	End time	Client IP	Client port	Server IP	Server port	Client bytes	Server bytes	Total bytes	Protocol
2014-04-28T15:03:22Z	2014-04-28T15:03:22Z	10.10.70.15	51617	192.168.10.10	80	10212	3606	13818	tcp

From this flow record, we can see that source host *10.10.70.15* made a 10212 byte TCP transfer from port 51617 to port 80 on destination host *192.168.10.10*.

Though at first glance this may look like a typical web connection, the flow record in and of itself doesn't necessarily indicate that a client connected to a web server on port 80. You need additional context to determine if this was actually an HTTP connection. Or do you?

Neither NetFlow nor IPFIX have built-in fields for the purpose of identifying applications. Application identification has historically been left to the collector, based on the flow's port. Attackers often obfuscate their network connections simply by running services on nonstandard ports, rendering port-based application techniques untrustworthy. Thankfully, the IPFIX authors, in the Information Model for IP Flow Information Export (RFC5102 (*https://tools.ietf.org/html/rfc5102*)), included the ability for vendors to implement proprietary information elements, beyond the standard elements such as port, source IP address, and protocol. Vendors can now use proprietary Deep Packet Inspection (DPI) engines to determine the application observed in a flow based on flow contents, and record that information in a flow record via custom information elements.

Cisco submitted RFC6759 (*http://www.ietf.org/rfc/rfc6759.txt.pdf*), an extension to IPFIX that includes new information elements identifying application information in flows such as the observed application description, application name, tunneling technology, and P2P technology. Cisco's vendor-specific NetFlow DPI application identification implementation is called Network-Based Application Recognition (NBAR (*http://www.cisco.com/c/en/us/products/collateral/ios-nx-os-software/network-based-application-recognition-nbar/prod_case_study09186a00800ad0ca.html*)). Palo Alto Networks offers a similar classification technology called App-ID (*https://www.paloal tonetworks.com/content/dam/paloaltonetworks-com/en_US/assets/pdf/tech-briefs/ techbrief-app-id.pdf*), Dell's SonicOS calls it Reassembly-Free DPI, and ntop's implementation is called nDPI (*http://www.ntop.org/products/ndpi/*).

What then, should you make of the previous example flow if one of the vendor-specific IPFIX application identification extensions instead identifies the traffic as FTP, TFTP, Telnet, or Secure FTP? Are the combination of `tcp 80` and those protocols an indicator of subversive data exfiltration, or simply a misconfigured service? At a minimum, it's worth contacting the host owner for follow-up, or setting up a packet capture in the hopes of collecting the entire transaction during a future occurrence.

Let's look at real-world examples

Limiting the usage of flow data to only post-incident investigations would sell short its potential as a means for detection and response. NetFlow works best for detecting threats where understanding the content of the communication is not paramount to identifying the attack. Simple NetFlow metadata provides enough detail to confirm the results from a play detecting any connections to known malicious IP addresses or networks.

NetFlow also performs well detecting policy violations. For example, let's presume we have PCI or HIPAA segregated data, or a datacenter policy explicitly defining allowed service ports. We can detect potentially malicious traffic to these networks by searching for connections from external or on disallowed ports. Although it seems trivial, these types of reports are amazingly helpful. Consider the play where we monitor NetFlow for any outbound/Internet TCP connections to blocked ports at the edge firewall. *Any* traffic that returns from this report demands immediate investigation as it might reveal the firewall has been misconfigured or is malfunctioning. The best thing about these plays is that with proper network administration, they should rarely generate an alert.

A slightly more complicated use of NetFlow for detection is to use the data to detect UDP amplification (DoS) attacks (*http://blogs.cisco.com/security/a-smorgasbord-of-*

denial-of-service/). Simply put, UDP amplification attacks abuse the ability to spoof the source address of UDP packets and to send a very small amount of data to a service which will respond with a disproportionately larger amount of data to the spoofed source. The more disproportionate the response, the larger the amplification factor, and the bigger the attack. The first step is to block all UDP services susceptible to amplification from your network entirely. The next step is to detect those services via vulnerability scans so that you can get them patched, shut down, or filtered. Yet another step is to prevent spoofing attacks via your networking gear. However, on a large and complex network, blocking and proactively scanning for unwanted services often isn't enough. For thorough defense in depth, you must also detect abuses of the UDP services. We'll discuss this concept further in Chapter 9.

Besides proactive monitoring, NetFlow excels during investigations, acting as the glue between different data sources and providing thorough timelines of network activity. No matter the initial source of an event—IDS, web proxy, external intel, employee notification—NetFlow can be used to identify all connections to or from a host or set of hosts around the time of the original event. The number of use cases is nearly limitless. NetFlow can identify outbound connections initiated after malware is dropped on a host, the possible origin of lateral movement, data exfiltration via abnormally large or sudden transfers, or additionally infected hosts communicating with a known C2 server. Even though attackers can host their infrastructure anywhere in the world, NetFlow can help detect connections to unexpected locations around the globe. If your goal is to understand what transpired on the network during a given timeframe, NetFlow is the data source you'll need.

Limitations (and workarounds)

As with all tools, none is perfect. NetFlow suffers from data expiration, directionality ambiguity, device support, and limitations from its use of UDP as a transfer protocol.

Realities of expiration

When a flow starts, the routing device stores information about the flow in a cache. When the flow is complete, the flow is removed from the cache and exported to any configured external collectors. There are five criteria a NetFlow exporter can recognize to know when a flow has completed and is ready for export to a collector:

- Idle flow (based on a specified time)
- Long-lived flows (30-minute Cisco IOS default)
- A cache approaching capacity
- TCP session termination
- Byte and packet counter overflow

Proper TCP session termination—FIN or RST—is the most obvious. This implies the router observed the initial TCP three-way handshake, all the way through to a proper teardown. In this case, you can be reasonably certain the connection was properly terminated, though there is also the possibility a TCP Reset attack terminated the connection prematurely. Counter overflow becomes an issue when using NetFlow v5 or v7, as those NetFlow configurations use a 32-bit counter instead of the optional 64-bit counter available in NetFlow v9. Consider lowering your cache timeout of long-lived flows if using an older version of NetFlow that doesn't support the 64-bit counters.

Long-lived flows, a cache near capacity, and idle flows all present somewhat of a problem when using NetFlow for analysis. Most NetFlow collectors can compensate for long-lived flows that have been expired from the exporting device, via an aggregation or stitching capability. This aggregation occurs during search time. For instance, the popular open source tool nfdump (*http://nfdump.sourceforge.net/*) will aggregate at the connection level by taking the five-tuple TCP/IP values—Protocol, Src IP Addr, [source] Port, Dst IP Addr, [destination] Port—and combining that into one result with the flow duration and packet count:

```
2005-08-30 06:59:54.324  250.498 TCP   63.183.112.97:9050  ->
   146.69.72.180:51899   12   2198   10
```

Why is this important and how might it affect your usage of NetFlow data? Consider a long-running flow for which you don't know the beginning or end. If you query NetFlow data for that flow, does your tool only query within the window you specified, or will it pad the beginning and end, looking for additional flows to aggregate into the result presented to you? If the former, how can you be certain that your results include flows outside the time-window for which you queried? Some tools will in fact go back in time to look for flows that should be aggregated. As a best practice, you should consider extending your search to include a larger time range or testing your infrastructure to see how it reacts when expired flows span a time range greater than your query.

Directionality

In the context of security monitoring or incident response, we must always be able to determine the source and destination of any connection. Recall that by definition, a flow is unidirectional. You can get an idea of a connection's direction by looking for the three-way handshake, and piecing together the source as the sender of the SYN and subsequent ACK, and the destination as the sender of the SYN-ACK. But what about UDP? What if the three-way handshake for the flow you're observing happened well outside of the query window for the results available to you?

Unfortunately, some tools determine directionality strictly on port usage. Ports less than 1024 are considered "server" ports, and those greater than 1024 are considered client ports. For the majority of connections, this common port allocation holds true. However, security monitoring means tracking hackers, who by definition like to break things. Let's refer back to the original NetFlow example discussed in the previous section. NetFlow identified the source host as *10.10.70.15* and the destination host as *192.168.10.10*. However, the NetFlow query indeed *incorrectly* identified the source and destination. The authors specifically crafted a simple scenario where the collector improperly assigned source and destination tags to hosts in the flow. How then do you know if the client/server designation is a result of the port usage (client port 51617; destination port 80), of seeing a TCP three-way handshake, or something else entirely? Ultimately, you can and should test your infrastructure, as we did for this example. But you can also look at some NetFlow metadata to give you a better idea of how flows traverse your network.

NetFlow v9 exports include field 61 (DIRECTION), a binary setting indicating whether the flow is ingress or egress on the interface exporting flow data. If you know your NetFlow exporters (you do know your network, right?), being able to determine whether a connection was incoming or outgoing from a particular interface will help you to establish directionality. If you export flows from one interface on a border gateway device, and the flow DIRECTION field says the flow was ingress, you can be fairly certain the flow was coming from external and is inbound to your network. You still have the problem of knowing whether or not all of the flows for that connection are aggregated. But repeating this process for all observed flows between the two hosts in a connection will help you to identify the true source and destination of the connection.

Device support

Not every piece of network gear you have will support NetFlow (full or sampled) or DPI capabilities, nor do you necessarily want exports from all devices that do. Like all other tools, at a minimum you need to have visibility of all ingress and egress traffic to and from your environment. Most organizations won't have enough storage and network capacity to collect flow data between all hosts on every subnet. But by all means, if you have a segment containing your crown jewels, consider exporting NetFlow data from the aggregation router of that environment. Where you lose visibility due to NAT, consider exporting NetFlow from both in front of and behind the NAT translation. Bear in mind, though, that depending on where you place your gear, you may end up exporting duplicate data. Can your collector aggregate and account for identical flows exported at different points in the network? Can you account for the increase in storage space due to duplicate flows?

UDP

NetFlow doesn't inherently provide any confidentiality, integrity, or availability (CIA) of your flow data. Flows are exported using UDP as a transport protocol, and all the limitations of UDP data transfer equally apply to your flows. A lack of sequencing, handshakes, flow control, and potential for spoofing all contribute to an inability to uphold the holy trinity of CIA. As a result, any precautions you take for other UDP services should be extended to your flow data. Monitor for network saturation, which could cause potential packet loss and incomplete flow records. Ensure you have controls like Universal Reverse Path Forwarding (uRPF) to prevent spoofing attempts on the networks where you export and collect flow data. Overall, be aware that your flow data is subject to the same limitations presented by any service utilizing UDP for transport.

The essential pros and cons of NetFlow come down to:

- Integral for both reactive investigative support and proactive detection plays.
- From a security perspective, full (i.e., unsampled) NetFlow is imperative to have any chance of understanding a complete timeline of activity.
- Modern features, such as DPI application identification, provide additional capabilities beyond those from basic NetFlow metadata.
- Vendor support for NetFlow varies, and there are few exhaustive solutions that go beyond just flow collection.
- Underlying NetFlow dependencies, such as UDP for transport and client search capabilities, introduce possible ambiguities and should be thoroughly understood to properly interpret and understand flow data.

DNS, the One True King

Let's just start by saying: DNS is awesome. It's fundamental to the Internet's success and operation and has so many uses in the context of security monitoring and incident response. Without going into excruciating detail about how the protocol works, think how difficult it would be if rather than getting a street address from someone, you had to use latitude and longitudinal coordinates to find their house. Sure, you can do it, but it's a lot easier to remember a simple street address. In much the same way, DNS provides us with an easier Internet location service. I can type *www.cisco.com* into my browser rather than *[2001:420:1101:1::a]*. If I'm using a search engine, searching for the DNS hostname of a website will get me there much faster. And to keep things interesting, it uses (mostly) UDP. Zone transfers (TCP) can be monitored through IDS logging or DNS server logs.

There are about forty DNS record types, many for obscure or not widely adopted DNS services. However, for our purposes we're interested in mostly:

- A (address record)
- AAAA (IPv6 address record)
- CNAME (record name alias)
- MX (mail exchange record)
- NS (nameserver zone record for authoritative servers)
- PTR (pointer record, for reverse DNS lookups—resolving an IP to a hostname)
- SOA (details about a zone's authoritative information)
- TXT (can be stuffed with all kinds of interesting info from malware)

These records provide the most usable information for data mining when looking for security events. Many of the other types related to Domain Name System Security Extensions (DNSSEC) or other applications are mostly relevant for troubleshooting, authentication, and DNS management.

Because malware authors are human like the rest of us, they too utilize DNS for much of their network communications. DNS hostnames are one of the most fruitful outputs of malware analysis. If we pick apart malware, we are not only looking to see what the program does to the victim's computer, but we are also looking to see what outbound connections are made. Most often, communications leverage DNS rather than a raw IP address. Hostnames reserved by attackers are easy indicators to search for. Attackers may leverage dynamic DNS services to stay more resilient to takedowns, or they may actually purchase and reserve a list of domains from a registrar. In either case, when we have basic controls over the organization's DNS infrastructure, we can detect and block any hostname or nameserver, including authoritative nameservers for huge swaths of domain names and hosts.

Leveraging DNS for incident response boils down to:

- Logging and analyzing DNS transactions
- Blocking DNS requests or responses

While many tools like IDS can be used for logging attempts by victims to resolve known bad hostnames (i.e., white/black list), the best approach is to log select DNS transactions using Passive (*http://blogs.cisco.com/security/tracking-malicious-activity-with-passive-dns-query-monitoring*) DNS (*http://blogs.cisco.com/security/tracking-malicious-activity-with-passive-dns-query-monitoring*), or pDNS. Passive DNS packet collection gives you visibility into the DNS activity on your network that you won't always get from the logs on your own recursive (caching) nameservers or from external DNS services.

To block requests to external (or even internal) hostnames, the most effective approach leverages BIND's response policy zone feature (RPZ). RPZ allows you to substitute a normal response for a response of your own or no answer at all. This lets you lie to a client requesting a known malicious domain and instead tell it the domain doesn't exist (NXDOMAIN). Taking it a step further, you can forge a response and point the client at a sinkhole hosting pseudoservices to collect even more information about malware that attempts to reach out to domains we redirect with RPZ. A honeypot approach combined with a DNS redirected sinkhole can be used to discover attack attributes useful for additional detection. For our purposes, we focus on pDNS and RPZ as the tools built on top of the DNS protocol, and leverage a sinkhole to collect additional intelligence as it unfolds.

Deployment considerations

Collecting DNS traffic or log data can be a challenge, particularly if you host your own DNS services or have a large network. There are also numerous ways to leverage the data once collected, and it all depends on your analyst capabilities and appetite for DNS-flavored metadata.

Little P, big DNS

Think for a moment how much network traffic crosses your organization's border to the Internet. Each new connection that leverages DNS (most likely all of them) will generate a request to the authoritative DNS server. If your laptop needs to reach *www.infosecplaybook.com*, it will ask your organization's DNS servers what IP address matches up with the hostname requested. If your DNS server doesn't already know the answer (that is, have the A and AAAA records cached), then the DNS server will recursively ask the authoritative upstream DNS servers for *www.infosecplaybook.com*. This lookup may in turn require that the DNS server looks up the authoritative server for *.com* and so forth. This leaves you with two possible locations to log your client's request: on the way in to your internal DNS servers, or on the way out, to DNS servers to external to you. Multiply this by the complexity of recursive lookups and all the clients attempting DNS resolution, and now you have millions of DNS queries and DNS responses. Even at a small organization, the number of DNS transactions can grow quickly.

There are a couple ways to tackle this mass of data. One way is to log the DNS transactions on the DNS server itself. Both BIND and Microsoft Active Directory (the two most common DNS server applications) provide options for logging client requests and server responses. With more logging comes additional burden on the server, including additional processing and configuration complexity. Server logging is certainly an option, but to remove any possibility of problems for the DNS admins brought on by your incident response team, the best solution is to capture DNS network traffic, extract the information you want, index it, and then make it available for searching. Just like a passive IDS, you can set up a pDNS sensor to collect specific traffic using something like libnmsg (*https://archive.farsightsecurity.com/nmsgtool/*), or ncap (*https://www.dns-oarc.net/tools/ncap*), which according to the DNS Operations, Analysis, and Research Center's (DNS-OARC) official site:

> is a network capture utility like libpcap (on which it is based) and tcpdump. It produces binary data in ncap(3) format, either on standard output (by default) or in successive dump files. This utility is similar to tcpdump(1), but performs IP reassembly and generates framing-independent portable output. ncap is expected to be used for gathering continuous research or audit traces.

There are two sides to DNS activity that you can passively capture. For the purposes of monitoring and incident detection, the most valuable packets to capture are the DNS queries made by your clients. With all the DNS query packets, you can determine all the domains the client attempted to resolve, or the number of clients attempting to resolve a specific domain. The other side of the DNS transaction is the responses sent back to your clients. Seeing the DNS responses can be valuable for investigating a specific malicious IP address, domain, or an infected client, as well as monitoring the evolution of an attack campaign.

With the DNS responses, you'll have responses for requests like "Show me all of the domains resolving to this IP" and "Show me all of the IPs this domain has resolved to." The difference between the client queries and nameserver responses is more significant than it may seem at first. Not only do they support different aspects of the security investigation and monitoring process, but they also tend to support semantically different queries.

Client queries

If you're going to successfully capture the query packets from clients, you have to capture as closely as possible to them. Most likely, the bulk of your client DNS traffic will be between your client and a "nearby" local nameserver. If the query packets can make it from the client to a nameserver without crossing a capture point, then instead of seeing the client make the query, you'll see the nameserver's data only when it queries recursively to upstream authoritative nameservers on behalf of the client. If your recursive DNS server deployment is relatively small, it may be possible to deploy a collector in front of every nameserver, and another collector at your network border to capture the stray DNS packets that weren't destined for your local nameservers (think Internet-hosted DNS services—8.8.8.8, for example). Hosts resolving addresses using external DNS servers may have something to hide. If you have a big network with a complex local recursive nameserver deployment, you'll need to take a more blended approach and capture DNS packets at network chokepoints just like the other tools. You may end up with good coverage of most DNS query activity, but still have some blind spots where clients are able to short-circuit your collectors and reach a recursive nameserver directly.

Server responses

Capturing the DNS query responses is a vastly simpler problem than capturing client queries. For the most part, every response you'll ever be interested in is for an external domain name. Because none of your local recursive nameservers will be authoritative for external domains, all DNS responses will originate from external nameservers and cross your network border into your network at least once before the response gets cached. If you deploy one collector for each Internet connection you have, you can get complete coverage for your organization. Unlike client queries, though, having complete visibility of all of the responses your organization has seen may not be enough for thorough investigations.

Broadly, there are two main reasons why. First, you may learn about domains via external intelligence feeds, but you've never seen your clients look up any of those domains. You don't have historical visibility into the responses received, which muddies the waters on whether the threat is still active. Second, the responses your clients are seeing may not be the same responses other organizations are seeing, and they may not be the same responses you'll see tomorrow. No single organization has enough data to piece together a complete picture for the current hostility of a given domain. Therefore, global visibility into DNS responses is quite valuable. Global DNS response visibility sheds light on emerging threats, as well as threat actor groups, by profiling the data. Constant changes in domain names, freshly registered and recently accessed names, domain registration patterns, and many other indicators can be analyzed and used to develop block lists and additional monitoring reports. There are a few services and intelligence feeds that provide visibility, but the current leader is Farsight Security's DNSDB service (*https://www.dnsdb.info/*).

RPZed

With the undeniable importance and power of DNS, the ability to block or subvert the DNS resolution process can be very powerful for incident investigation, mitigation, and containment. Just as IP addresses are clumsy for human usage (can you imagine "Visit our website at 173.37.145.84 today!"), they're also a clumsy mitigation measure for trying to block activity related to a domain name. The natural choice for blocking or redirecting a hostname is at the recursive nameserver used by the client. DNS RPZ provides a fast, flexible, and scalable mechanism for controlling the responses returned to clients, based on security policy triggers loaded into the nameservers configuration dynamically. Think of DNS RPZ as a DNS firewall that can filter out certain requests from ever succeeding, depending on your block or redirect criteria.

Four policy triggers to rule them all

For maximum flexibility, RPZ provides four different types of policies for triggering a security response instead of the intended DNS response (see Table 7-3). The most straightforward policy trigger is based on the name being queried by the client (QNAME). A QNAME policy for *www.bad.com* will tell the nameserver to not provide the normal response back to the client. The remaining three policy triggers are based on data learned by the nameserver in the process of recursing to resolve the queried domain. The IP policy trigger allows you to provide a RPZ response for any domain that resolves to a particular IP address. The other two policy triggers enable blocking of domains, based on the IP address of their authoritative nameserver or their authoritative nameserver's name (the NS record).

Table 7-3. Four types of policy triggers

	Client request	Server IP address	Nameserver IP address	Nameserver hostname
QNAME	X			
NSIP			X	
IP Address		X		
NSDNAME				X

With these four policy trigger types, you can block or intercept the queries for huge blocks of malicious domains. For example, if your organization blocks any known malicious IP addresses or classless interdomain routing (CIDR) ranges, you can also RPZ all of the domains that would resolve to blocked IPs or that use nameservers you have blocked. Doing this means you can RPZ domains you didn't even know your clients were looking up. Your RPZ logs provide great context for some of the domains in your pDNS Query logs. That is, if internal clients are repeatedly resolving known bad sites, there may be lingering infections or callbacks trying to succeed.

Don't block; subvert

The real power of DNS RPZ isn't just the ability to block queries your clients make. Because RPZ happens in the nameservers you control, you can configure RPZ to forge a fake response to the query and redirect the client to a machine you control (a sinkhole). With a sinkhole, you can emulate common services like HTTP, set up network detections in front of it, and collect logs of the requests being made or the data being sent. This is like giving a police department the ability to swap out a drug dealer for an undercover cop mid-transaction. With data like that, the police would be much better at tracking criminal drug organizations! The actual technical way DNS RPZ redirects queries to a sinkhole is by forging a CNAME record claiming the domain looked up is actually an alias to your sinkhole machine. When you combine the data recorded in your RPZ logs with the data in your sinkhole and pDNS systems, you can monitor for incidents much better than you'd be able to do without any DNS visibility or control. For example, you can set up HTTP, SMTP, IRC, or any listeners to intercept any communication attempts to these services on the intended domain, the one you redirected with RPZ to your sinkhole.

Let's look at real-world examples

There are many useful plays available through mining pDNS and RPZ/Sinkhole log data. With some additional metadata, you can find new infections by analyzing sinkhole logs for potentially compromised systems querying for previously RPZ filtered domains. DNS filtering hampers the malware by preventing successful connections to C2 servers, but also leaves a log trail of compromised hosts still trying to connect to defunct attackers. Further investigation into common indicators and unusual DNS activity will yield additional conclusive results. Sinkhole log analysis could involve looking for:

Results with no HTTP referer
   From the sinkhole HTTP service logs

Results to seemingly random hostnames (i.e., domain generation algorithms [DGA])
   The following table breaks down the event into metadata elements (source, hit count, domains, URL, time range) and values (*192.168.21.83, 64, /wpad.dat*, etc.) Note the request for *wpad.dat*, or the Web Proxy AutoDiscovery JavaScript file, from these seemingly random domains:

Source	Hit count	Domains	URL	Time range
192.168.21.83	64	eumeiwqo.com	/wpad.dat	4h
		frtqgzjuoxprjon.com		
		idppqjvwwtfoj.com		
		jarigtvffhkgrvz.com		
		ohvxvkytfr.com		
		oisjuopdi.com		
		qrjnenmjz.com		
		qvcquqvjl.com		
		rqtdkahvoeg.com		
		uzmgyvgqctou.com		
		vdicplctstkpmjm.com		
		xmbeuctllq.com		

Source	Hit count	Domains	URL	Time range
		xqflbszk.com		
		ygyfzxkkn.com		
		ysiefuwipz.com		

We could reasonably assume that malware on *192.168.21.83* is attempting to reach out to those domains, and that the event most likely does not represent normal activity on that system.

Clues in the URL_String *that point to data beaconing or data exfiltration*

For example, URLs containing *in.php*, *id=*, lots of base64 encoding, weak encryption/XOR, configuration file downloads, tracking scripts, authentication parameters, and others. In this example, you can actually see a binary file called *cfg.bin* posted by the likely infected client to an unusual remote web server:

```
2015-07-09 01:38:58.064865 src=192.168.21.183 client_bytes=5403
    dest="dunacheka.meo.ut" dest_port=tcp/80 url="/admin/cfg.bin"
    http_method="POST" "http_user_agent="Mozilla/4.0 (compatible;
    MSIE 7.0; Windows NT 6.1; Trident/4.0; SLCC2; .NET CLR 2.0.50727;
    .NET CLR 3.5.30729; .NET CLR 3.0.30729; .NET4.0C; .NET4.0E;
    InfoPath.2)"
```

This table provides additional examples of potentially malicious URL parameters:

Source	Hit count	Domains	URL	Time range
192.168.21.89	32	bro.dubaiii.net	/pagetracer/duba/__utm.gif?param=RURJSxAAAAB KAAAAAQAAAHicSOwuyczPyOvMTbVNzMksS1UrqS xItTU3MrCwNFMrLc1MsTWyMDJ2cjE2MHQxc3ZxdHU0dnJ2 dDY0NzQ1dnZxMjZOAgDVEhNK	4h

Note the "pagetracer" in this example, followed by the "param" parameter loaded with a base64 value. Although having large base64 values for URL parameters is commonplace, looking at the name of the script combined with an idea on the validity of the domain can help shake out potential attackers or fraudulent activity.

The following table shows the client host *192.168.21.52* attempting connections to oddly named domains at presumptively obfuscated scripts. Most likely, these connections are not legitimate nor requested by a human:

Source	Hit count	Domains	URL	Time range
192.168.21.52	14	4jun3vxnu2o376llv4ynuydu5xhgwtvjq qfagcm7rfclhiwe7rmpz6eify.wonderful -nature.org	/x/?AFwVKo11t4mJnU2lWxFQtOc=	4h
			/x/?RQHbZiOsJ5/n7yP4hq+HyWM=	
		ezwobvb2qivshlekef2ti4v7ia7tz7jhjtk mguk5yjoxhvklc32y27klde.wonderful-nature.org	/x/?Y/lOzY7y81Fqwd/u5nS0jlo=	
			/x/?ddCCQjRTxrdPgtuUx5l5wjc=	
		hp7xx2csnhfoo2iw5izgv235tdfiag4w mq3cmdysnhcxa6zhbhgh7ktoum.won derful-nature.org	/x/?eKhqTJcoo/plZ117fSOqDGQ=	
			/x/?hZ4qsvawxTVnlb9bNxN+c54=	
		l2aajjixxjspq7los7r2ebweo37at5ywiop fzf7mrwomnwp7fyin2seaby.wonderful -nature.org	/x/?loNtE6yuyk1Tuxn3XZ1WJAc=	

A higher count of lookups to that domain over time

Spikes in requests for a particular domain, particularly for domains that are rarely seen in your environment, could indicate a rash of new system compromises and C2 traffic.

Details known about the domain

For example, sourced from internal data, Google, Urlquery, threat feeds, or others. Researching domains and URLs with third-party feeds, or by enriching your DNS source with threat intelligence, can significantly improve your detection rate. Knowing what requests (and clients) to flag as suspicious based on confirmed reports of malicious activity makes the approach no more than simple pattern matching. In any case, blocking bad domains and waiting for victims to resolve them again may also enable you to collect additional indicator information from their clients such as the hostnames they have recently resolved or unusual flows they may have created.

As with any investigative play, the query must be tuned, removing confirmed false positives each time it's analyzed and compared with other data sources for corroboration. Additionally, correlating the source IP, source host, or username with additional data sources (HIDS, AV, IDS, web proxy) may also show more suspicious activity and help confirm or refute the activity.

RPZ and sinkhole monitoring is also valuable when a malware outbreak or massive campaign-based attack occurs. Many exploit kits bundle and drop ransomware like Cryptolocker, Cryptowall, CTB-Locker, and others, or deploy them shortly after other infection vectors have succeeded. It infects a computer, encrypts personal files, and then demands ransom be paid in a short period of time before the attackers/ extortionists delete the files. All the Cryptolocker-style infections call back to a DNS hostname; however, due to their huge infrastructure, there can be thousands of possible names to check against. Their domain name generation algorithm was eventually discovered, and we were able to proactively RPZ all the Cryptolocker callback domains to minimize the damage.

RPZ can also help with accidental data leakage and sneaky tricks by blocking typo'd versions of your domain name or partners. It can also reduce some adware served up by domain parking services that leave a token advertisement at the site of an unpurchased/inactive domain. Dynamic DNS services, very popular with attackers, are easy to block entirely by simply adding the authoritative nameserver for those domains to your RPZ filter.

Finally, we also track and measure our team against how many infections or problems we detect internally before an external entity reports something. For this reason, we generally sinkhole third-party sinkhole nameservers to get access to the same data in our local RPZ. When we see internal clients attempting to resolve a domain that's attached to a known sinkhole, we know the client is infected and don't pass that information externally. Microsoft and U.S. federal agencies have shut down large botnets, widespread malware campaigns, and have sinkholed thousands of domains. Blocking the nameserver for the sinkhole with RPZ keeps any infection data we have local, offers us some additional privacy, and gives us the benefit of additional and measurable protection.

Limitations

The pDNS data provides domain name metadata analogous to how NetFlow serves up IP metadata. However, just because a client resolves a known bad domain doesn't always mean the cause of the lookup is malicious, or that the client is infected. It also doesn't mean any traffic was ever sent to the domain by the client. Although having only one bit of metadata from DNS can be a smoking gun, it isn't always, and more context is usually needed. To confirm an event was malicious, pDNS/RPZ logs must be used in conjunction with other defense-in-depth data sources like your NetFlow or sinkhole logs.

It's also important to realize that you still have to maintain a DNS collection infrastructure, even if you already have a log management system in place. Much like the web security proxies, DNS data, along with RPZ mitigation capabilities, offers a precise view into a commonplace protocol. Still, it is a disparate source to maintain in conjunction with your IT groups. After all, DNS is a critical and foundational service. Moving around zone files, editing configurations, and adding new services needs to be done with a circumspect approach and in communication with all the DNS stakeholders in IT and the organization.

Another major limitation with pDNS deployments for large networks arises when there are multiple tiers of DNS services behind an organization's primary nameservers. Take, for example, a university department (say, biology) providing name resolution services to members of their domain through departmental Active Directory servers. Rather than querying the central IT network's authoritative DNS servers for the school, clients in the biology department request name resolution to the nameserver provided to them by Active Directory. Generally, this is the domain controller itself, and if you detect resolution of known bad or RPZ'd domains from this session, you will only see the source IP address of the domain controller, and not the client who initially made the request. Naturally, this makes attribution difficult, especially if the domain controllers are not logging their DNS requests. There is no current solution for pDNS collection on Windows Domain Controllers. The only option is to log the DNS service and its transactions.

The essential pros and cons of DNS monitoring and RPZ detection come down to:

- DNS provides a fundamental source of data used in most communications, and therefore provides a wealth of information for security monitoring.

- RPZ can shut down attacker C2 services and provide insight into your internal client activity.

- Domain names are very common indicators shared by various groups, and it's important to have the capability to know where and what your clients are resolving.

- Because DNS is a critical (and deceptively complex) service, you must take caution in changing the configuration parameters, BIND versions, or any components of your DNS architecture to avoid outages.

- Not every organization runs their own DNS servers, but packet capture can still intercept request and responses from internal clients to Internet-provided DNS services.

HTTP Is the Platform: Web Proxies

A few years ago, we took a hard look at our detection infrastructure to determine where we might improve our capabilities. Realizing that 33% of outbound packets used HTTP, it became abundantly obvious that an investment in this area would have the biggest impact. At the time, the only web proxies on the network served as caching services to improve WAN link performance and to reduce bandwidth costs. If a client can load common files from a local HTTP cache and avoid using an expensive WAN or Internet connection, performance improves and bandwidth is conserved. However, the caching proxies only improved performance, and offered no additional security protections. In fact, the proxies actually masked the true client source IP address behind the proxy, increasing our time to respond. That is, when our IDS or other tools alerted on outbound HTTP traffic, we could only trace back to the proxy's IP address rather than the original client host.

Configuring and adding the Via and X-Forwarded-For headers can help upstream detection determine the original client IP behind a web proxy.

Pairing our TCP utilization numbers with the fact that increasing volumes of exploits were sourced from compromised websites, it was an obvious choice to expand our detection capabilities beyond IDS to more precise and flexible web monitoring.

It's critical to ensure a safe web browsing environment for employees to protect the business, intellectual property, and communications with each other and customers. The weakest link in our security defense-in-depth strategy was our lack of controls around Internet web browsing. Some IP enabled embedded devices, unreachable by client security software, were often not under IT control or even patchable, meaning malware and outsider control could have manifested itself in these hard-to-protect areas. Balancing web and browser security versus openness and a culture of research, development, engineering, and well, Internet, made it a difficult but rewarding process in the end.

Deployment considerations

Web proxies allow you to solve additional security problems at a more precise and scalable layer than NetFlow, or IDS, but still on the network level. Web proxies collect only web browsing information, which means client requests and server responses. Their narrow focus affords capacity and confidence that more attack patterns and traffic can be identified than broader scoped tools. At some point, every attack must have a callback component to notify the attacker of their success. Most commonly, callbacks occur over HTTP and on TCP port 80. Many organizations allow outbound TCP port 80 on their firewalls; therefore, the callback has a better chance of connecting and avoids filtering.

Many callbacks also occur on TCP port 443 over SSL. Some proxies have the ability to inspect SSL sessions, but only after requiring their own SSL certificate to install the client, who must agree to allow their SSL traffic to be decrypted once before it reaches its destination.

Even if an authenticated proxy is required to access outbound Internet resources, malware can take advantage of existing sessions and proxy settings on the victim's system. Because callbacks are leaving via HTTP, you need a proxy in place that can detect, log, and if possible, block incoming malware or outbound callbacks. A web proxy brings the ability to block web objects (HTML, plaintext, images, executables, scripts, etc.) based on preconfigured rules (signatures), intelligence feeds, or custom lists and regular expressions. This last component is key: any regular expression you can develop that identifies a malicious HTTP transaction can be used to develop a playbook report. The vast majority of our playbook centers on our web proxy logging and analysis.

Depending on the proxy product, there will be several possible configuration options. Most all professional grade proxies support:

- Web caching and proxy
- Numerous redirection methods
- High availability or failover
- Substantial logging facility
- SSL inspection (man-in-the-middle)
- Malware detection and blocking
- Threat intelligence feeds
- Custom policies and filters

For a smoother transition and easier support, inline transparent proxies offer the best approach. Transparent means the proxies are unknown to the web browsing clients as they pass through typical Internet web traffic. There are no client settings to modify, no proxy auto-config (PAC) files to create and distribute, and little to no support issues for configuration. To transparently proxy, however, you must employ either an HTTP load balancer or content routing protocol like Cisco's Web Cache Communication Protocol (WCCP) on a chokepoint router. WCCP can intercept outbound HTTP requests (or other protocols depending on what service groups and ports are configured) and redirect them anywhere, most likely to your web proxy anxiously waiting to make a decision to forward or drop the request. The client has no idea their HTTP request has hit a proxy, and won't know unless they look up their IP address on a remote web server and see it's actually the proxy's IP address. Other clues that you are behind a proxy can be found in the outbound HTTP headers. Properly configured, a web proxy can append additional headers like Via or X-Forwarded-For to each request, indicating the original client source IP. Configuring these headers also helps to identify client traffic from behind other proxies. When the Internet-facing security web proxy receives a web request from an internal caching proxy, if the caching proxy includes one of the client identification headers, the security proxy can recognize, log, and allow or deny that traffic. In any case, you now have a true source IP to investigate versus a possible dead end with just a caching proxy server IP.

```
GET / HTTP/1.1
Host: www.oreilly.com
User-Agent: Mozilla/5.0 (Macintosh; Intel Mac OS X 10.9; rv:29.0)
  Gecko/20100101 Firefox/29.0
```

```
Accept: text/html,application/xhtml+xml,application/xml;q=0.2,*/*;q=0.5
Accept-Language: en-US,en;q=0.5
Accept-Encoding: gzip, deflate
Connection: keep-alive
HTTP/1.1 200 OK
Server: Apache
Accept-Ranges: bytes
Vary: Accept-Encoding
Content-Encoding: gzip
Content-Type: text/html; charset=utf-8
Cache-Control: max-age=14400
Expires: Sat, 17 May 2015 07:08:42 GMT
Date: Sat, 17 May 2015 03:08:42 GMT
Content-Length: 18271
Last-Modified: Fri, 16 May 2014 18:43:57 GMT
Via: 1.1 newyork-1-dmz-proxy.company.com:80
Connection: keep-alive
and
Connection: keep-alive
Host: query.yahooapis.com
Cache-Control: max-age=0
Accept: */*
User-Agent: Mozilla/5.0 (Macintosh; Intel Mac OS X 10_8_5) AppleWebKit/537.
  36 (KHTML, like Gecko) Chrome/34.0.1847.131 Safari/537.36
Referer: http://detroit.curbed.com/archives/2014/09/the-silverdome-54-photos-
  inside-the-ruined-nfl-stadium.php
Accept-Encoding: gzip,deflate,sdch
Accept-Language: en-US,en;q=0.8
Cookie: X-AC=ixJG0Qqmq9R; BX=923h6vl88u22kr&b=4&d=_mbiZA5pYEI5A0OR2p
  6p_g45v8y9reARiupeHw--&s=83&i=mSeKQNWKVRy3IESGPi5i
X-IMForwards: 20
X-Forwarded-For: 10.116.215.244
```

Transparency is a critical part of a successful and accepted deployment, but where to deploy the proxy also makes a big difference (Figure 7-3). Deploying to an Internet facing connection reduces the total amount of proxies necessary for internal scrubbing, and can simplify configuration. Placing web proxies at the outer layer can also avoid conflicts with internal caching proxies that are now downstream.

 An added benefit of deploying directly at the Internet uplinks for all internal networks are the layer two performance boosts offered by WCCP. Connecting your proxies directly to the device running WCCP can significantly improve performance in layer two mode, as redirection processing is accelerated in the switching hardware and avoids the overhead of software switched, Layer 3 generic routing encapsulation (GRE).

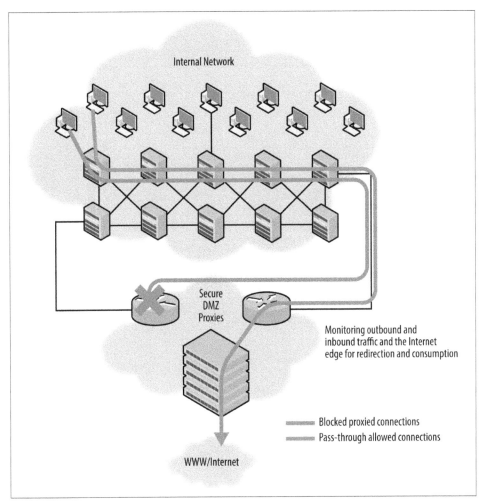

Figure 7-3. Web proxy deployment

The one primary side effect to a transparent security proxy is that clients will not receive certain pages or objects they requested in their browser. Depending on the proxy, a configurable error message might appear, or simply a blank space on the browser window. It's important to remember that this is a great chance to put text in front of a user for basic security awareness, with links to why the site or object was blocked and how to get support. We spent almost as much time crafting the language on the error pages (returned by the proxy with an HTTP 403 error) as we did in the project's design (Figure 7-4).

Based on Cisco security threat information, access to the web site http://ihaveabadreputation.com/ has been blocked by the Web Security Appliance (WSA) to prevent an attack on your browser. The Cisco Security Intelligence Operations (CSIO) Web Reputation Score for this site indicates that it is associated with malware/spyware, and poses a security threat to your computer or the corporate network.

In order to cater for a growing number and variety of devices on the Cisco network, malware protection has shifted from the endpoint, deeper into the network. In order to offer the most effective protection to computing assets on the Cisco network, CSIRT and Cisco IT jointly rolled out the Cisco Ironport WSA solution on all Cisco Internet Points of Presence (IPoPs). These WSAs are configured to block access to sites whose Web Based Reputation Score (WBRS) shows that they are serving malware or content otherwise harmful to users of the Cisco corporate network.

If you believe this page was incorrectly blocked, please open a case with Infosec, providing the corresponding debug information below, and an analyst will determine whether the block was due to a misclassification. Please note that Cisco Infosec does not add sites to the WSA allowed-list on demand, and may require the end-user to contact Senderbase directly in order to submit a request to have a site removed from the WSA blocked-list.

Debug information to include when opening a case:

Date:	Sat, 17 May 2014 03:56:58 GMT
Time:	1400299018.290
Client IP address:	
Request URL:	http://ihaveabadreputation.com/
User-Agent:	Mozilla/5.0 (Macintosh; Intel Mac OS X 10_9_2) AppleWebKit/537.36 (KHTML, like Gecko) Chrome/34.0.1847.137 Safari/537.36
Transaction ID:	0x1e8f21e1
Request Method:	GET
Blocking reason:	BLOCK-MALWARE
Web Reputation Score:	-9.5
Malware threat name:	
Malware category name:	
Web reputation threat reason:	Researchers or users identified possible threats.
Web reputation threat type:	othermalware
Proxy hostname:	

As a matter of good practice, you may check whether your browser or any component plugin is vulnerable by visiting browsercheck.qualys.com. The UID at the end of the browsercheck.qualys.com URL does not uniquely identify your machine to Qualys; it is a shared UID to group all requests originating from Cisco IP ranges.

FAQ

⊞ Question: How do I access the page I'm trying to reach?
⊞ Question: Why am I seeing this page? Why didn't my page load?
⊞ Question: Can I view a list of all the Internet sites that are blocked?
⊞ Question: How do I learn more about Cisco Ironport's Web Security Product?
⊞ Question: None of these questions address my issue, where can I get more help?

Figure 7-4. Web proxy blocked request notification

Logging is another major consideration when deploying the secure web proxies. As mentioned earlier, 33% of all our traffic is HTTP. Each day, we log and index around one terabyte of HTTP browsing metadata. Be prepared to store, index, and recall large volumes of HTTP transaction data. It turns out that only between 1%–3% of all traffic is automatically blocked by threat intelligence feeds and anti-malware blocking. However, that small percentage represents millions of blocked objects that could have otherwise negatively impacted the web browsing clients. The rest of the transaction data is still extremely valuable, as it now can be searched and profiled for what reputation scoring and signatures could not detect. Applying self-discovered intelligence to the web proxy log data will yield surprising results. If you create a generic query, you can find even more versions of the same attacks from different entities. Beyond malware, browsing data is a gold mine for investigating data loss, fraud, harassment, or other abuse issues. If you can see what sites are being used by what people, you can collect evidence of unsavory activity through the log data.

Threat prevention

Security proxies should provide several methods for preventing the import of malware through the network borders. They should also provide adequate protection and detection of suspicious outbound traffic. Callbacks represent a particularly valuable piece of information when it comes to a phishing response. If sysadmins or executives are successfully phished, the link they click will go through a proxy that can either stop the damage from occurring, or at least provide a log for future investigation. Blocking access to phishing-referenced links can protect some of the most valuable assets through the high-risk vectors of email and curiosity. Other important callbacks to detect are made by infected clients responding to check-in or health scripts run by the attacker. When a host is successfully compromised with an exploit kit or otherwise, to extract data or send commands to the victim, the attack must have some connection to deliver its instructions. In some cases, systems sit idle, periodically checking in until access to them is sold to another attacker. In both cases, a check-in status almost always appears to let the attackers know the host is still on, up, and under control.

A web proxy can distinguish and detect watering hole attacks, drive-by downloads, and other HTTP attack types. Simply put, any attack involving HTTP will go through your proxies and create a log file that can be used to develop reports. The more common a pattern and the easier to distill into a regular expression, the easier detecting exploit attempts will be. Most commonly used exploit kits attempt to foist as many exploits as possible or relevant onto a victim host in the hopes of getting a successful load. The exploit detection is best handled by client software as it attempts to execute. This only comes into play, however, if the proxy failed to block the exploit download attempt. To actually deliver an exploit, the kit must have a landing and subsequent loading page, typically via PHP or HTML, often in iframes. It's at this point where the web proxy can detect and block the connection.

Let's look at real-world examples

Like pDNS collection, because web proxies provide so much meta detail about ubiquitous network traffic, they provide the perfect test lab for discovering security incidents. Web proxy data is a great place to start developing effective plays.

Backdoor downloads and check-ins

The venerable password-stealing Zeus Trojan provides an excellent example of how best to leverage the security web proxy. Even from its earliest versions, the Zeus bot downloader was served from an exploit kit hosted on a compromised website. Once an exploit successfully compromised a client system, the host would soon after make an HTTP "POST" to a check-in script hosted by the attackers. Most commonly, Zeus authors named the script *gate.php*. To detect a successful compromise, all one has to do is look for this specially crafted POST to any URL ending in *gate.php*. Of course, there may be legitimate sites that also run scripts called *gate.php*, so a bit of investigation is necessary; however, we further improved the detection by alarming only when a POST goes to *gate.php* and there was no HTTP referer. That means there was no previous link leading to the *gate.php* script, and the client connected directly to the script. HTTP requests with no referrer only occur when someone types a web address directly into their browser navigation bar, or if an application creates a web request. In this way, it's much easier to distinguish between human-generated traffic and computer-created traffic (the latter potentially representing malware, like Zeus bot).

To further improve precision, we can add additional regular expressions on fields like URL or User-Agent, based on how the exploit kits are reconfigured or shifted around. In this example, we can see the query we developed to find common Zeus bot compromises in the web proxy logs:

```
"gate" AND "php" AND cs_url="*/gate.php" AND "POST" (NOT (cs_referer="*"))
```

Here's the result:

```
1430317674.205 - 10.20.12.87 63020 255.255.255.255 80 -5.8
http://evalift0hus.nut.cc/Spindilat/Sh0px/gate.php - 17039 798 0
  "Mozilla/4.0 (compatible; MSIE 7.0; Windows NT 6.1; Trident/5.0;
  SLCC2; .NET CLR 2.0.50727; .NET CLR 3.5.30729; .NET CLR 3.0.30729;
  Media Center PC 6.0; .NET CLR 1.1.4322; InfoPath.3)" - 503 POST
```

In this case, host *10.20.12.87* attempted an HTTP POST to a *gate.php* script hosted on *evalift0hus.nut.cc* with no apparent referer. Looking at the novel domain name (recently registered), examining the site itself (does not look like a legitimate website someone would type into their browser bar), and factoring in other web browsing data from the client, it's clear this is an example of a true positive, a Zeus infection. To contrast with this example, we've removed the no HTTP referrer requirement and have run the report again. The following example shows a hit that represents a false positive:

```
1403077567.205 10.20.12.61 15873 199.107.64.171 80 - 4.9
  http://www.idsoftware.com/gate.php - 263 607 2589 "Mozilla/5.0
  (Windows NT 5.1; rv:28.0) Gecko/20100101 Firefox/28.0"
  text/html 302 TCP_MISS "http://www.idsoftware.com/gate.php" POST
```

The client *10.20.12.61* attempted an HTTP POST to a *gate.php* script hosted on *http://www.idsoftware.com*. On further investigation, we can see that there is actually a referer (*http://www.idsoftware.com/gate.php*) that sends an HTTP redirect (error code 302) to itself. Visiting the site itself (from a secured lab browser), it's clear that *gate.php* is a script that requires visitors to register their age before proceeding through "the gate" to the main website. The site is completely benign and harbors no threat of malware attack.

The differentiator here is the absence or presence of a referer. Certainly, attackers can modify their code to include benign referers in their check-in requests, but at the moment, there are plenty of exploit kits that don't include this additional layer. It's easy to find Zeus bot check-ins using this method, and in fact, we have successfully detected other malware families with the same report. Lazy attackers often use their exploit kit default settings, and *gate.php* is a common, if not default, script name.

This might seem like an overly simplistic example, yet this query is extremely effective in finding this particular malware, and its logic and methods can be easily adapted to detect additional malware strains using a similar exploit vector. It's also important to understand that the hosts making these connections are infected with malware already. The source hosts need to be completely reinstalled to ensure all traces of the backdoors and installers are removed.

Exploit kits

A web security proxy   can also be used to detect attacks at earlier stages of exploitation. We already know it can detect callback traffic, but it also can detect exploit attempts. Detecting an exploit attempt is only partially useful. Only when we can confirm an exploit attempt has succeeded can we take significant action. Simply put, we expect exploit attempts—it's why we deploy monitoring gear and people interpret its data. We log all exploit attempts and analyze them for veracity and their impact, but a single alarm of an exploit attempt doesn't provoke any action besides further investigation. However, combined with multiple other security event sources at various layers, proxy logs are indispensable.

For the common exploit kits deployed by those in the crimeware ecosystem, the proxy will hold its ground and deliver plenty of investigative detail. In the preceding example, we detected a post-infection callback. We could also detect the actual exploit kit infection attempt. Websites can be compromised by attackers through a variety of vulnerabilities and techniques.

 For hundreds of victims to fall prey to web-based attacks, websites themselves must first be compromised. Trojans like Gumblar, ASProx, and others have attacked website administrator credentials, as well as exploited vulnerabilities in content management software.

When a victim visits a compromised site, conveniently modified by the attacker to include an exploit kit, the process begins again, only this time the clients are the targets. The exploit kit will test the visiting client's browser for plug-ins and plug-in versions to determine what exploits to use, or simply try them all regardless to see which ones work. It's at this point we can leverage the web proxy for detection. Because we don't control the compromised website, we can look at client behavior to find the attacks.

The following example shows an internal client browsing the web and then getting redirected to an exploit kit.

The client (based in Singapore) begins by intentionally browsing to the WordPress-powered site for a preschool in Singapore, *shaws.com.sg*. As soon as they reach the site, some interesting connections are made to *lifestyleatlanta.com* and *www.co-z-comfort.com* hosted on the same IP address:

```
1399951489.150 - 10.20.87.12 53142 202.150.215.42 80 - 0.0
  http://www.shaws.com.sg/wp-content/uploads/2013/03/charity-carnival.png
  - 329 452 331 "Mozilla/5.0 (compatible; MSIE 10.0; Windows NT 6.1; WOW64;
  Trident/6.0)" - 304 TCP_MISS "http://www.shaws.com.sg/"
  - - - - - 0 GET

1399951490.538 - 10.20.87.12 53146 46.182.30.95 80 - ns
  http://www.lifestyleatlanta.com/hidecounter.php
  - 990 316 548 "Mozilla/5.0 (compatible; MSIE 10.0; Windows NT 6.1; WOW64;
  Trident/6.0)" text/html 404 TCP_MISS "http://www.shaws.com.sg/"
  - - - - - 0 GET

1399951492.419 - 10.20.87.12 53145 46.182.30.95 80 - ns
  http://www.co-z-comfort.com/hidecounter2.php -
  3055 313 10835 "Mozilla/5.0 (compatible; MSIE 10.0; Windows NT 6.1; WOW64;
  Trident/6.0)" text/html 200 TCP_MISS "http://www.shaws.com.sg/"
   - - - - - 0 GET

1399951493.305 - 10.20.87.12 53142 202.150.215.42 80 - 0.0
  http://www.shaws.com.sg/favicon.ico - 304
  215 370 "Mozilla/5.0 (compatible; MSIE 10.0; Windows NT 6.1; WOW64;
  Trident/6.0)" image/vnd.microsoft.icon 200 TCP_MISS
  - - - - - - 0 GET
```

Shortly after those connections (as coded on the hacked WordPress site), you can see the client *10.20.87.12* attempting to GET the *proxy.php* script from yet another domain with a few parameters like req, num, and PHPSESSID:

```
1399951719.307 - 10.20.87.12 53187 255.255.255.255 80 - ns
  http://yoyostylemy.ml/proxy.php?req=swf&num=5982&PHPSSESID=
  njrMNruDMlmbScafcaqfH7sWaBLPThnJkpDZw-
  4|MGUyZmI5MDNlMzJhMTIxYTgxN2Y5MTViMTJkZmQ0Y2I 1260 576 6531
  "Mozilla/5.0 (compatible; MSIE 10.0; Windows NT 6.1; WOW64; Trident/6.0)"
  application/octet-stream 200 TCP_MISS
  "http://yoyostylemy.ml/proxy.php?PHPSSESID=
  njrMNruDMlmbScafcaqfH7sWaBLPThnJkpDZw-
  4|MGUyZmI5MDNlMzJhMTIxYTgxN2Y5MTViMTJkZmQ0Y2I" GET
```

The last log indicates PHP's session-tracking mechanism, and num likely references either a random number or a number assigned to the victim. The interesting option is the req, and in this case, req=swf. Most likely, this means the exploit kit was attempting to attack the client browser's Adobe Flash plug-in with a malicious Small Web Format (SWF) file. The 200 code indicates that the client successfully connected to the remote site; however, there's no additional data in the request, or even subsequent HTTP requests that show a successful compromise. All we know is that the client connected:

```
1399951499.025 - 10.20.87.12 53148 108.162.198.157 80 - ns
http://yoyostylemy.ml/proxy.php?req=swfIE&&num=3840&PHPSSESID=
njrMNruDMlmbScafcaqfH7sWaBLPThnJkpDZw-
4|MGUyZmI5MDNlMzJhMTIxYTgxN2Y5MTViMTJkZmQ0Y2I - 1274 514 6430
"Mozilla/5.0 (compatible; MSIE 10.0; Windows NT 6.1; WOW64; Trident/6.0)"
application/octet-stream 200 TCP_MISS
"http://yoyostylemy.ml/proxy.php?PHPSSESID=
njrMNruDMlmbScafcaqfH7sWaBLPThnJkpDZw-
4|MGUyZmI5MDNlMzJhMTIxYTgxN2Y5MTViMTJkZmQ0Y2I"
- - - - - 0 GET
```

Next, let's add to the investigation information from a host-based log:

```
AnalyzerHostName=ERO-PC1|
AnalyzerIPV4=10.20.87.12|
DetectedUTC=2014-05-13 03:54:05.000|
SourceProcessName=C:\Program
Files\InternetExplorer\iexplore.exe|TargetFileName=
C:\Users\epaxton\AppData\Loca\Temp\~DF43538044D73DACA6.™|
```

We can see that the file made it through, was executed, and detected by the host IPS. Now that we have confirmed this is indeed an exploit kit, and that the attacks are almost successful, we can create a report to look for this same activity using a regular expression to match up with the URL/kit parameters. Additionally, we can add any domains we find to a DNS RPZ, block all connections to the IP address hosting these names, or simply add the hostnames to the proxy block list.

Limitations

Like all the tools discussed here, there are significant limitations to using a security web proxy. However, in the spirit of defense in depth, and because of their high yield rate, we advocate deploying web proxies wherever it makes sense. Keep in mind that there are still limitations and challenges to any organization considering a proxy solution. A proxy has to go in front of everyone's traffic: performance problems and outages are more obvious. When email goes down in an organization, everyone notices. It's almost as bad as the power going out. Today, the same goes for HTTP. If employees cannot use the web for business applications, operations will grind to a halt. If there are significant delays watching broadcast video because of the proxy, most people will notice. There's also the chance that someone is using an application that's incompatible with an HTTP proxy.

Depending on the configuration, WCCP and the proxy can miss HTTP on nonstandard ports. WCCP and other techniques can redirect HTTP on any TCP port to your proxy. Although the vast majority of HTTP occurs over port 80, many applications opt for alternative HTTP ports. Malware is no different, and some samples will make HTTP connections on any random port. Because of their prevalence in malware callback communication, ports 80, 81, 1080, 8000, and 8080 are good choices to include in the redirect service group toward the proxy. It's not scalable to add all 65536 TCP ports to your redirect list for the proxy. In these cases, an IDS or NetFlow (with NBAR or the equivalent) may serve a better purpose. Many proxy applications will support more than HTTP as well, and application proxies like for FTP or SOCKS are great places to retrieve even more log data.

SSL inspection will also cause issues. Intercepting and logging encrypted web traffic means breaking the fundamental trust model in SSL and inserting your organization between your clients and remote web servers' encrypted communications. This brings up a whole host of potential issues. Performance issues notwithstanding, compatibility issues (e.g., Shared Spanning Tree Protocol), configuration complexity issues (additional certificate authorities), certificate management, and potentially privacy, legal, or regulatory issues are all part of the baggage. In general, it's great to have the capability to read encrypted traffic streams for the purposes of incident response; however, it's not without significant disruption to normal web and SSL services.

Another limitation is that it's possible the proxy may not get the full HTTP session headers like an IDS or pcap would. To cope with scalability and decrease log complexity and size, many proxies only log and alert on top layer components in the HTTP headers, such as URL, host IP, referer, and HTTP actions. IDS is a better fit for lower-level header inspection when a precise signature is available.

The essential pros and cons of web proxy log monitoring come down to:

- HTTP data is fundamental to modern networks and many applications offer control and visibility into HTTP traffic.
- HTTP traffic's prevalence makes it a worthwhile log source to target.
- Many simple reports can find malicious activity using web proxy data alone.
- Deploying a proxy between users and their web content can require configuration overhead.
- Even with WCCP, visibility into HTTP traffic on nonstandard web ports may be missed.
- Performance issues or outages as a result of the proxy are highly visible to end users.

- SSL inspection has issues beyond a technological aspect.
- A proxy may not be able to capture full session headers.

[rolling] Packet Capture

In a perfect world, we would have full packet capture everywhere. In fact, in many small environments, this capability exists. What better way to provide evidence for an investigation than to simply study or even replay a network conversation that has already occurred? However, implementing successful ubiquitous packet capture demands great resources and engineering effort to achieve.

Deployment considerations

As with the other event sources, specifically where to deploy remains a key question. Packet captures are helpful anywhere we want to re-create an attack scenario or determine what already happened. Logging all packets into and out of the internal network can work, with proper filtering, storage, indexing, and recall capabilities. A rolling (constant) packet capture can be an acceptable solution for querying near-time packet data, with the option of searching historical data in more long-term storage. Beyond the basic ideas of capturing and storing packet data, the recall of data is just as important as other event sources. Will you be able to not only capture packets, but also index their contents to make searching and log mining possible? If so, consider the additional size imposed by building an index or loading the packets into a database.

For rolling packet capture to work, you must also filter out unreadable or unusable data. If you are looking for payload information, IPsec or SSL traffic (unless you already have, or later discover, the private keys) is practically worthless from a packet capture standpoint. If you are only looking for network metadata, you are better off leveraging NetFlow. Broadcast, multicast, and other chatty network protocols can also be filtered to reduce the total size of the packet capture.

Let's look at real world examples

Using a network packet capture appliance or switch module, you can set up packet triggers to only log data when a particular condition occurs, or you can preconfigure a capture filter and wait for it to fire again. In either packet capture scenario, by definition, it must be a reactive approach. Rather than attempting to record all conversations, the bulk of which are meaningless, having an ad hoc solution deployed in key areas (Internet edge, client networks, datacenter gateways, partner gateways, etc.) will provide you with precise data, as well as a solid foundation for developing detection methods, based on packet data, on other event sources. There have been many times where we have taken sampled packet data and developed reports using NetFlow or IDS based on the original packets.

Rather than spend the millions it would take for a robust commercial packet capture, storage, and retrieval system, we opted for the ad hoc solution with the option to develop reports based on metadata we pulled from packet data investigations into other event sources. We still use packet capture on a regular basis, but depend on log data from our other systems and detection logic to study or re-create attack scenarios. If an attack works once, it will probably be attempted again, and when our ad hoc packet capture is standing by, we can use its output to enhance our other widely deployed monitoring tools by replaying captured traffic and testing our detection capabilities.

Limitations

While packet capture can provide the full, historical record of an incident, there are some prohibitive overhead components and technical concerns that can make it a less attractive event source. In most cases, the cost of a full packet capture program for a large organization is astronomical when factoring in all the computing horsepower and storage requirements. Small environments or targeted areas work best to avoid an expensive storage and recall system. Also remember that packet captures, while complete, are still just raw data. Without knowledge of what to look for and where, it doesn't offer the instantaneous response possibilities present in other, more metadata-focused event sources.

As with other event sources, encryption can partially thwart your efforts. While you can deduce certain assumptions based on simple ideas like the fact that a flow occurred between two hosts, or that a single host had a long-running connection, without the decryption keys (and in some cases without the right timing), encryption still prevents analysis of packet contents.

The essential pros and cons of full packet inspection come down to:

- Packet captures provide a full, historical record of a network event or an attack. No other data source can offer this level of detail.

- Packet data has not been summarized or contextualized automatically and requires understanding and analysis capabilities.

- Collecting and saving packet data takes a lot of storage, depending on archival requirements, and can be expensive.

Applied Intelligence

The U.S. Department of Homeland Security maintains the National Terrorism Advisory System (*http://www.dhs.gov/national-terrorism-advisory-system*). This system attempts to inform the American populace of imminent or elevated threats to their personal safety as a result of potential terrorist aggression. This is a physical security threat intelligence system. However, if there's a credible threat, what are you supposed to do? What does elevated or red mean? There are no specific instructions other than basically, "stay tuned for more details." This is an unfortunate tautology. If this were part of the security incident response process, we'd be stuck on the preparation phase. To have effective threat intelligence, you need more than just colors and strong words. You need to know what threat intelligence feeds or digests are available to you. You'll need to consider how to manage threat indicators after you've received them. You need a system to manage the repository of intelligence data, as well as a way to manage contextual information like indicator relationships. Intelligence data on its own is not terribly helpful, but when used to color network events from your organization, it can be enlightening.

Threat intelligence is tactical information about adversaries, tools, techniques, and procedures (TTPs) that can be applied to security monitoring and incident response.

The hope, when subscribing to a threat intelligence feed, is that you will receive vetted, actionable information about specific threats to your organization. This means that you can take the threat intelligence data and actually use it for incident response. Threat intelligence alone is like the National Terrorism Advisory System—you have information on credible (possibly even confirmed) threats, but no real information or strategy on what to do. It's up to you to decide what to do with the intelligence when you receive it. Does the data overlap with your other commercial or freely available feeds? Do you trust their results and can you corroborate the detection? If you are automatically blocking hosts based on third-party intelligence, what happens if you get bad data? If you are sending your CTO's laptop up for remediation, you'd better be confident you made the right call. If it comes down to a decision to reimage 5,000 hosts on your network, are you prepared to put full trust into this feed and defend its findings?

Deployment considerations

To supplement the intelligence you are developing internally, you can use third-party threat intelligence feeds to let you know what problems you already have on your network and to prepare for future incidents. This can be helpful, especially for organizations with no CSIRT, or an under-resourced security or IT operations group with no time to research on their own. Intelligence feeds typically come as a list of known indicators of malicious activity broken out into metadata such as IP address, DNS hostnames, filenames, commands, and URLs. Using feeds will enhance your existing data with additional context that can be used for detection. For example, if an IP address fires a seemingly benign alarm in your IDS events, yet it is tagged as belonging to a blacklist of IP addresses from a threat intelligence feed, your analysts have reason to take a closer look to ensure the event doesn't have more sinister intentions. Perhaps a system account has logged in from an IP address included in a list of threat actor group subnets, or you have detected HTTP connections to watering hole sites already discovered by researchers and shared in an intelligence feed.

There are three types of intelligence feeds: public, private, and commercial. Finding good intelligence feeds (usually private) generally requires collaboration among industry peers willing to share information on indicators they have discovered in their operations. Some threat intel exchange groups like Defense Security Information Exchange (DSIE), Cyber Information Sharing and Collaboration Program (CISCP), and the various Information Sharing and Analysis Centers (*http://www.isac council.org/memberisacs.html*) (ISACs) are industry (sometimes country) specific—and in a few cases, public/private collaborations.

 The National Council of ISACs publishes a list of member ISACs, including such groups as the following (to name a few):

- Financial Services: FS-ISAC
- Defense Industrial Base: DIB-ISAC
- National Health: NH-ISAC
- Real Estate: REN-ISAC

However, there are dozens of feed providers, generally available to the public like: Abuse.ch, Shadowserver, Team Cymru, Malc0de, DShield, Alienvault, Blocklist.de, Malwaredomains, and many others. Selecting a feed really boils down to the trust you put in the organization and the quality of the feed. This is why industry partnerships and ISACs work well, as long as everyone within the groups is sharing information. Free online feeds are useful for broader coverage of less sophisticated or targeted attacks, but will never be specific to temporal and advanced threat actors.

It's also important to understand that different organizations share different types of data at different levels of classification or sensitivity. This is one reason for the Traffic Light Protocol (TLP). This protocol allows organizations to score intelligence information on a shareability scale. In other words, threat intelligence can be coded red, amber, green, or white, depending on the perceived sensitivity. The US-CERT provides the following guidance on leveraging the protocol (Figure 7-5).

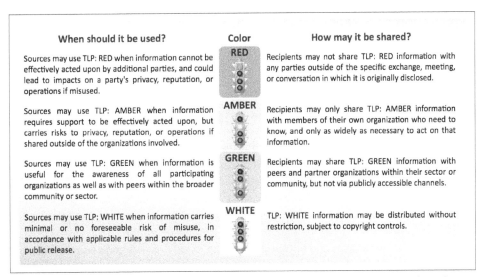

When should it be used?	Color	How may it be shared?
Sources may use TLP: RED when information cannot be effectively acted upon by additional parties, and could lead to impacts on a party's privacy, reputation, or operations if misused.	RED	Recipients may not share TLP: RED information with any parties outside of the specific exchange, meeting, or conversation in which it is originally disclosed.
Sources may use TLP: AMBER when information requires support to be effectively acted upon, but carries risks to privacy, reputation, or operations if shared outside of the organizations involved.	AMBER	Recipients may only share TLP: AMBER information with members of their own organization who need to know, and only as widely as necessary to act on that information.
Sources may use TLP: GREEN when information is useful for the awareness of all participating organizations as well as with peers within the broader community or sector.	GREEN	Recipients may share TLP: GREEN information with peers and partner organizations within their sector or community, but not via publicly accessible channels.
Sources may use TLP: WHITE when information carries minimal or no foreseeable risk of misuse, in accordance with applicable rules and procedures for public release.	WHITE	TLP: WHITE information may be distributed without restriction, subject to copyright controls.

Figure 7-5. Traffic Light Protocol (source: US-CERT, https://www.us-cert.gov/sites/ default/files/TLP.pdf)

After you have found the feeds you intend to consume, you'll need to prepare for importing and analysis. One of the biggest problems with threat intelligence sharing is the lack of any fully accepted standard for indicator format. There are a variety of options:

- Structured Threat Information Expression (STIX)
- Incident Object Description and Exchange Format (IODEF)
- Collective Intelligence Framework (CIF)
- OpenIOC
- CybOX

The challenge is to build a system that can handle multiple metadata formats, as well as multiple file formats. Threat feeds can come in via XML/RSS, PDF, CSV, or HTML. Some intelligence sources are not even aggregated and have to be distilled from blog posts, email lists, bulletin boards, or even Twitter feeds.

After the threat data is collected and standardized (not unlike how we standardized log features), the indicators need to tie in to your security monitoring infrastructure. Applying the indicators to your existing log data delivers a broader set of previously unknown data to enable better report building for your playbook. Like with all tools, there are many ways of managing indicators. Databases, flat files, or even commercial and open source management systems can store and recall indicators that can be leveraged by your log monitoring and alerting systems. Intelligence indicators can be used to both detect and prevent threats—it all depends on which security tools you enhance with indicator data. For example, you could add hostname-based indicators to your DNS RPZ configuration to prevent any internal hosts from resolving known bad hosts. You could also add IP-based indicators to your firewall policies to prevent any communications. On the detection side, you could simply watch for indicators flagged in your monitoring systems and then follow up with a more intensive investigation.

Like the other tools and processes, you'll want to measure the efficacy of your applied intelligence. Knowing which feeds provide the best value can help you determine the priority in handling their outputs, the source's trustworthiness in terms of data fidelity, and how effective the intel sources are at enhancing your log data. Therefore, it's always a good idea to tie your intelligence indicators to their source. As you analyze events through reports in your playbook, you should be able to determine not only where an indicator was sourced, but also why an event was flagged as malicious. You can also graph relationships (e.g., trends, outliers, repetitive patterns) between disparate investigations if a common intelligence source prompted the investigations. These relationships can help to discover future incidents and highlight security architecture improvement opportunities.

Let's look at real-world examples

A threat intelligence system feeds a playbook nicely. It will help find known threats, and provide information about your exposure and vulnerability to those threats. You can automate threat intelligence data analysis by running queries across your security log information against reported indicators. Intelligence indicators enhance the DNS, HTTP, NetFlow, host security, and IDS event sources. You could:

- Take a feed of known bad C2 domains and run an automatic report looking to see what internal hosts attempt to resolve them
- Auto-block some senders/domains based on phishing and spam feeds (prevention), and then query for any internal users afflicted by these campaigns by looking at callbacks and other indicators (detection)
- Log and report when any internal host tries to contact a malicious URI
- Take a specific policy-based action on a domain or URL that clients have resolved, which has been flagged in a feed with a low "reputation score"
- Automatically create incident tracking and remediation cases based on feed data about your compromised internal hosts

Feeds automate the dirty work of detecting common threats and provide the security team with additional context that helps improve incident response decisions. Judgments about an external host can help analysts better understand a potential incident by providing some peer-reviewed bias. Ultimately, the intelligence can lead to new reports in your incident response playbook. However, only subscribing to a variety of feeds is not a comprehensive answer to your internal security.

Limitations

Locally sourced intelligence is also highly effective, doesn't have any of the disadvantages of a giant statistical cloud, and it can be more precise and effective for your organization. This is particularly true when responding to a targeted attack. If you have gathered evidence from a prior attack, you can leverage that information to detect additional attacks in the future. If they are targeted and unique, there may be no feed available to tell you about the threat. The other advantage to internal intelligence is that it is much more context aware than a third-party feed.

You and the rest of your IT organization—hopefully—know the function and location of your systems. With proper context (that can only be developed internally), the feed data could be extremely helpful, or worthless, depending on your response process and capabilities.

The most effective attackers will also monitor external threat feeds. If their versions of exploit kits, their hosts, or any of their assets are implicated by a threat feed, it's time to change tactics. Attackers run their own malware hashes through various online detectors to see if their campaign has been exposed and detected. After the attackers change their tactics, the threat feed is moot until the new tactics are analyzed.

Reputation scores, malware lists, spam lists, and others can never be fully current. They are completely reactionary because of gathering and analyzing events that have already happened. How many attacks have you detected where the exploit kit, the dropper, and the latter stage attacks were always hosted at the same location for weeks? Initial attacks want to hit and run. It is trivial for an attacker to bring online a brand new domain and website, install an exploit kit, and when the victims are compromised, discard the domain once satisfied with the bot count. A dynamic DNS provider service offers a simple and common technique to burn through thousands of unique, one-time hostnames for attack campaigns. Regardless of the attack methods, a reputation score or vetted evidence cannot instantly be calculated. There will always be a lag in detection and propagation time of threat information. Because your team understands internally developed intelligence so much better, you can create higher-level, broad patterns rather than just using specific lists of known bad indicators.

To be fair to reactive threat feeds, it is called *incident response*, meaning we respond to an event after the fact. The key is to take action as fast as possible for situations where threats cannot be prevented.

The essential pros and cons of integrating threat intelligence come down to:

- Your historical data and data researched by other security experts gives you additional detection capabilities.

- Legitimate threat data can be used to block attack campaigns before they reach your organization, shortening the window of opportunity for attackers.

- Deploying threat intelligence collection requires a system to manage, prepare, and potentially share threat data.

- Proper threat research takes a lot of time, which can be challenging for a security operations team to keep up.

- Valuable threat intelligence is only good if it's fresh. Attackers change tactics and hosts so often that intelligence-based indicators only work well for a short period of time.

Shutting the Toolbox

In Figure 7-6, the rings represent various common security monitoring tools. Each 120-degree slice represents a particular threat. The green shaded areas identify tools that specialize or excel in detecting the threat listed in the slices. This doesn't necessarily mean that the unshaded tools are unable to perform in those threat areas. It simply highlights the strengths and relative weakness of each tool in the context of these three common threats: network, host, or user anomalies; command-and-control traffic or data exfiltration; and compromised (infected) systems. It also confirms that the more data you have access to, the better your potential to detect threats.

There are so many security tools and technologies that it's difficult to figure out the best manageable architecture. Selecting a broad group of tools with niche capabilities enables you to understand what's most effective for your network and what's redundant or unhelpful. It's also important to keep in mind that tools and technologies come and go. All of us remember very helpful detection tools we've used in the past that have ceased development or were owned by a company that went out of business; competitive pressures have sometimes forced our hand in other ways as well.

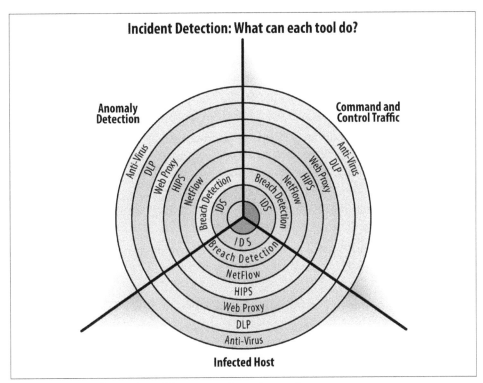

Figure 7-6. Sample overlay of threats per detection tool

Many of us are constantly testing and trying new products, or enabling and testing features of existing products to deliver the best blend of monitoring capabilities and performance. It seems the combinations of approaches to security monitoring are innumerable. However, while any defense-in-depth architecture could provide the proper data for monitoring, the strategy and operation truly makes incident response work. The playbook is the documented strategy that's simply fed by event data from your monitoring tools. The tools are really just that—implements to help you accomplish work.

Putting It All Together

Your work, as incident responders, is defined and prescribed in the playbook. Therefore, if you put garbage into your playbook, you get garbage out of your playbook (and tools). You can create a better playbook with an appropriate toolset, a fundamental understanding of your network architecture, and an awareness of your security risk profile.

Chapter Summary

- The right tools for your environment depend on a myriad of factors including budget, scale, familiarity with the products, and detection strategy.

- Network-based detection systems obviate many problems with unmanaged systems, but log data or host security data is the closest to the source of trouble.

- There are as many tools for security monitoring as there are different approaches, but tools should be selected not based on their ability to do more, but rather to do at least one thing well, while providing adequate details as to why something was detected or blocked.

- Target individuals and critical systems with additional monitoring and technology as necessary.

- Host and network intrusion detection will always have a place in the security monitoring toolkit, but they are only valuable if they are tuned to match your organization.

- Focus on fundamental network traffic and applications like DNS and HTTP for highly effective monitoring.

- NetFlow can be both a powerful detection and correlation tool.

- Threat intelligence can be developed internally, as well as sourced from third parties. The key is to integrate validated intelligence into your playbook development and operation.

CHAPTER 8

Queries and Reports

"Truth, like gold, is to be obtained not by its growth, but by washing away from it all that is not gold."

—Leo Tolstoy

If this book were about gold mining, you'd have your mining plan all laid out at this point. You'd have your tools, a sluice box, a scale, and everything else you need to begin. You'd even have an idea of what to do with the gold once you've found it. Even though gold is everywhere, how are you going to separate it from the rest of the dirt? A random shovelful of dirt does contain gold, but obviously digging at random isn't a very efficient or cost-effective strategy—you need a better plan. Just like finding gold, identifying actionable security events requires good queries to sort through a mountain of data to yield those incident and monitoring nuggets.

This chapter will help to equip you with basic ideas for creating valuable reports and the queries that power them. Keep in mind that the key to success is knowing how to ask the right questions about your log data. Explicitly define the problem you are trying to solve and then use the data to arrive at an answer. Like anything, developing effective queries becomes easier the more you practice and familiarize yourself with the data. Specifically, you need to know:

- What makes a good report
- Cost-benefit analysis of running a report
- What makes up a good high-fidelity report, and how to decide when to make a report investigative or high fidelity
- How to avoid great-but-impossible ideas and other pitfalls

- How to work backward from an event to get a query that can effectively find more of the same and beyond

- How to integrate security threat intelligence into your playbook

This chapter will help you get started creating the first few easy playbook reports. As you build a corpus of simple reports and familiarize yourself with your data and the report creation process, you'll be ready for the more exploratory report creation process laid out later in the chapter, eventually making use of the more advanced query styles in Chapter 9.

False Positives: Every Playbook's Mortal Enemy

The limiting factor in any searching endeavor is the amount of useless information you have to search through before you find whatever you're looking for. In the needle-in-a-haystack problem, the useless content is the hay. In gold mining, it's the dirt. All the extra content you have to sort through and discard on your way to finding what you're looking for slows you down, and this ultimately limits the efficiency and effectiveness of your searches. The results returned from your searches broadly fall into three categories: the results you were looking for (which we usually call "true positives"), the results that really look like the bad stuff but turn out not to be bad (which we call "false positives"), and the rest of the events (which we call "benign" results, or hay). Hay can make the haystack really big and laborious for an analyst to sort through. There is no true delineation between benign results and false positives, and the definition will vary from analyst to analyst. Experts that are very familiar with a data source or the results from a query may easily be able to sort through most of the benign results at a glance, whereas to the untrained eye, every benign result may look like a true positive that turns out to be a false positive. The more you refine and tune a report query, the fewer obviously benign results you'll have to sort through. With extensive tuning, you may be able to eliminate all the benign results so that every result looks like a true positive, even if some turn out to be false positives.

The real trouble with benign results is that each one takes a tiny bit of time and resources to analyze and discard, which draws you away from spotting the suspicious events. False positives are even worse, because they absorb your analysis time on a false lead. With enough benign events and false positives, the amount of analysis time adds up to a nontrivial drain on resources. This is why a needle in a haystack is such a hard problem. Even hay that doesn't look like a needle can waste time when there is a lot of it. If a query returns too many benign events, there is a good chance you'll spend so much time discarding hay that you just won't have time to find the needles.

The majority of your logs are just like gold in dirt or needles in hay. The actionable events with useful security information are there in your logs, and they may even stand out when you see them, but finding what you want still requires a lot of time and effort. Creating good, effective plays is really about finding a way to identify and separate actionable events from the surrounding chaff to reduce benign events and false positives and the costly analysis time they bring.

There Ain't No Such Thing as a Free Report

In a magical fairy-tale world without false positives, you could just have one report that extracts all actionable events in one step. In the real world, such all-encompassing and effective queries don't exist. Creating successful reports is about striking the right balance between a query that's broad enough to return the events you're looking for, while not being so broad that your analysts spend all of their time sorting out benign events or worse, false positives. In general, analysis time is the primary cost of running a report. You need to do everything in your power to make sure result analysis is easy and efficient, and doesn't get bogged down with junk data.

Because the analysis time cost can make or break a report, as you are writing the query, think about what the *analysis* section of the report will contain and how involved the processing of the report results will be. If every result that precipitates from the query requires significant human analysis, you must ensure that the query is narrow and doesn't produce very many results or else your report will be too costly to analyze. Reports whose results require additional analysis, either by correlating with activity in other data sources or by building timelines of activity around the event's occurrence, are especially costly in terms of resource utilization. Results that require detailed analysis aren't necessarily bad, and sometimes they are unavoidable, but their additional cost does mean you need to keep them to a minimum.

Think of a report's value in terms of a cost-benefit balance. You derive value from a report for every valid and actionable event it detects. If those events indicate a machine is infected with some common malware, possibly already thwarted by anti-virus, then the benefit may be modest. However, if the events indicate some sophisticated hacking campaign, the benefit of even one detection may be very high. Of course, there isn't an objective numerical measure of cost or value, so you must estimate the trade-offs of running a report based on three criteria:

- The report's objective
- Analysis time for each true positive detection
- The relevance/value of the results examined in the context of your environment

Your tolerance for potentially wasting time analyzing false positives will vary between reports because the risk and severity of the issue targeted by the report varies. A true positive alert for a critical issue may be so valuable that you can reasonably accept more analysis time on false positives.

Fortunately, in cases where a report can be made extremely precise, the difficult cost-benefit analysis does not have to be done. We call these *high-fidelity* reports. What sets high-fidelity reports apart from all the others is that they're essentially free. High-fidelity reports are the "Holy Grail" of your playbook because the only cost to running them is the (often negligible) load to your systems performing the query. A high-fidelity report produces results that don't need human verification—each result is directly actionable, doesn't require a human to sort out the true positives from all other events, and is therefore a prime candidate for further automated processing. In other words, every result is a true positive.

An Inch Deep and a Mile Wide

You may be thinking, "Great, I'll make all of my reports high fidelity so I don't have to deal with the costs of dealing with false positives." Unfortunately, the reality is that not every report can be high fidelity. You'll find that the bulk of your good reports are investigative in nature because a highly specific query is usually what makes a report high fidelity. You'll run out of highly specific, yet highly useful query criteria fast. There is no harm in looking for some specific behavior, but usually organizations face so many threats that detecting or preventing just one doesn't significantly reduce their overall threat exposure. Most high-fidelity reports are built on specific indicators like a known-malicious IP address, domain name, file hash, or something similar. A common pitfall is to broaden the scope of a high-fidelity report by adding more indicators as they're found. Soon, reports end up as a hodge-podge list of criteria, and report maintenance becomes unwieldy and burdensome fast. Worse yet, reports with lots of criteria lure you into a false sense of security because they seem comprehensive when they often just cover a small, imprecise subset of all of the indicators. They also tend to be deceptively tricky about their accuracy. Indicators such as IP addresses, domain names, and other hyper specific criteria may be malicious this week, but not next month or next year. Once a report based on dozens or hundreds of indicators starts generating false positives, it often requires extensive review and analysis work to re-vet all of these atomic indicators. Your threat intelligence management system and process is a much better place to handle lists of indicators. Without the benefit of threat intel management and curation, a report based on lists will become stale and may eventually lead to additional investigation time for false positive issues.

Take the example of the virtual hosts running on a remote web server. It's completely normal for a single IP address to host hundreds of virtual hosts and domains. If you intend to detect attempts to contact an IP address reported as malicious, it's likely that some of the connections are completely benign and legitimate (especially if more than a few weeks have passed since the IP address was flagged as malicious). If you start trying to exclude the benign events by adding more logic to narrow down an already poor query, you'll end up adding complexity that won't pay off in the long run. Normally, the cost in terms of time and effort to create a report is negligible, but trying to maintain a messy high-fidelity report can easily outweigh the benefit of the report. Don't fall into the pitfall of clinging onto a messy and poor high-fidelity report if you can do better with an investigative one!

A Million Monkeys with a Million Typewriters

For some reports, there are other costs beyond analysis time. Just like reports, not all of your analysts are created equal. If a report requires sophisticated or skilled analysis such that only your top analysts can effectively process it, then the report has a higher cost. In some cases, it's unavoidable to deploy reports that require highly repetitive analysis or a lot of manual analysis labor. Your analysts aren't human machinery to be chained to a spot in the report analysis assembly line, so be wary of reports that are too repetitive. Carelessness is an unfortunate side effect of analyzing reports of this type. High stakes reports can also inflict analysts with general stress and anxiety. You likely don't have reports looking for nuclear launches or Ebola outbreaks, but to your analysts, analyzing mission-critical reports or reports with high-level visibility can impart a similar fear. If the fallout of missing a true positive or accidentally flagging a false positive as a true positive is extremely high, every effort must be made to keep the report's quality high.

Above all, don't be afraid to reject or retire reports when it seems the costs outweigh the benefits. The security landscape is constantly shifting, and threats don't last forever. Even reports that were once very good can stop producing enough results to justify the cost of running them. You also shouldn't feel like there needs to be some quota on the number of reports you run. If you disable or reject an underperforming report, the resources that are freed up can easily be put to good use elsewhere, perhaps even creating newer and more salient reports. The number of reports doesn't matter as much as actionable and comprehensive results do.

A Chain Is Only as Strong as Its Weakest Link

Malicious activity is rarely a singular set of behaviors to detect. Most real-world malicious behavior is an exceptionally complex system with many "moving parts" that work together to achieve a nefarious goal. The complexity of real attacks and malware is often a necessity because the software, computers, and networks subject to attack are themselves quite complex. Although this attack complexity can be quite daunting to a defender, it creates an asymmetry that we as defenders can take advantage of to help us detect or even prevent attacks.

Just as attackers don't have to understand the inner workings of our systems to attack pieces of the system, we don't have to understand all of the inner workings of their attacks to still detect the attack.

For even a technically modest operation like conducting click-fraud with malware (see Figure 8-1), attackers need a staggering amount of infrastructure to get their attack started and keep it going:

Some sort of malware delivery system to infect victim hosts
This usually involves developing or buying exploits, sending spam, setting up malicious advertisements, or actively scanning for vulnerable systems.

A way to trick or force the victim into downloading the malware
This usually involves (registering or hosting) domain names and their resolving IP addresses.

Bought or developed malware to infect hosts
The malware needs command and control infrastructure to receive lists of domains to click or other commands related to the fraud.

A robust system
The system needs the flexibility to include methods to update the malware and to add features, fix bugs, or change how the command and control works.

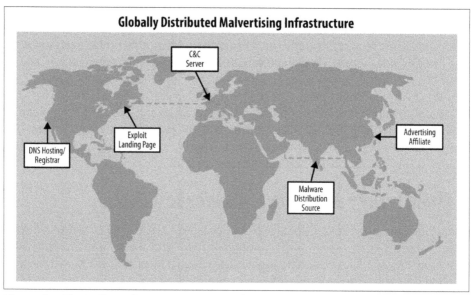

Figure 8-1. Typically, malware campaigns make use of globally spread infrastructure for successful exploitation and bot delivery. Often infrastructure is used based on availability and opportunity in response to the defender's actions, forcing the attackers to constantly shift techniques. By splitting up the infrastructure into components, attackers are able to constantly work on standing up replacement infrastructure as needed.

In short, most real attacks are complex and require attackers to develop and maintain a lot of infrastructure. There are numerous points at which the defender can fight back. Just like in the Lockheed Martin kill chain model, you can detect an attack if you can detect even one of:

- The exploit
- The malware delivery process
- The malware on the host
- The callback to malicious controllers

If you can reliably detect any aspect of the long chain of events that happen over the course of an attack, then there is a report development opportunity.

Detect the Chain Links, Not the Chain

The motivation behind thinking about attacks in terms of a chain of events is not so you can try to detect the whole chain. Detecting the chain by looking at how the various links relate or correlate with each other is the stuff of marketing fluff. Rarely is something so complex that trying to detect the whole chain is the best, or even a good detection strategy. Instead, you should look for the easiest or most reliable-to-detect aspect of an attack—the weakest links in the chain.

If the malware authors have put a lot of time and effort into making it difficult to detect their bot because it's polymorphic, packed, encrypted, and constantly changing, then don't bother trying to detect the bot; instead, go after the command and control communications. If the communication is hard to detect, go after some other aspect like the domains or IP addresses involved in the attack. After all, at some point, the malware must use the network to have any profound effect for the attacker. If you can find more than one weak link in the attack chain that you can detect with high-fidelity methods, don't build a report that looks for them to occur at the same time; instead, take a defense-in-depth strategy and create a report that looks for either.

Attacks change; if you build a complex report that requires every indicator in the chain of events to happen in sequence, even minor permutations on the attack can break your report. If your report can detect any of the weak links in the attack, you're more likely to trigger on variations of the attack where not every indicator has changed.

Simplicity should be your goal in detecting any specific malicious activity. The simpler the aspect of an attack you're trying to detect, the simpler the report and query logic must be. A query like "A and B" is more complex and much less likely to produce results than "A or B"; therefore, as long as event A and event B are both high-quality indicators, your report is likely to be more robust.

Getting Started Creating Queries

One of the hardest things about developing a playbook with efficient reports is getting the first few reports developed. It's easy to think up big ideas but have only a vague idea of how to actually implement them. Don't let this discourage you or bog you down. Although counterintuitive, in your initial efforts at getting started making reports, it's easier to go for a few easy high-fidelity reports. The main reason why high-fidelity reports are often easier to make is that they're often very specific. High-fidelity reports are usually based on a single, very reliable indicator, like a request to some malicious domain that matches a precise pattern. If you can find an indicator that demonstrates something is compromised beyond a reasonable doubt, then creating a report looking for that indicator is easy and no analysis of the query results is needed. Creating investigative reports requires a certain amount of subjective gut feeling about the cost of the report and the efficacy of the results, which high-fidelity reports sidestep.

The easiest thing to do is pick some simple, concrete idea and jump right in. If you don't have any concrete ideas, don't worry—there are many places to get them. No algorithm can adequately perform the task of objectively and empirically knowing what to search for. Trust your human brain and your security instincts. Here are some of the things you can do to get started:

Review existing or historical case investigation data
> Have you had a machine compromised in the past? How did you investigate the issue and ultimately determine how the machine was compromised? Was there a "smoking gun" indicator in your logs that would have pointed to a security incident? Particularly good indicators for getting started are things like malicious domain names or IP addresses that the compromised machine was looking up or communicating with. If antivirus software was installed, the specific names of malware flagged by AV software can be used to locate additional infections in your logs, which can lead to finding indicators on other hosts or finding indicators associated with the malware published online. If samples of network traffic from the incident are available, those indicators can often be used to write IDS signatures. Similarly, if you have a searchable full-packet-capture system, the same indicators can be used to search through that traffic. Authentication logs can provide additional context around if a login was unexpected as a result of this incident. On their own, authentication logs are also great at detecting egregious abuse, like brute-force login attempts.

Search for indicators published online
> InfoSec has matured to the point where there is a lot of content published online about monitoring and incident response. Most major researchers and companies have blogs they use to publish current research and recent security trends. This research often comes with example indicators or other technical information

about specific emerging threats. There is no comprehensive list of places to look, but it's a good idea to start with major security and antivirus companies and then branch out based on current security trends and researchers focusing on areas relevant to you. Eventually, you'll build a lengthy list of excellent sources from mailing lists, blogs, Twitter, and other places where security engineers discuss and write about attacks. After you've found some technical information, you can search your data for any of the indicators mentioned. It often only takes one indicator such as a domain, IP address, or regular expression to find many other related indicators. You can search your own network logs for the indicators to better understand your organization's exposure, or you can search for the indicators online to stitch together a complete picture based on information published in many different places.

Search your security logs for malicious activity

When you don't have many reports, it's often easy to find low-hanging fruit in your logs. If you begin with logs that are already good at detecting malicious activity like AV or HIPS logs, you won't have to sort through as much benign activity before finding a good indicator to use as the basis of a report. For example, host security software might successfully identify malware or unwanted software on a client and report this information through its logs. Rarely does AV or HIPS software detect and stop an entire attack. Where there's smoke, there's fire. Activity in other event sources from around the same time as when AV or HIPS software logs malicious activity is a great place to find other indicators. Building reports that detect attacks using indicators in any of several data sources is critical to a good defense-in-depth monitoring strategy.

After you have a corpus of reports built up, creating new reports will feel natural. You'll also have a good feel for what sort of indicators make for high-fidelity reports. Whatever you do, avoid pie-in-the-sky report ideas early on. It can be very tempting to try to create a sophisticated report to detect a major security threat. For example, if your idea involves multiple events across multiple, different data sources in a specific sequence, then it's probably too sophisticated to start with. Also, if your idea is very generic, it can be hard to create a reliable report that doesn't generate too many benign events or require too much human analysis time. Your initial report should be both *specific* and *simple*. Only after you've made several specific and simple reports should you expand your scope to include more sophisticated report ideas based on all of the patterns you'll start to see lurking in your data.

When we were getting started, one of our first fruitful high-fidelity reports was based on highly specific intel from the Swiss *abuse.ch* service for tracking the ZeuS family of information stealers. The ZeuS Tracker service provides a highly curated list of ZeuS-related domains, IP addresses, and URLs. Their compromised URL list at *https://zeus-tracker.abuse.ch/blocklist.php?download=compromised* contains a long list of URLs associated with ZeuS downloads and C2 servers. At the time of writing, the list contains entries such as *http://anlacviettravel.com.vn/home/plugins/system/tmp/bot.scr* and *http://albrecht-pie.net/new/gate.php*. With such a highly specific and high-quality list of URLs available, the report logic is already done for you. We regularly (automatically) rebuild our report query to reflect the ongoing changes to the ZeuS tracker URL list and integrated it into the following query:

- **HTTP Request**
- **URL of request matches any of:**
  - **— <Full ZeuS Tracker URL list>**

Because this query is based on a list of specific criteria, it falls into our intel-based report category, which we discuss in more depth at the end of this chapter.

Turning Samples of Malicious Activity into Queries for Reports

In the children's board game *Guess Who?*, two players each choose a character from a grid of pictures and try to guess the other player's chosen character by asking simple "yes" or "no" questions. The pictures in the grid are each attached to a little plastic hinge that allows pictures to be flipped down when an answer to a question eliminates that character. By process of elimination, when only one photo remains standing, that character must be the other player's choice. Typical questions include "Does your person have a red shirt?" "Is your person a woman?" and "Does your person have any facial hair?" Although many characters share traits like facial hair and shirt color, each character's total set of traits is unique. In many ways, finding specific events in your security logs is like a giant game of *Guess Who?* where your goal is to find the right set of questions to ask in order to find logs with actionable security information in them.

In the world of data science, an object's traits are often called *attributes*. More generally, in the world of machine learning, any tidbit that can be used to make something stand out is called a *feature*. The term *feature* tends to be a bit more generic and all encompassing, so that's the word we'll stick with. The following is an example of a Conficker malware HTTP C2 callback request:

```
GET /search?q=149 HTTP/1.0
User-Agent: Mozilla/4.0 (compatible; MSIE 6.0; Windows NT 5.1; SV1)
Host: 38.229.185.125
Pragma: no-cache
```

One feature of the request is that it uses HTTP/1.0. Another is the Host header with the value 38.229.185.125. Features can be much broader in scope, though, and make use of less obvious traits like metadata. When searching for a needle in a haystack, one feature of the needle is that it is made of a metal that is attracted to a magnet. In the preceding Conficker example, some of the features include:

- There are exactly three HTTP headers
- The question mark in the URL follows a filename that does not have an extension
- The host is an IP address rather than a domain name

The first step to finding an event is to identify what features the event has. When you have a list of features, you can use a combination of the less common of those features to uniquely define the pattern of what you're looking for.

To illustrate the power of identifying a pattern by using a combination of event features, first it is worthwhile to look at naive approaches to see why they fail. One naive approach would be to search your HTTP logs for requests to the exact URL *http://38.229.185.125/search?q=149*—but if you do that, you'll find just the one request you were looking for and no other Conficker requests. Such an absurdly specific high-fidelity report isn't going to be very useful. A slightly less naive approach would be to search for URLs that contain *search?=*. In addition to turning up Conficker requests, this query will find other events including the following:

```
GET /search?q=modi&prmd=ivnsl&source=lnms&tbm=nws HTTP/1.1
Host: www.google.com
User-Agent: Mozilla/5.0 (compatible; MSIE 10.0; Windows Phone 8.0; Trident/6.0;
   IEMobile/10.0; ARM; Touch; NOKIA; Lumia 820)
Referer: http://www.google.com/m/search?=client=ms-nokia-wp&q=%6D%6F%64%69
```

This result is a false positive. The more false positives a query returns, the more effort is needed to analyze the results. To create a good, high-fidelity query for Conficker, you should list the request features and estimate how common those features are. If you aren't very familiar with a data source or you can't estimate how unique a feature is, you can always query your data source for just that feature to see what kind of results are returned with that feature. In fact, this is exactly what you should do to determine how unique a feature is to a particular threat. It's usually a good idea to do this even when you do have an estimate, because finding results with the same feature often gives you a better picture of what a false positive could look like. One ancillary benefit to this searching is that you'll likely find other malicious activity with some features in common. When you find leads to other reports while working on an initial report, you can feel like a miner that just struck a big vein of gold with nuggets everywhere!

The following is an example of a feature list for the Conficker HTTP request, sorted by the likelihood of seeing that feature in the entirety of your web proxy data:

Very Common:

- Uses HTTP
- GET request

Common:

- Internet Explorer User-Agent string

Uncommon:

- HTTP protocol 1.0
- Does not contain a Referer header
- Takes a "*q=*" parameter
- Filename in URL doesn't contain an extension
- Request is directly to an IP address
- File path in URL is in base directory

The common versus uncommon categories aren't scientific in nature, and there isn't some cutoff that separates the two. Instead, the groupings between common and uncommon are there for you to estimate how useful a particular feature is likely to be. The more uncommon features you can identify, the more likely you're going to be able to weave together enough of them into a great report. By querying the logs for some of the uncommon features, you can focus on just the right set of features so that the query isn't too specific that it misses malicious activity, while also not so general that it catches harmless activity. This step is very important, because if you go straight to writing a very specific query, you'll likely miss slight permutations on the request like this one that some Conficker variants make:

```
GET /search?q=0&aq=7 HTTP/1.0
User-Agent: Mozilla/4.0 (compatible; MSIE 6.0; Windows NT 5.1; SV1;
  .NET CLR 1.1.4322; .NET CLR 2.0.50727)
Host: 216.38.198.78
Pragma: no-cache
```

After testing various features and combinations of features, you will hone in on a high-fidelity query for detecting Conficker. Our query includes the following:

- **Does not have a Referer header**
- **Contains "/search?q=" in URL**
- **Request uses HTTP 1.0**
- **Full URL matches the regular expression "^http://[0-9]+\.[0-9]+\.[0-9]+\.[0-9]+/search\?q=[0-9]{1,3}(&aq=[^&]*)?$"**

 This regular expression is looking for URLs that start (^) with *http://* and then an IP address by looking for four sections of numbers split up by three periods (dotted quad). There is no need for the regular expression to be more precise about checking for valid IP addresses.

The remainder of the regular expression looks for a one- to three-digit value for *q=* and then an optional *aq=* parameter with any value before the end of the URL ($).

For much more detailed information about regular expressions, see Jeffrey Friedl's *Mastering Regular Expressions* (O'Reilly).

The Conficker example is a classic easy-to-find event with a unique enough set of features that building high-fidelity detection for it is relatively straightforward. Conficker is currently a static target, though—there are only a few variants, and they aren't being updated. In most cases, the activity you're trying to detect is a moving target that's constantly using new domains and new IP addresses, and the bad guys are changing tactics and updating the malware on a continual basis with additional features or functionality.

Reports Are Patterns, Patterns Are Reports

When you're first getting into the report creation mindset, you're bound to run into the question of what the threshold for creating a report should be. The general approach we take for determining what should become a report is that reports should look for *patterns* of activity instead of specific indicators. That is, if you're searching through your data and you see a request to a malicious domain, you shouldn't create a report based on a query like:

- **HTTP GET Request**
- **Domain is *verybaddomain.com***

One of the problems with a report like this is that there is no end in sight. There are thousands of new malicious domains every single day, and you could never hope to keep up creating reports like this. It isn't just domains that are troublesome either. Malicious IP addresses, known-bad User-Agent headers, cryptographic hashes of files, and other highly specific indicators are all too specific to create individual reports based entirely on a single indicator. It isn't that specific indicators aren't reliable—they often are—it's that a playbook filled with highly specific reports becomes unwieldy and hard to manage, and the time spent creating new reports will outweigh the value of the reports. Specific indicators like known bad domains and IPs are useful for finding malicious patterns, and they do play an important role in detecting malicious events, but detection logic based entirely on them requires special handling. At the end of this chapter, in the section titled "Intelligence: A smart addition to your playbook" on page 189, we discuss ways of integrating indicators into your playbook in a maintainable way.

The Goldilocks-Fidelity

In the classic children's story *Goldilocks and the Three Bears*, a trespassing child tastes the porridge of a family of three bears before determining which bowl was the perfect eating temperature. When building a query for a report to detect an evolving threat, you want to shoot for the "Goldilocks-fidelity"—not too specific that you only catch a few events and not too generic that you catch too many other events. Finding the Goldilocks-fidelity is more of an art than a science, as there is a certain amount of unavoidable experience-based gut feeling that guides the report creation. Your tolerance for false positives and false negatives in a report is based in part on the value of finding the event you're looking for and the amount of analysis time you can spend sifting through results.

A good example of less straightforward events are the requests made by Java falling victim to a version of the Nuclear Exploit Pack (*http://blog.spiderlabs.com/2012/04/a-new-neighbor-in-town-the-nuclear-pack-v20-exploit-kit.html*). The following are examples of exploit requests:

```
GET /f/1/1394255520/1269354546/2 HTTP/1.1
Host: bfeverb.nwdsystems.com.ar
User-Agent: Mozilla/4.0 (Windows 7 6.1) Java/1.7.0_09
```

And in another event:

```
GET /f/3/1395062100/1826964273/2/2 HTTP/1.1
Host: interrupt.laurencarddesign.com
User-Agent: Mozilla/4.0 (Windows 7 6.1) Java/1.7.0_05
```

It is possible to make a feature list for these requests, but there aren't a lot of features to go on:

Very Common:

- Uses HTTP 1.1
- GET request

Common:

- User-Agent is Java

Uncommon:

- URL contains a lot of numbers
- URL contains a lot of slashes
- URL starts with */f/*
- URL ends with *2*

Very Uncommon:

- URL contains a Unix timestamp between slashes

With a feature list like this, it can be hard to determine where to start in locating other events. Do all malicious requests start with */f/* or end in *2*? In most cases, you'll have no idea, so you'll need to do exploratory queries to find out. Unfortunately, even if all past malicious activity contained both, there is a reasonable chance that future ones won't. If you build features like that into the query, you could end up missing a lot of malicious events. You'll need to rely on your experience with a data source and go with your gut. In cases like this, it can be tempting to go another route, like making a list of domains or IP addresses and watching those instead. For example, in a 90-day period, there were only six domains in the logs for the Nuclear Exploit Pack requests, so a query like the following might seem reasonable:

- **User-Agent contains "Java"**
- **Domain is any one of (OR):**
    - **"edge.stroudland.com"**
    - **"interrupt.laurencarddesign.com"**
    - **"instruct.laurencard.com"**
    - **"lawyer.actionuniforms.com"**

— "bfeverb.nwdsystems.com.ar"
— "jbps61lz.djempress.pw"

Remember, though, domains and IP addresses are usually treated as disposable resources, so what's used today (or in the past) is often a poor predictor of what will be used in the future. For this reason, it can be very hard to maintain a query and keep it updated with whatever the domain or IP du jour happens to be. Queries based on lists of values are very useful for manual exploring to get an idea of the variety and variation of events related to some security incident, but they should only be put into production reports as an absolute last resort. It is very common to see the specifics of security events like the domain or IP address change frequently while the overall pattern of the events stays the same. Instead of building up lists of domains and other specific indicators in a single unwieldy report, you can take the specific indicators you run into and add them to your security intelligence management system so that they get picked up by your intel-based reports.

With that in mind, the goal should be to create a query that looks for a *pattern* rather than a query that looks for the same specifics every time. Using the features identified in the two preceding sample Nuclear Exploit Pack requests, a reasonable query could tease out the pattern with an approach like the following:

- **User-Agent matches a typical Java request string**
- **URL contains at least four / characters after the *http://* portion**
- **URL contains a run of between 20 and 30 numbers bounded by / and optionally with / between numbers**
- **URL contains numbers that look like a Unix timestamp between / characters**
- **URL only contains letters, numbers, and slashes (excludes common URL characters such as periods, questions marks, etc.)**

This query is highly effective at detecting the example variant of the Nuclear Exploit pack while still being generic enough that the domains and IP addresses it's hosted at can change without affecting the report. Even future versions of the exploit pack are likely going to match the query, which will make the query effective for a longer period. Because the query is based on a unique enough set of features, it is very unlikely that it will produce false positives, and if it does, there probably won't be many. When there is only one or a few false positives, it's usually possible to identify the unique features the false positives have and then explicitly exclude those features from the query. However, this can be a dangerous game if the number or type of false positives grows. If tuning out false positives by explicitly excluding them becomes unwieldy, instead of negating event features, you may need to add yet another unique feature the malicious events have that the false positives don't.

 In general, positive features (ones required for an event to match) tend to be more powerful and less finicky than negative features (ones excluded for an event to match). One trick to creating high-quality queries is finding ways of using positive features to make the event you're looking for stand out from all of the other events in your logs. After you have a set of traits (features) that describe the event you're looking for, it's just a matter of constructing a query that selects those features all at the same time. If the events you're looking for don't have enough unique features to make them stand out, there is little you can do.

Exploring Out of Sight of Land

Up to this point, most of the discussions and examples of report creation strategies have all involved building off a sample of the malicious activity. You've learned how to identify unique features of a particular event and build queries to find other events with those same features. However, you won't always have examples of malicious activity. Sometimes, you will want to find things based only on an *idea* of what the malicious activity might look like rather than anything concrete. The most obvious strategy is to just guess at some specific set of features you think malicious activity would likely have and then write a query to detect those features. More often than not, though, you'll find that jumping straight to a fully defined query based on guessed features won't return anything useful. Instead, you need to be smart but methodical about building new reports without the benefit of examples. There are many ways to do this, but we will focus on a few we find particularly effective.

Sticking with What You Know

By the time you're at a stage where you're creating reports based on hunches rather than concrete examples, you should already have quite a few reports under your belt. Often, your existing reports are the best source of ideas for new reports. In the process of identifying features for specific events and building queries for those events, you spent a lot of time finding a unique set of features for an event. If you leave out the most specific features but include some general indicators of "badness," you can search through logs that are similar but much broader and more inclusive than events you already know about. These sorts of queries would usually make for poor investigative reports due to the number of benign events and false positives, but they can make great exploratory queries for you to try to find previously unknown events.

For example, if you've made a good set of reports based on HTTP logs, you'll probably find a few reports looking for POSTs without a Referer header. The circumstances under which a web browser would legitimately POST to a server without a Referer header are rare and often convoluted. However, exclusively looking for matches with both features produces too many false positives for a playbook report. If you spot a suspect event with a broad query, you can then pivot and use that event for further exploration. The specific way to pivot is going to depend on the data source and the event(s) you find. Often, there are multiple possibilities, and you will have to select the likely best ones based on your experience and understanding of your data. The following query is an example of broad searching using the HTTP POST with no Referer header:

- **HTTP POST**
- **No Referer header**
- **Deduplicated events by the source host**

As you can imagine, many results are returned. Sifting by hand through the first 50 results quickly turns up:

```
POST /index.php HTTP/1.1
Host: m0nplatin.ru
User-Agent: Mozilla/4.0 (compatible; MSIE 7.0; Windows NT 5.2; WOW64;
    .NET CLR 1.1.4322; .NET CLR 2.0.50727; .NET CLR 3.0.4506.2152;
    .NET CLR 3.5.30729; InfoPath.1)
```

Although there is nothing specifically malicious about this event, the domain looks highly suspect. By itself, the *.ru* TLD isn't inherently malicious, but it has built up a relatively low reputation because a lot of malicious actors abuse it. Unless you're a Russian-based organization, uses of *.ru* won't be very common, so using it as a possible indicator of malice is reasonable. More significant than the *.ru* TLD, though, is the actual domain name text *m0nplatin*. Humans are expected to type, and usually don't make use of l33t spe4k, so the zero in place of an "o" is unusual. Many common fonts used don't have much difference between a zero and capital O, which can trick users (or security analysts!) into thinking they're seeing one name when they're actually seeing another. When you combine the suspect domain with a HTTP POST and no Referer, the event as a whole stands out as highly suspicious.

Other than the domain, though, there aren't a lot of other identifying features that would make this event particularly great for a report. Without a useful pattern, you'd probably have to build a query looking for the specific domain. Even though the results would likely be a high-fidelity report, it'd also be highly specific and likely not useful for long. There is nothing intrinsically wrong with a highly specific report like this, but without more evidence that it's a significant or prevalent threat, creating a report for it will just be a drop in the bucket. Instead of trying to build a one-off report for this event, adding the domain to your locally generated intelligence list should be effective enough at detecting identical subsequent infections.

You don't have to stop at the most obvious indicators, though. Yes, a report looking for a POST with no Referer to the domain would work, but when you're exploring, you should try to pivot on other features to see where they lead. One way to pivot on this event would be to notice that the POST is to a PHP script and add that criteria to your exploratory query to see what it gets you. We know from experience that this query is a good way to start exploring your HTTP logs for possible malicious activity:

- **HTTP POST**
- **No Referer**
- **File on server is a PHP script**
- **Deduplicate by client host**

Doing so would still be awfully generic, though, and wouldn't take you much closer to the malicious activity the previous query returned. Another option would be to look at any similar activity from the same host to see if any other events have more features for identification:

- **HTTP POST**
- **No Referer**
- **Same source host seen performing previous malicious event to *m0nplatin.ru***

This query returns many interesting malicious events, including the following:

```
POST / HTTP/1.1
Host: pluginz.ru
User-Agent: Mozilla/4.0 (compatible; MSIE 6.0; Windows NT 5.1; SV1)

POST / HTTP/1.1
Host: yellowstarcarpet.com
User-Agent: Mozilla/4.0 (compatible; MSIE 6.0; Windows NT 5.1; SV1)
```

Of course, there are events showing connections to many other domains, too. The vast majority of the events use the same Internet Explorer 6 User-Agent string, though (for historical reasons, Internet Explorer and almost all other browsers claim to be a version of Mozilla). Experience will tell you IE 6 is ancient and has almost no legitimate deployment anymore. The same is rapidly becoming true of Windows NT 5.1 (XP). Adding these features to the initial query is quite effective:

- **HTTP POST**
- **No Referer**
- **User-Agent claims "MSIE 6.0" and "Windows NT 5.1"**

Almost all of the results of this query look quite suspect, if not outright malicious. Depending on your data, you might find the results good enough to turn that query directly into an investigative report. It's pretty easy for an experienced human to pick out the obviously unusual or malicious activity from the results, and many of the other results can be pivoted to turn other report-worthy activity. There is something to be said for the power of the human brain to spot unusual activity! The more events you look at, the more familiar you become with normal activity for your organization. Of course, if you're a Russian organization with a big deployment of Internet Explorer 6 on Windows XP, your experience will probably be looking for other events that stand out. However, you should use other information to influence your analysis of activity. For example, if the system you use to collect HTTP logs can provide additional context like IP or domain or URL reputation, you can draw conclusions about the nature of the activity faster. If you augment the query to look for low reputation requests, you can further reduce the total number of results to explore. Another option would be to add features known to be common among malicious activity, like restricting the POSTS to just PHP scripts as a clause to create a new exploratory query:

- **HTTP POST**
- **No Referer**
- **User-Agent claims "MSIE 6.0" and "Windows NT 5.1"**
- **URL uses IP address instead of domain name**
- **File extension on URL is .php**

As you go through the results this query digs up, you're bound to spot patterns that can be further developed into reports of their own.

Inverting "Known Good"

When searching for unknown malicious activity, consider the sage advice of fictional character Sherlock Holmes: "When you have eliminated the impossible, whatever remains, however improbable, must be the truth." The events in some data sources are much more regular and predictable. This regularity can be very useful for detecting anomalous activity because it sets an expectation for what events *should* look like. When it's easy to quantify what a regular event is, then events that don't match the expected pattern can also easily be found. This regularity can take on many different forms, and the type of regularity will vary from data source to data source. In some data sources, it's easy to identify certain properties that all events of a particular type should always have. In other data sources, all legitimate events may use a specific format. Sometimes, data sources mostly have nonpatterned data, but a subset of events related to a specific behavior takes on a specific form.

For example, a common trick used by malware is to name itself the same thing other common processes are named on a system. On Windows, one of these common process names is *explorer.exe* (also *svchost.exe*, *winlogon.exe*, *rundll32.exe*, etc.), which on a standard install is always located at *c:\windows*. All legitimate copies of *explorer.exe* that happen to generate host-based alerts in HIPS or AV software should match the known pattern; therefore, looking for all *explorer.exe* alerts where *explorer.exe* is not in *c:\windows* can be quite useful:

- **Process name ends with *explorer.exe***
- **Process directory is not *c:\windows***

The results of this query will find malware masquerading as legitimate activity without perfectly matching all of the traits you'd expect from actual legitimate activity. Anytime you have events where two features should always coincide, there is an opportunity for a report that checks for one feature without the other.

Looking for Things Labeled as "Bad"

Oftentimes, a data source will have some reputation, threat, or severity metadata associated with events. For example, IDS events usually contain an alert level or severity score, HTTP proxy logs often contain domain or IP reputation information, HIPS or AV logs are only supposed to trigger on malicious activity, and so forth. If you were to throw all of your data in a SIEM, it is primarily the reputation metadata that would get used for alerting and prioritizing of security events. Building reports solely based on this metadata is fraught with pitfalls because most reputation scoring or other metadata changes over time, or the process used to generate it is a black box. Without intimate knowledge of how reputation metadata is built, you don't have any ability to estimate the fidelity of a report if the report relies exclusively on black box threat scores.

Reputation metadata isn't useless, though—it can often serve as a big red flag in your data saying "look here!" When you're looking for new examples of malicious activity, a great place to start is by looking at the events another system already thinks is malicious. The actual value of looking at the low-reputation or high-threat events will depend a lot on the quality of whatever scoring/reputation source you have. The obvious place to start is to look for the events with the lowest reputation or highest threat score. When you've built a solid understanding and "gut feeling" about your data, you'll be in a much better position to judge the reputation system associated with that data.

Taking the naive initial approach may pay off, and you may find actionable events that you can use as the source material for new reports, especially at the beginning. Even if your reputation metadata doesn't yield good results all by itself, there are always ways to take a "blended approach." A blended approach mixes the exploration tricks and techniques already discussed with reputation data to help further filter/prioritize what to review.

For example, in our HTTP proxy logs, domains are scored on a sigmoid curve in the range [-10, +10], where a score of 0 is a neutral reputation and a null score means no reputation data is available. Combining reputation information with another general query for unusual features can yield useful results. Suppose you have an exploratory query like the following:

> - **HTTP POST**
> - **No Referer header**
> - **User-Agent header does not contain "MSIE" or "Firefox" or "Chrome" or "Safari"**

A query like this is going to return a lot of results. Some of the events will be malicious, but many of them won't be. Domain reputation metadata can help filter out many of the events and help you prioritize which events to look at first:

> - **HTTP POST**
> - **No Referer header**
> - **User-Agent header does not contain "MSIE" or "Firefox" or "Chrome" or "Safari"**
> - **Domain has a reputation less than -3**

For this query, the very first event turned up was:

```
POST /dron/g.php HTTP/1.1
Host: marmedladkos.com
User-Agent: Mozilla/4.0
```

For this request, the domain reputation score is `-7.1`, and the note accompanying the reputation is "`Domain has unusually high traffic volume for a very recent registration.`" Further investigation shows that the activity is actually the result of GameOver ZeuS, a sophisticated information stealing bot. By itself, the reputation score metadata isn't high enough quality to be worth the time to sort through results where a low reputation score is the sole criteria. Although -7.1 is rather low, there are hundreds of thousands of requests every day with worse scores. When the reputation score is used to augment other features, though, the results can be quite actionable.

Whether you use the tricks outlined here or you come up with other ways of finding new malicious activity in your logs, log exploration is virtually guaranteed to lead to new reports. Don't be afraid to go deep into the gold mine in pursuit of malicious activity, but understand that there isn't always a nugget at the bottom. Even when you have no idea where to start, you can just look at the first dozen or even hundred events and pull things out of them at random to explore. There is no "right way" to do it; letting the data take you down interesting paths is likely to open up lots of areas for further exploration. An ancillary benefit of exploratory queries is an increased familiarity with a data source, and you're likely to improve your ability to search and understand the events it contains, too. The more you explore a data source, the more efficient and effective you'll be at creating reports based on the data source.

Intelligence: A smart addition to your playbook

As we discussed in Chapter 3, attacks and attackers are evolving at a frantic pace. To keep up, a vast landscape of data aggregators, indicator curators, and information sharing organizations have sprung up to fill the information void. Usually, the huge array of information available about individual attacks is referred to as *intel*. Whole books could be written about security intel management, preparation, vetting, automation, organization, sharing, and curation—intel is a rapidly evolving aspect of security monitoring. Intel isn't a replacement for your playbook, and all of your playbook reports aren't substitutes for using intel in your playbook.

To fit security intel and indicators into your playbook, the "rule" that all reports are based on *patterns* must be broken. Our approach to breaking the pattern rule, while retaining the easy maintainability of the playbook, is to group intel by fields or features such as domain names, IP addresses, or known malware MD5s, and then build designated intel-based reports for each category. For example, you'll likely have many different data feeds providing information on malicious domains. To integrate all of the intel we have on malicious domains into the playbook, we programmatically extract all domains from our intel management system and build a single report with a query:

- **ANY of the following:**
  — Domain is *baddomain1.com*
  — Domain is *otherbadomain.org*
  — Domain is *verymaliciousdomain.biz*
  — Domain is *yetanotherbaddomain.com*
  — [....]

The important difference between this report and most of the other reports in your playbook is that the query is not meant to be maintained by a human, and tuning the report doesn't involve directly changing the query. Instead, all curation of the domain list for this report happens in the intel management system, and the query for this report is regenerated as needed. This approach works well for your own homegrown intel, too. As you're hunting through your data looking to create new reports, any malicious indicators you see that don't rise to the pattern level can still be added to your intel management system where they will be pulled into your playbook through your intel-based reports.

Basics are 90% of the game

None of the concepts covered in this chapter have been particularly sophisticated and yet, you will likely find the bulk of your playbook reports only make use of the basics covered in this chapter. It's not that advanced plays are too hard to create—it's that query simplicity often beats complexity for creating reports with good result fidelity. The simple tricks for exploring your data to find examples of malicious activity for the basis of new reports are effective and get the job done.

For a playbook to be effective, it must be *your* playbook tailored to *your* organization's needs by detecting the threats *your* organization faces. By starting with specific examples of malicious activity, you can become familiar with the process and get comfortable with your data and creating plays. After you've built up a set of initial high-fidelity reports, you can branch off into uncharted territory by exploring your logs and trying to build more generic investigative reports. A corpus of high-fidelity detection logic utilizes your infrastructure to detect threats, freeing time for your human resources to create, analyze, and tune lower-fidelity detection techniques. You'll never *need* advanced queries, but sometimes the basic ideas covered in this chapter aren't the best way to find attacks. In that case, you may want to rely on statistics, correlated data, and other tricks to uncover malicious activity. Chapter 9 will help get you started building more advanced queries.

Chapter Summary

- There are many ways to search through data, but starting with simple and broad queries can help to reduce large data sets to functional and actionable components.

- False positives slow down your analysis, but with careful adjustment, they can be reduced.

- Attacks happen in multiple stages with detection possibilities available in most of them.

- Researching and developing unique features in your data will aid in constructing efficient queries.

- Avoid serially processed indicators, as well as overly complex logical contingencies for plays that are easy to understand and execute.

- Most reports should detect patterns and turn the highly specific items into indicators.

- Specific indicators are better handled through an intel management system rather than being spread out in lists across many different reports.

CHAPTER 9

Advanced Querying

"The world is full of obvious things which nobody by any chance ever observes."
—Sherlock Holmes

In the preceding chapter, we laid out the basic foundations of creating queries for reports based on the data available. Most of the query ideas presented were limited, based on looking for specific indicators and previously known activity. Additionally, most of the queries were based on looking at events in a single data source, or events related to the activity of a single host. Certainly, using known indicators or finding indicators in your data to create new reports goes a long way. However, you can dig a little deeper by applying more sophisticated analysis to your event data to uncover indicators and additional patterns not evident through basic searching. Statistics provide tools and methods for sorting through your security event data in ways that are less obvious than matching an event to a single, static indicator. It will also help to find the outliers and the commonalities in the data, which can also yield valuable information.

In this chapter, we'll cover:

- More false positive elimination strategies
- How to identify and filter common traffic
- How to detect anomalous traffic
- How to pair statistical formulae with security event data to discover incidents

Basic Versus Advanced

It probably comes as no surprise that there is no specific, objective "dividing line" between what makes a query basic or more advanced. It doesn't matter either way, so long as the query achieves your report objective efficiently and effectively. For the purposes of this chapter, the general divider for advanced queries is that the query isn't based on a specific known indicator or simple pattern. Queries that use multiple data sources in nonrelational ways or look for commonalities in behavior across multiple hosts are examples. Added query complexity can provide a lot more flexibility to find nuanced suspicious activity, but greater complexity often means more analysis and investigative work to understand and analyze the query results.

It is difficult to estimate the fidelity of an advanced query because instead of looking at one narrow set of indicators, the results are often woven together from multiple events, sometimes across multiple hosts or multiple data sources. Understanding the interaction between numerous, diverse events is nontrivial in the general case. With advanced queries, you often can't predict all of the real-world scenarios that could manifest in your query results, so you can't easily get a handle on the likelihood of false positives or estimate fidelity.

Other differences between basic queries and advanced queries are the nature, type, and impact of false positives on the results. When you build a basic report using known malicious indicators like domains, user agents, specific requests, or other unique data, you generally end up with a high-fidelity report. Even when an amalgamation of features in a basic query produce false positives, the analysis of those false positives can be easily tracked back to one or more of the features not being specific or unique enough. A lack of specificity in simple queries leads to a trade-off between generality and fidelity (see Figure 9-1). For most basic queries that make use of several unusual event features, the generality of the query tends to go up at the cost of the fidelity of the report going down.

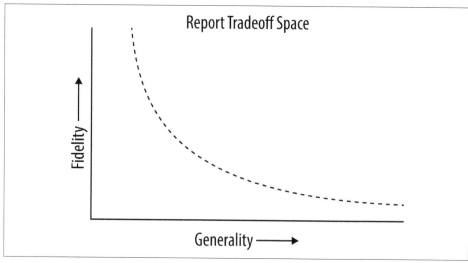

Figure 9-1. Most reports can be tweaked to be more general at the cost of a lower fidelity or more specific in return for a higher fidelity

Reports tend to lie on a curve where if you make them more generic, you increase the chance of false positives creeping in and reducing the overall fidelity of the results. There is no correct choice in this trade-off, and there is room in your playbook for highly specific high-fidelity reports as well as somewhat generic lower-fidelity reports. An added complication to this trade-off curve is that there is no way to know exactly where on the curve a report lies. False positives can sneak into reports in surprising ways. More advanced queries have to contend with false positives to a much greater extent, so a theoretical basis for the expected base rate of false positives is in order.

The False Positive Paradox

False positives and lots of benign results are the mortal enemy of your playbook, because they drown out true positive results and waste a lot of analysis time. Estimating the likelihood of false positives can be a tricky business and isn't as easy as you may think. Statistics are a great tool in your report creation arsenal, but the math is not always on your side when it comes to avoiding false positives.

Suppose you have a busy web server under attack. As a result, you decide to write an IDS signature to detect the attack. The attack is easily detectable when real attack traffic goes by and your IDS signature successfully detects the attack 90% of the time. However, sometimes legitimate requests also look like the attack, so your signature triggers a false positive on legitimate nonmalicious traffic 0.015% of the time. Assuming only one in a million requests to your server are part of the malicious attack, what's the probability that an alert from your signature is an actual attack? Intuition based on the 90% accuracy of your IDS signature would suggest it's close to 90%; however, the actual probability that the detection is a true positive is only 0.59%. That is, there will be about 165 false positives for every true positive in your million results. Faced with a result like this, you may try to make the IDS signature 100% accurate at detecting true positives. However, if the false positive rate stays at 0.015%, this will only improve the chances of an alert being a true positive to 0.66%. If you reduce the false positive rate to 0.001%, the chance an alert is a true positive only rises to 9%. False positives seem a lot more treacherous now, don't they!

If you overestimate the accuracy of a report because you neglect the expected rate of false positives, you're committing what's known as a *base rate fallacy*. When trying to estimate the overall efficacy of a query, the most important factor to consider is the chance that the query produces a false positive on benign events. In the preceding example, only one in a million events is malicious. Unless benign events trigger the query less frequently than about once in a million, the overall quality of the results will be very poor. In practice, though, you rarely know the actual percentage of malicious events in your logs (the *base rate*), and you're even less likely to know the chance that a nonmalicious event could falsely trigger your query. Without knowing both of these values, you're mostly left to guessing how accurate a query will be. Likely the only thing you'll be certain of is that false positives defy intuition and sneak into results in unexpected ways.

InfoSec isn't the only field that has to deal with the treachery of Bayesian statistics. Doctors know the chance of a false positive test on a rare disease is much more likely than an actual case of that disease. This is one of the reasons why doctors are often reluctant to report initial test results to patients without follow-up tests. Airport security is another glaring example of false positives drowning out true positives. There aren't that many terrorists flying daily in comparison to the number of total nonterrorist passengers that pass through security. Factoring in the poor detection rate for true terrorists with the occasional flagging of an innocent traveler, nearly 100% of all passengers detained or questioned further are false positives.

Good Indications

When you're creating a report, you must be mindful to minimize false positives. If you don't have a good way to estimate the quality of a query, always assume it's less accurate than your gut tells you it will be. Usually, the bulk of your query development effort will be carefully crafting a query that doesn't return the nonmalicious events, but still captures the malicious ones. Put another way, most of your time won't be spent in finding the malicious events, it will be spent avoiding the nonmalicious ones. Above all, the best indicator of the quality of a query is to run it against historical data to estimate the accuracy.

 If you have historical logs to search against, you have a report "time machine" that can tell you how a query would have performed had it been in place in the past. Even for brand-new attacks with no historical data containing traces of the attack, queries on historical data can help you estimate the number of benign and false positive results that could turn up.

Consensus as an Indicator (Set Operations and Outlier Finding)

Not all data sources are created equal. Even data sources that are rich in information may not be rich in useful features to aid in finding needles in the haystack. Information and feature-rich data sources like HTTP logs give you more query possibilities than what you get with feature-poor data sources. Feature-poor data sources tend to be the ones that provide sparse, record keeping-like information without nuance or flair. DNS query logs, NetFlow, DHCP logs, authentication logs, and firewall logs are all usually feature poor. Without many features to aid in query development, it's easy to dismiss the data source as either not useful or only useful in specific circumstances, but fortunately there are query strategies that can work even without many features.

Just as you can't look at individual spoonfuls of dirt to tell how bountiful a gold mine is, without specific known malicious indicators, it's hard to look at events individually and gain much insight. In feature-poor data sources, it's better to step back and look at events in aggregate to get a big picture view of activity. There are lots of ways to do this, so this chapter will only cover a few of the ones we've found to have a good effort-to-payoff ratio.

Set Operations for Finding Commonalities

Suppose during an investigation of DoS activity sourced from your network you learn that several machines have all been compromised, without knowing the specifics of the malware used or how it is controlled. It would be natural if your next step were to look for commonalities in the behavior of the hosts. This is where set operations come in.

Set operations are overly complicated mathematical constructs for what is a very simple idea: to manipulate groups of items (called *sets*) to form new groups based on some properties of the elements in the groups. The three most common set operations are:

- Union
- Intersection
- Difference

Union combines two groups into one larger group comprised of all of the elements in each. *Intersection* produces a new group that only has items that are in both groups. *Difference* gives you all of the items in the first group that are not contained in the second group. Using these set operations, it's easier to handle large amounts of data automatically, and that's exactly what you want if you're going to find what compromised hosts have in common.

To find what two DoSing hosts have in common, the intersection operation will be most useful. First, choose a data source to search for common behaviors and then gather the activity of each host into host-specific groups. For DNS queries, they may look something like:

Host 1	Host 2
accounts.google.com	*a.adroll.com*
ad.wsod.com	*a.disquscdn.com*
adfarm.mediaplex.com	*a.visualrevenue.com*

Host 1	Host 2
adserver.wenxuecity.com	*about.bgov.com*
aph.ppstream.com	*about.bloomberg.co.jp*
api-public.addthis.com	*about.bloomberglaw.com*
[...]	[...]

For most active hosts, the groups of activity will be quite large. Taking the intersection of the two cuts the results down significantly:

Host 1 *intersect* Host 2
accounts.google.com
apis.google.com
br.pps.tv.iqiyi.com
cdn.api.twitter.com
clients1.google.com
cm.g.doubleclick.net
connect.facebook.net
edge.quantserve.com
googleads.g.doubleclick.net
ib.adnxs.com
lh4.googleusercontent.com
[...]

Although the intersection in activity between the two hosts is usually much less data than the complete activity of either host, it's often still too much to go through by hand. You can manually discard some of the more obviously nonmalicious domains (e.g., commonly known sites and content networks); however, that approach is slow, error-prone, and not scalable. Again, set operations can help. Uninfected (good) hosts lack the malicious behavior exhibited by malware infected hosts. This difference provides an opportunity for identifying the malicious activity common among infected hosts that isn't shared with uninfected ones. Good hosts make it easy to build a whitelist of domains to ignore by taking the union of activity from several hosts you don't suspect of being compromised.

How you select *good* hosts for the whitelist is only marginally important. Good hosts are most helpful when they have lots of nonmalicious activity in common with the hosts you're investigating. The more legitimate activity they have in common, the better your good hosts will be at eliminating nonmalicious results from your query results. After you've grouped a bunch of benign activity together (union operation), take the set and subtract out the legitimate activity with a set difference operation.

For the DoSing hosts, that results in only two domains: *www.frade8c.com* and *vh12.ppstream.com*.

Pictorially, this operation looks like Figure 9-2.

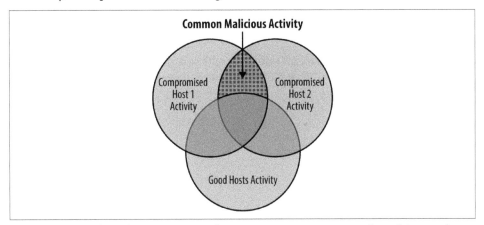

Figure 9-2. By taking the intersection of activity on two compromised machines and removing the activity also exhibited by hosts that aren't compromised, you can quickly narrow in on what the malicious machines have in common

Any events from a similar "intersection + difference" operation must be confirmed to be malicious. From the preceding results, a web search reveals that *www.frade8c.com* is a known command-and-control domain for a DoS malware variant. Armed with this knowledge, you can find other compromised hosts exhibiting similar behaviors, deploy mitigation measures, and look for other related activity found in subsequent sets.

Finding Black Sheep

Another method of profiling unusual behavior is looking at a single host's network activity. Newly infected hosts will deviate from their own regular pre-infection behavior enough to be actionable. For example, most client hosts are configured to use a small number of DNS nameservers (two or three is most common) for their query needs. There isn't just one pattern of query behavior, because of differences in how machines are configured and how different operating systems balance their queries among nameservers. Even though there can be large differences between machines, the query pattern of individual machines should stay consistent over time. A typical host pattern might be something like:

Nameserver	Queries
172.30.87.157	1344
172.30.115.191	110
172.29.131.10	88

Though the query distribution isn't uniform, there is no extreme outlier. For a host infected with malware that uses a hardcoded nameserver, the distribution does have an outlier:

Nameserver	Queries
172.30.166.165	1438
10.70.168.183	286
172.30.136.148	179
8.8.8.8	1

As you can see, even though query activity is highly uneven, a single query to 8.8.8.8 stands out. In this example, the domain queried is *qwe.affairedhonneur.us*, and the host shows many signs of malicious activity. The specific query criteria and thresholds to find this activity will depend on the type of hosts on your network and how they're configured. If all of your hosts are to use a single nameserver, then detection is easy—any host querying two nameservers is doing something unusual. For other configurations, you'll need to play with the query knobs to find something that works well. For nonuniform data like in the example table, you may want to look at the logarithm of the query counts to each nameserver instead of the absolute number of queries. Using the logarithm of the numbers, a reasonable threshold might be to look at the difference between the most queried and least queried nameserver, and if there is a difference above some threshold, flag the queries to the rare nameserver for further review.

 Using the log() of data works well when your data has an exponential distribution. In the case of nameserver query patterns, oftentimes the most queried nameserver is queried many times more often than the second most queried nameserver. Using the log() of data like this smooths out the big differences and works better than the absolute difference between two data points.

There are additional DNS abuse detection methods beyond nameserver query counts. A common DoS strategy is the DNS amplification attack. These attacks send spoofed DNS query packets that appear to come from the chosen victim, to any nameserver that will respond. When the nameserver receives the query, it processes the request and responds to the victim with the answer. From the view of the nameserver, it received a query and provided the answer. From the perspective of the victim, there is a nameserver flooding it with DNS answers to queries it never sent. Besides hiding the actual attacker from the victim, this technique is popular because DNS questions can be very small, but DNS answers can be very large. This allows attackers to amplify their DoS ability by flooding their victim with more traffic than they actually sent. Amplification factors of better than 25-to-1 are common.

This sort of attack is easy to detect with NetFlow. The hallmark of a successful DNS amplification attack is a significant imbalance in traffic toward a DNS server compared to traffic out. If you look at historical activity to your authoritative nameservers, you'll find that DNS responses out are, in general, about twice as big as the queries in. That is, about 33% of the total bytes across all flows will be queries in and about 66% of the total bytes will be answers out. Of course, there can be significant variation from server to server, depending on the types of queries it sees, but you'd never expect a server to account for more than 95% of the bytes out. However, for a DNS amplification DoS attack, you'll likely see your server's answers accounting for more than 95% of the total bytes. This is depicted in Figure 9-3.

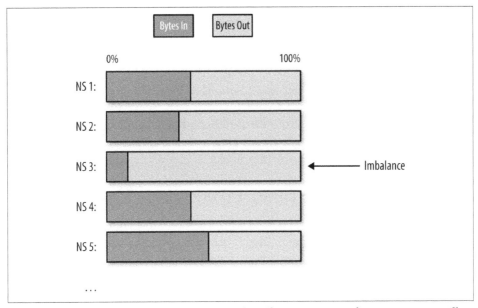

Figure 9-3. A breakdown of the percentage of traffic in versus out for nameservers will show an imbalance towards traffic sent out when a nameserver is being abused in a DNS amplification attack

Using NetFlow, there are a few signs you can look for to detect UDP amplification attacks:

- A sudden positive deviation in the total packet count
- A disproportionate number of UDP server response bytes compared to the client bytes sent
- A positive deviation of the total amount of UDP service traffic
- Any of the above indicators associated with deprecated services (chargen, daytime, echo, etc.)

Here is an example query using this technique:

- **UDP traffic with local network host using port 53**
- **For each unique pair of outside host to inside host**
  - **— Total packets between hosts is at least 1000**
  - **— Total traffic between hosts is at least 1 megabyte**
  - **— Server traffic accounts for at least 95% of total flow bytes**

The fidelity of this query is quite high. It would be unusual to see your server sending significantly more traffic than the client. For small flows, the ratio can easily deviate from the norm a lot; however, for flows with many packets and bytes, normal behavior will average out and won't cross the threshold. Some people like to call this the "law of large numbers," but whether you think of this as a law or not, the more data you have, the more the statistics are on your side.

Statistics: 60% of the Time, It Works Every Time

Statistics and data aggregation are especially useful because high-fidelity "smoking gun" events are so infrequent and limited in scope. Statistics can get complicated fast, and a report that no one can understand is a real problem. As with basic queries, simplicity should be your goal wherever possible. In many cases, sums, averages, and standard deviations are often powerful enough to be useful in reports without the need for more sophisticated statistical machinery.

Some data sources benefit from statistical analysis more than others. Data sources where each individual event is relatively low fidelity are a prime target for statistics like counting events, unique event value aggregation, or finding event outliers. Even when a data sources contains events that are entirely unactionable individually, aggregating events together may still provide useful results. Two common data sources where statistics are often quite helpful are IDS events and NetFlow. Alerts from an IDS span a huge range of fidelities from purely informational events to highly specific malware signatures. After you've created reports containing the high-fidelity events, you're left with—and will need to start looking at—noisy behavior: often the result of lower-quality signatures firing across large numbers of hosts.

Skimming the IDS Flotsam Off the Top

Traditional IDS signatures for exploit detection are notoriously noisy and often provide little value on their own. But taken in aggregate, even a bunch of very low-quality events can be a good indicator that *something* bad is happening. For the purposes of detecting malicious host activity on your network, you should prioritize hosts that are the source of attacks rather than the victim of attacks. One of the biggest flaws of exploit-detection signatures is that they're usually very poor at telling you when a host has actually been exploited. No doubt every day your IDS sees hundreds of exploit attempts, such as Unix passwd file grab attempts, SQL embedded in web traffic, or port probes against your Internet-facing hosts. Instead of trying to guess at the success of attacks, you can look for IDS events where your hosts are the source of the attacks as an indicator of when hosts have been compromised on your network.

Even so, many IDS signatures trigger false positives enough that in some cases the false positives will obscure the actual malicious behavior. You still need a way of identifying the most suspect hosts. A great strategy for doing that is to aggregate your events in a one-to-many relationship. The idea behind aggregating events is to group all events from a single attacker into a summary of the behavior rather than getting bogged down with each individual event on its own. A lot of detailed information is lost when you aggregate events, but for a high-level overview of activity, details like the sequence of events aren't very important. Often, thousands of events from a single source can be compressed into an easily digestible summary of what that machine is doing. Here is an example query using this technique:

- **IDS event attacker (usually source) is internal network host**
- **For each unique attacker, aggregate all events sourced by that attacker**
    - **Count and record each unique IDS signature triggered with timestamp**
    - **Count and record each unique victim host**
    - **Count the total number of events fired**

Instead of looking for some specific threat or activity pattern, this query is simply grouping results together for easier analysis of the high-level details. For the results to be useful, you still need a way to prioritize looking at the groups. Start by sorting the group from the most total events fired to the least total events fired. This will give you a feel for some of the noisiest and most invaluable signatures, which should be disabled or tuned. You can follow up by sorting the results by unique victim hosts, unique signatures, network location, host sensitivity, or other contextual factors for additional prioritization and detection possibilities.

When you've aggregated a bunch of different events from several hosts, your method of sorting will determine which hosts rise to the top of your results. If you sort by the total event count, the noisiest hosts by total event volume show up at the top. If you sort by the total number of unique victim hosts, then attackers scanning across a whole network will rise to the top. There are many ways to slice the data through sorting, but in many cases there isn't a "best" choice for which aggregated field to sort on. What's more likely is that none of the fields are particularly great for sorting on their own. In these situations, you'll find yourself wanting to weigh each field equally, so hosts that stand out in multiple categories rise above hosts that stand out in just one. You could try averaging the values of various fields together, but you'll find that usually just one number, total events, completely dominates the other numbers. This makes the average value useless. The same is true if you just add all the values together and sort by the sum. For example, 10 unique signatures might be a lot of signatures for a single host to fire, but 10 total events may not be that many at all. If a host fired 1,000 events with only one signature, the sum is 1,001. A host that fired 900 events and 6 unique signatures sums to 906. Sorting this way favors the first host, even though the latter host is more concerning because of the breadth of their attack profile (six signatures, lots of hosts). Instead of simple sums or averages, a good statistic to use for data like this is the geometric mean.

A geometric mean works best when you want to find an average-like value for a set of data but each element of the data uses completely different ranges. The geometric mean of the three items is the third root of the three items multiplied together. In general, the geometric mean of n items is the nth root of the product of all n items. The geometric mean of data is much less sensitive to one element dominating all of the others and naturally weighs each element equally.

Computing the geometric mean and sorting the preceding query by it produces actionable results near the top, as in the example shown in Table 9-1.

Table 9-1. Example of sorting report results by geometric mean

Attacker	Event count	Sig count	Signatures	Victim count	Victims	Gmean
10.129.63.43	99	4	(DNS lookup and TCP/445 sigs)	87	12.109.104.145	33
					12.109.104.146	
					[...]	
172.27.3.12	83	2	(TCP/445 sigs)	82	128.79.103.57	24
					128.79.103.58	
					[...]	
172.17.20.151	972	1	(Active Directory Password Failure)	2	64.100.10.100	12
					64.100.10.101	
72.163.4.161	1330	1	(ICMP Flood)	1	89.64.128.5	11

Notice that in this table the top two results are more balanced because they have a high number of events, signatures, and victims. The noise of a single signature firing repeatedly (like in the last result) doesn't drown out other interesting results. The result with 972 password failures is a great example of the power of a geometric mean to normalize down highly repetitive events. Just sorting on the event count would place the most repetitive events at the top, which is likely to distract the analyst away from the behavior with more variety. It's not uncommon to see a broken script or misconfiguration in an environment trigger thousands or millions of events. Even legitimate activity can sometimes generate a flood of events. In a lightly tuned report, analyzing noisy, repetitive events prevents you from getting to the more nuanced activity. Events regularly fire in a loop, but an event that fires ten times more often as another doesn't equate to that event being ten times as bad. Where averaging and other naive sorting methods have trouble with extremely noisy events, the geometric mean may excel.

IDS events aren't the only noisy data source. NetFlow benefits from statistics for useful detection. Rarely is a single flow a good indicator of anything. Instead, behaviors like P2P participation, port scanning (both vertical and horizontal), and various worm activities can all be detected by analyzing a large number of related flows.

Another hurdle when using statistics can be your data storage and query system. Does your query system support simple statistics like computing an average or standard deviation? If you can't apply the statistical function to the data in the way you want, you must be creative, sometimes working around your query system. Sometimes, the most reasonable way to apply statistics to your data is to export the data from the system. Once beyond the limitations of the query system, you can use alternative tools to apply the statistical functions. The practicality of this approach is specific to the data source, query system, and case. If you cannot pre-filter a very large data source before statistically processing it, the resulting output may be unreliable enough to be of no use. Where possible, your strategy should be to pre-filter the data by creating a query that only produces results directly useful as input to the statistics stage of the processing.

Pulling Patterns Out of NetFlow

Like any technical endeavor, to use statistics effectively, you must first carefully lay out the problem and your detection goals. This will allow you to clearly reason about how to detect a behavior and the limitations of that detection. For example, suppose that you want to detect port scanning behavior with your NetFlow data source. Before you can begin to think about any sort of detection logic based on statistics, you need to understand what the behavior looks like and how events could be aggregated to find that behavior. A few different activities fall under the port scanning umbrella.

Horizontal Scanning

A horizontal scanning host tries to connect to the same destination port on a large number of other hosts. For example, for SSH scanning, the destination port would be 22. Horizontal scanning isn't limited to single port scans, though; many Windows-based worms scan on both ports 139 and 445 and sometimes even more. Horizontal scanning also isn't restricted to trying IP addresses sequentially or in a small CIDR range; targets could be chosen at random. That said, sequential IP addresses are a dead giveaway of horizontal scanning, and sequential scanning is still quite common, even though random scanning tends to be less obvious and more stealthy.

Vertical Scanning

A vertical scanning host tries to connect to a large number of destination ports on another host. The port numbers may be noncontiguous, and the scan target can be more than one host.

Horizontal and vertical scans are idealized versions of the possible scanning behavior variations. A more complex scenario could involve horizontally scanning on port 445 and any host that responds with 445, open has all their ports vertically scanned. Applying detection logic to something as diverse as port scanning first requires that you carve out a specific pattern that you think is worthwhile to look for from all possible behaviors. Perhaps you want to detect "worm-like" rapid horizontal scanning from one host to a large number of other hosts. With that subset in mind, make a list of features:

- Short period of time
- For a given single source host
- For a given single destination port and protocol
  - Large number of destination hosts
  - Relatively small packets

Notice that none of these features are highly specific concrete values to look for. Instead of searching for a specific string of bytes or some number, the features useful for statistical analysis are often fuzzy. To make them concrete, you need to pick a range of threshold for their values. With some features in hand, you can begin to construct a query to get at the interesting behaviors lurking in your data.

Looking for Beaconing with Statistics

One of the hallmarks of human behavior is that it's mostly random. If you ask someone to press a button once per second, they'll come close, but no matter how hard they try, there will still be significant random deviations from a regular interval. If, on the other hand, you program a computer to click a button once per second, it's going to come darn close to perfect. The amount of effort needed to program the computer to emulate the imprecision of a human pressing a button is actually surprisingly significant. The contrast between humans and computer behavior is so stark that it offers a great way to detect automated behavior for further analysis.

Of course, not all automated behavior is malicious. Much of the background activity and network traffic is not human initiated. Software checking for updates is a prime example. Plenty of other software like stock tickers or weather forecast applets also periodically check in. Even though malware isn't the only source of automated activity, by combining with other features, it's possible to make reasonable fidelity investigative reports. Detecting automated communications to C2 servers, or beaconing, will quickly identify compromised hosts. Beaconing refers to malware's regular and periodic "checking in," "calling back," or "phoning home" to a remote location. Fortunately, most beaconing is easy to detect with basic statistics.

To detect beaconing, you need a way of identifying the highly precise nature of computers. The first step is to measure the intervals between actions, which can be done with a lagged difference operator. Each operation has a timestamp associated with it; call them T1, T2, T3, etc. Then, using a lagged difference, the intervals I1, I2, etc. are I1 = T2 - T1, I2 = T3 - T2, and so forth. For automated beaconing traffic, these intervals will be consistent. To measure their consistency, you can use the intervals' standard deviation normalized by their mean (the coefficient of variation). Normalization allows the comparison of the values derived from different activity.

Once normalized, sort the activity from most regularly periodic to least regular. After throwing in a few additional features, the following query works well:

- **HTTP POST**
- **No Referer header**
- **For each host**
    - **For each destination domain**
        - **Domain has at least 11 requests**
        - **Requests are spaced out at least 1 second**
            - **Compute lagged difference values**
            - **Compute coefficient of variation of lagged difference values**
                - **Sort output by coefficient of variation (low to high)**

For a four-hour interval, many of the top results are as shown in Table 9-2.

Table 9-2. Example of beaconing hosts sorted by least precise to most precise time deviation

Source	Destination	Request count	Average	Standard deviation	Coefficient of variance
10.19.34.140	204.176.49.2	14	903.122571	0.13807	0.000152881
10.79.126.41	portal.wandoujia.com	14	299.976571	0.113251	0.000377533
10.99.107.11	militarysurpluspotsandpans.com	14	617.416429	0.249535	0.00040416
10.51.15.199	6.1.1.111	48	149.470979	0.06968	0.00046618
172.20.14.241	militarysurpluspotsandpans.com	21	616.192143	0.291051	0.000472338
10.99.38.68	militarysurpluspotsandpans.com	17	616.951059	0.317271	0.000514256
10.21.70.121	addonlist.sync.maxthon.com	10	601.6654	0.310379	0.000515866
10.155.1.142	militarysurpluspotsandpans.com	21	616.27919	0.356551	0.000578554

After some digging, you'll determine the requests to *militarysurpluspotsandpans.com* are associated with known malware. With a bit of tuning to ignore the nonmalicious beaconing, this query could be used by itself in an investigative play. It's also a great start for exploratory querying to find additional malicious activity and indicators by searching for activity related to the beaconing results.

Is Seven a Random Number?

We saw in the previous section that spotting periodic behavior is easy when the behavior is regular. Of course, data isn't always so clean. Sometimes, automated behavior involves multiple timers or some element of randomness like human activity mixed with automated activity. Event intervals can identify some types of regular or automated behavior, but there are many times when another test is needed. One such test is Pearson's chi-squared test (for more information, see "Detecting and Analyzing Automated Activity on Twitter" by Chao Michael Zhang and Vern Paxson). This test can tell you how well one element of data correlates with another element, or how well a set of data matches an expected distribution.

For example, when a human browses the Web, you wouldn't expect the specific second of the minute to have any relationship with which minute in the hour a web page is visited. The same goes with clicking links on pages, posting comments, sending emails, sending instant messages, and other common activity. If you gather enough activity from a host, you can start to look at the relationship between things that shouldn't be correlated. Here is a graph of the activity of a bot's C2 server where the specific minute of the hour is plotted along the vertical axis and the specific second of the minute is plotted along the horizontal axis. Each event from the bot is then plotted as a single circle (Figure 9-4).

Visual inspection alone identifies this activity as highly nonrandom. This type of analysis works well for detecting computer imposter activity masquerading as human activity. Malware posting blog comment spam or fake Twitter tweets is a common situation where this is the case.

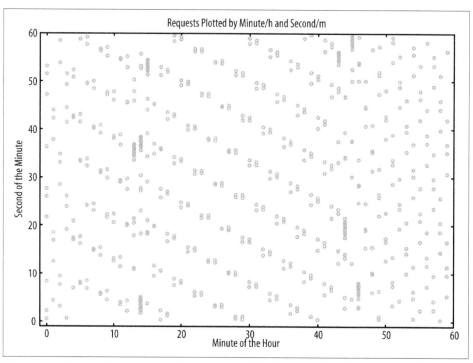

Figure 9-4. Automated request behavior plotted by the second of the minute and by the minute of the hour

There are more ways than just behavioral analysis to distinguish humans from computers. When you want to give a person your email address it's much easier to say and share when it's *mikehockey85@gmail.com* versus *ythuaydiavdqvwu@gmail.com*. The first looks normal, and the second looks random. The same goes for domain names. If you want anyone to remember a domain name, it should be something pronounceable or short, but certainly not long and random. If malware tried to generate real-looking email addresses or domain names, a frequent problem would be that they're already registered. Random long strings are much easier to program and are less likely to collide with existing ones. One such type of evasive behavior is a domain generation algorithm (DGA). As we discussed in Chapter 3, the idea behind a DGA is that if the botmasters used *www.mycommand-domain.com* and coded their malware to look for that domain, as soon as the domain is taken down, the malware is useless. In the escalating malware arms race, some malware periodically generates new domains to use to stay one step ahead of the defenders. Today the malware may use *www.ydyaihqwu.com*, and tomorrow it might switch to *www.fvjkpcmv.net*. When the attackers employ a strategy like this, it limits the effectiveness of taking down or blocking a domain.

In one extreme example, in 2009, a variant of the Conficker malware family switched to a DGA that produced 50,000 new domains across eight different TLDs every day. To thwart Conficker, defenders had to work with many countries and registrars across the globe to register or block every single domain.

The benefit to defenders when attackers use random-looking domains is that the domains stand out from most other domains—most domains look particularly random! To tease out random data from nonrandom, Markov chains are an ideal tool. Markov chains apply well to a wide variety of problem, but one area they particularly excel in is modelling the complexity of languages and identify the "randomness" of a string of text. A Markov chain is a probability table that describes the likelihood that a state will follow from a previous state. For natural language processing, each letter in a word is a state and then a probability table is created to describe which letters are most likely to come after others. For example, "h" is likely to come after "t," but "b" isn't very likely to come after "t." The table for "q" is especially lopsided because "u" is the only likely letter to follow. A Markov chain encodes all of these relationships and then can detect how well a piece of input text matches the table. It is easy to train a Markov model with sample text like English words, common names, common domain names, and other sources of text. Then you can score domains against the model to determine how the sequence of letters matched the model. A domain like *babybottles.com* will have a relatively low score (high probability of matching the model), while *fvjkpcmv.net* will have a high score, meaning it doesn't match the training set very well at all.

Markov chains can be applied anywhere text appears and a training set can be found. Domain names are easy because basic words, names, and common domain names can be used as training material. Other places Markov chains can apply are filenames, email addresses, scripts, page names in URLs, and other human-generated or human-consumed content. Malware commonly generate random filenames or random registry keys because randomness makes signature writing and artifact removal harder on defenders. If you don't know what to search for, how will you have anything to write a signature against? When building a report using host data like HIPS logs, spotting random filenames can help prioritize analysis. You can create a training set by installing common software on a clean system and using all the filenames on the system to train the Markov model. While this method won't catch malware named *system32.exe*, it will absolutely catch malware named *yfd458jwk.exe*.

Randomness (or a lack thereof when it is expected) doesn't have to be a detection method on its own. You certainly could build an investigative report that just looks for the most random-looking domain names in your DNS or HTTP logs, but that's likely to be only moderately effective because measuring randomness is highly dependent on your measurement model. Randomness measures work best when used in tandem with other features. Identifying or scoring behavior on a scale from not random to highly random can be integrated into a report as another feature. A common way you might use a random score as a feature alongside other nonstatistical features would be the following query:

- **HTTP POST**
- **No HTTP Referer Header**
- **Domain name looks highly random**

Or even something like:

- **HIPS event detecting creation of new system service**
- **AND ANY of:**
  - **Service name looks highly random**
  - **Executable name looks highly random**

Correlation Through Contingent Data

The idea that there are hidden relationships between data is more prevalent than ever. Often, when data science or big data is explained (or marketed!), the word *correlation* is thrown around without a lot of time spent on what it really means. Pushing the idea that a product contains magical secret algorithms for finding hidden correlations in your data might sell better, but it isn't a very accurate picture of reality. Most actionable reports are going to be based on queries that look at explicit relationships in data. Explicit relationships are easier to find, they're easier to understand, and they're less likely to be misleading or produce false positives. Even though data correlation isn't all it's marketed as, there are definitely situations where it can be very effective.

Feature-rich data sources usually have more possible hidden relationships in the data, but sometimes even low-feature data sources like NetFlow can have correlations between the features. For example, the transport protocol (TCP or UDP) is moderately correlated with the port. So, if you know the destination port is 80, it's much more likely the protocol is TCP than UDP. It would be unusual to see UDP/80 traffic. If you know the destination port is 53, it's much more likely the protocol is UDP. In fact, DNS is one of the biggest users of UDP, so if you know the protocol is UDP, then there is a high chance either the source or destination port for the flow is 53.

Hidden relationships in data are often advantageous for the defender. If you're able to find data relationships hidden even to an attacker, surely you have the upper hand in detection. HTTP is an especially feature-rich data source where attackers regularly fail to adhere to hidden relationships. The HTTP specification is very forgiving and a lot of things just don't matter. For example, HTTP request headers can be in any order. If the browser puts the User-Agent header above the Accept-Language header that will work just as well as if they're reversed. If you have N headers, this results in $N!$ (N factorial) possible orderings and usually any ordering is equally as good as any other, so the choice is arbitrary. But, if you built a profile of a specific version of Firefox, you'd find that in reality just a few different orders are actually present. This isn't unique to Firefox—almost all code that makes HTTP requests is consistent in how it constructs the requests.

By sorting through your HTTP proxy data, you could build a header-order profile of all of the major browser versions. When a malware author tries to hide by masquerading as a browser, if the author uses different headers or the same headers in a different order, their HTTP request won't match your profile for that browser. If you know Internet Explorer 9 always lists the Referer after the User-Agent header, if you see a request claiming to be from IE 9 listing the User-Agent first, the request isn't actually from IE 9. Catching software in a lie doesn't necessarily mean it's malicious, but if you combine the knowledge that the request is spoofing IE 9 with other suspicious features, you'll likely get a report that produces quality results.

Browsers tend to be consistent with their header ordering because software doesn't do anything without being explicitly coded. So unless browser developers put in extra effort to randomize the header permutation, consistent orderings are a given. Heading ordering is a rather trivial feature that can be found through simple visual inspection of requests. For more complex relationships, other tricks are needed.

One such trick is to build a contingency table. The basic idea behind a contingency table is that if there is a correlation between two different features, then given the value of one, you will see a difference in the likelihood of the other. Suppose you're looking at HTTP requests with Internet Explorer User-Agent strings, and you see a few different variations:

- `Mozilla/4.0 (compatible; MSIE 8.0; Windows NT 6.1; Trident/4.0)`
- `Mozilla/5.0 (compatible; MSIE 9.0; Windows NT 6.1; WOW64; Trident/5.0)`
- `Mozilla/5.0 (compatible; MSIE 10.0; Windows NT 6.2; WOW64; Trident/6.0)`

There seem to be four different features that vary within the User-Agent header for IE: Mozilla version, IE version, Windows version, and Trident version. You may ask,

"Is there any relationship between these version numbers?" Contingency tables are helpful at answering that question, as shown in Table 9-3.

Table 9-3. ~30k requests claiming to be IE plotted by the Mozilla version vertically and the IE version horizontally

Mozilla Version	Internet Explorer Version									
	1.0	4.0	5.0	5.5	6.0	7.0	8.0	9.0	10.0	11.0
3.0	0	27	0	0	0	0	0	0	0	0
4.0	0	0	30	504	1052	16912	902	520	24	1
5.0	1	0	0	0	0	0	7	8510	2842	0
TOTAL	1	27	30	504	1052	16912	909	9030	2866	1

A few things should stand out right away. First, versions of IE before 6 are so old they are not legitimately seen any more, so anything claiming to be these old versions of IE should automatically be suspicious. Second, IE versions 6 through 8 always claim to be Mozilla 4.0, making the 7 requests claiming to be IE 8 with Mozilla 5.0 suspicious. IE 10 always claims to be Mozilla 5.0, so the 24 requests that listed Mozilla 4.0 are suspicious. IE 9 is less conclusive, because 520 isn't that small compared to 8510, so it may be that there is some normal variation in IE 9. There is no reason to stop at a single contingency table. Table 9-4 shows the IE version versus the Trident version.

Table 9-4. ~30k requests claiming to be IE plotted by the IE version vertically and the Trident version horizontally

IE Version	Trident Version				
	3.1	4.0	5.0	6.0	7.0
4.0	0	0	0	0	0
5.0	0	0	0	0	0
5.5	0	0	0	0	0
6.0	0	3	0	0	0
7.0	2	574	6075	3891	55
8.0	0	453	5	1	0
9.0	0	0	4784	22	1
10.0	0	0	1	1727	0
TOTAL	2	1034	10865	5641	56

In Table 9-4, you can see IE 8 should only claim to be Trident 4. IE 9 should only claim to be Trident 5. IE 10 should only claim to be Trident 6. IE 7 is oddly inconsistent with the Trident version, but you can be sure that anything claiming to be Trident 3.1 or Trident 7 is bogus.

After you've found how various pieces of data relate to other pieces, you can start building logic to check for these relationships. Part of your query decision tree to check for impersonation of IE might look like this partial query:

- **If IE version is 7.0**
  - **If Mozilla version is not 4.0**
- **If IE version is 8.0**
  - **If any of the following are true**
    - **Mozilla version is not 4.0**
    - **Trident version is not 4.0**
- **If IE version is 9.0**
  - **If Trident version is not 5.0**

If you built a contingency table between the IE version and the Windows NT version, the logic in the decision tree could be even more complicated. After you've built out your whole decision tree for IE User-Agent strings, you have a powerful tool for detecting obvious impersonations of IE. Combine that with other suspicious features in an event, and you'll have a solid report for detecting activity warranting closer inspection.

Generating a contingency table for simple correlations involving a pair or few pairs of features in your events is easy to do by hand, as seen in the preceding query. What made reading the contingency table so easy was the strong correlation between versions. You could say with certainty and with no need for nuance that if you see IE version N, then the Mozilla version must be M. Sometimes, though, the relationships defining correlated data are murkier, and the breakdowns more difficult. Suppose you have a dataset with two parameters, as in Figure 9-5.

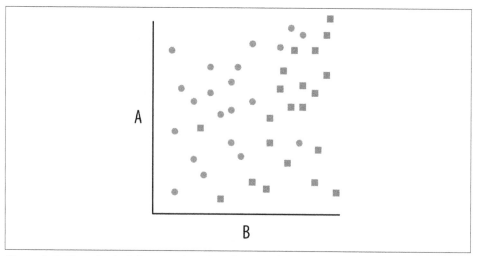

Figure 9-5. Hypothetical features A and B plot revealing their relationship

Here the A and B are two separate features and the circle and square points are malicious and nonmalicious activity. The division between the two groups is not a simple horizontal or vertical line, so you can't build a decision tree with simple logic like *if A > x, or B > y*. There is a line that divides them, but it's difficult to describe in simple Boolean logic and thresholds. You could build logic that does some simple algebra to figure out on which side of the line a point falls, but as your data sets grow or if you add additional parameters, this math quickly gets unwieldy. The machine learning tool of choice for classifying data separated like this is the support vector machine (SVM).

An SVM finds a linear divider between data even when the relationship is hard to pick out by hand. The divider for datasets with only two features, like the example shown, is a line. When you have three parameters, the divider is a plane, and when you have four or more, the divider is a multidimensional hyperplane. The biggest benefit to an SVM over a contingency table and manually built logic is that an SVM is automated and handles many parameters at the same time. Even indirect relationships between the parameters are easily handled by SVMs. Contingency tables are useful for visual inspection and spotting simple relationships, but SVMs can help you build a classifier when you have many parameters or the relationships between the parameters are hard to manually identify.

On the topic of machine learning, SVMs are not the only tool or even the best or most powerful tool for all situations. In the User-Agent example, we showed a manually built decision tree, but there are many machine learning algorithms for building decision trees automatically. If data doesn't lend itself to plotting (e.g., if some of the parameters aren't numeric), you may want to use decision-tree learning. If you have several different categories of activity and you want to group data into those categories based on similar behavior, a clustering algorithm may be the best option.

No one book could ever hope to cover the vast landscape of machine learning. The right machine learning model for your security events and your problems is best determined by you through experience and experimentation. Your playbook certainly won't be built exclusively out of reports that use machine learning for all their logic. However, once in a while when you run into a tricky problem, looking for hidden relationships in the data and using machine learning to act on them will help you create a very powerful report.

Who Is Keyser Söze?

A great cliché from many crime investigation films is the obsessed detective with a wall covered in photos of people arranged by how they connect to each other. Law enforcement calls this a *link chart*, and their usefulness extends beyond just fictional crime fighting. The abstract idea behind a link chart is that events or pieces of data can be represented by nodes in a graph, and the way the events link or relate to one another are the edges in the graph. Viewing data as a graph is useful for a few fundamental reasons:

- Connections between nodes mean they share some property
- Individual nodes are rarely directly connected to all other related nodes

For security event data analysis, nodes can be any number of things:

- Hosts causing an event to be fired (e.g., IDS or HIPS events)
- Event targets
- Domain names being looked up
- IP addresses
- Malware samples (by name, MD5 hash, AV hit, etc.)
- Users
- Individual features of events (User-Agent header, TCP port, etc.)

The primary property nodes should have is that they can be reused or may appear in multiple events. If a node doesn't appear in multiple events, it won't be connected to any nodes associated with other events, so placing it in a graph isn't useful. For example, an exact timestamp makes a poor node because a specific timestamp will only be associated with one event. The more events a node is associated with, the more connected it will be. The edges in the graph that connect nodes reflect how the nodes relate to one another. For example, if you want to make a graph of HTTP activity, your nodes will include client IP addresses, server domain names, server IP addresses, User-Agent strings, and Referer domains. Then, a request by a client would have an edge from the client IP node pointing to the requested domain node, the server IP node, and the User-Agent and Referer nodes. In turn, the User-Agent node would also point to the Domain, Referer, server IP address, and domain nodes. Each event would have a tightly connected set of nodes associated with it. As more and more events are added to the graph, many events will reuse nodes already in the graph. The graph encodes all of the complex relationships between events in a highly structured format that can support sophisticated queries that are hard to perform without a graph.

Sticking with HTTP as an example, after you've built a graph out of your HTTP events, your graph traversal queries can range from simple to quite complex. On the simple side, for most normal HTTP activity, you'd expect most clients to be using only a small number of User-Agent strings. Considering the variability in User-Agent strings, you'd expect most clients making a request to a domain to be using unique User-Agent strings. Querying the graph for all User-Agent nodes and computing the median connectedness of User-Agent nodes to client nodes shows that most User-Agent nodes are only connected to a few clients. So, if most clients use a unique User-Agent string, it would be particularly odd if there was a big imbalance between the number of clients and the number of User-Agents talking to a domain (Figure 9-6).

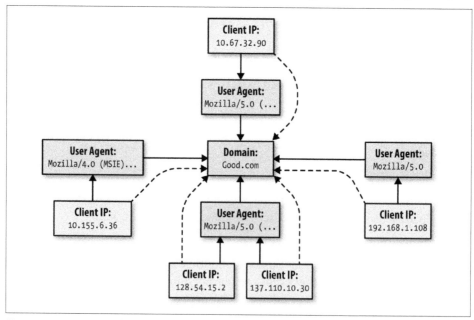

Figure 9-6. A typical domain doesn't see a lot of overlap in User-Agent strings across many clients; shown here are five unique clients and four unique User-Agent strings associated with activity to a single domain (compare with Figure 9-7)

This translates naturally into a query:

- **For each Domain node in graph**
  - **— Count the number of connected Client nodes as *N***
  - **— Count the number of connected User-Agent nodes as *M***
    - **— Compute the ratio *N:M***
      - **— If *N:M* is greater than 1.33 or less than 0.75, flag the domain for an imbalance**

Of course, the threshold values of 1.33 and 0.75 values were chosen arbitrarily for illustrative purposes, and the actual thresholds would need to be adjusted for your data. Additional thresholds like a minimum number of connected client nodes would also be needed for real datasets. Although very simple, domains returned from this query have an unexpected imbalance between unique User-Agents that when coupled with additional information can make an actionable report. A domain being visited by the same malware on many machines may show an imbalance in the client to User-Agent ratio (Figure 9-7).

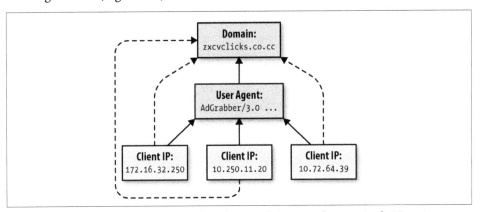

Figure 9-7. Many malware command-and-control domains have a single User-Agent string hardcoded into malware; shown here is one unique User-Agent and three unique clients making requests to a domain (compare with Figure 9-6)

One of the reasons why this type of query is so simple is that it doesn't fully exploit the highly connected nature of the graph. The query only looks at the nodes directly connected to domain nodes and doesn't explore the connections beyond that. Queries that traverse many nodes on the graph often require small amounts of code and a data structure to keep track of already visited nodes.

Guilty by Association

With your data in a graph, queries that make use of the interconnected structure are easy to implement, too. In many real-world scenarios, if you know an item like a domain is malicious, there is a good chance that related items like the IP addresses it points to are also malicious or the clients looking it up are compromised. In a simple case, if you assume all IP addresses associated with a malicious domain are also malicious, and you assume all domains that point to a malicious IP address are malicious, then starting from the known bad domains, you can find other bad domains by using the IP address they have in common. Using the HTTP graph described previously, a natural query for finding more malicious domains would be:

- **For each Domain node in known malicious set**
  - **For each connected server IP node**
    - **For each Domain node connected to IP node**
      - **Report found domain if domain is not already in known malicious set**

This query finds all of the domains that share an IP address with a known malicious domain. As long as the malicious by association holds true, this query can find new malicious domains that would be incredibly time-consuming to find by hand. This type of query works for many other node relationships besides just domain and IP addresses. This query isn't limited by a single step either. The newly found domains can be added to the malicious domain set, and the query repeated for the newly found domains until no more domains are found. This type of searching is known as *breadth-first search*, or BFS, and it allows you to find whole connected regions of malicious activity.

One of the trickiest aspects of graph-based queries is being cognizant about which edges you follow in well-connected graphs. Following all edges haphazardly can quickly expand the scope of your query. For the previous example, if a single "popular" or nonmalicious domain or IP slips into or is connected with the known malicious set, large numbers of nonmalicious domains may be found. For that reason, the malicious data set used with BFS-based queries needs careful curation. Instead of letting the algorithm extend the sets, a reasonable report may produce the next step of results in from the query for human analysis. Then as your analysts look at results, they can mark them as malicious or nonmalicious. After several iterations, a good set of malicious IP addresses and domains is created, and anytime a new IP address or domain is added, your report can fire an alert. We've found that queries like this are particularly well suited for tracking specific hacking groups, exploit kits, and pieces of malware.

Exploiting the interconnected nature of graphs extends beyond just hand-curated lists of malicious activity. BFS can produce too many results when edges between nodes don't indicate a malicious connection. Connections that are less black-and-white can get tricky. When you're building a graph of your data, it's tempting to want to look for nodes that are connected to lots of different, possibly malicious nodes. That is, if you have a list of domains you think might be malicious, IP addresses pointed to by several of these domains are probably more suspicious than IP addresses pointed to by only one suspect domain.

In general, if you believe something about one node, you may want to propagate some of that belief to the nodes that connect to it. This is called *belief propagation*, and these algorithms can be powerful tools for finding malicious activity. The specifics are highly dependent on the data sources in your graph and the types of information you want to propagate between nodes. When properly implemented and carefully tuned, you can propagate negative and positive reputation data throughout the graph to assign other nodes a reputation based on the reputation of their peers, their peers' peers, and so on. The specifics on how to implement belief propagation algorithms are well beyond the scope of this book.

Chapter Summary

- Avoiding false positives aids your detection success rate by lowering the total time of analysis required for detecting and responding to security incidents.
- Set operations can quickly reveal common activities hidden in large sets of data.
- Contingency tables are a powerful tool for measuring correlations between event features and detecting forged or spoofed events.
- Graph analysis, statistical relationships, and machine learning can take your playbook to the next level, giving you detection capabilities beyond simple event-by-event analysis.
- Visualizing data through graphs and relationships makes it easier to detect unusual patterns that can lead to explicit malicious indicators or are pointers to additional indicators to research.

CHAPTER 10

I've Got Incidents Now! How Do I Respond?

> *"We kill people based on metadata."*
> —General Michael Hayden, former
> Director of NSA

Up to this point, we've explained how to understand threats, how to build and operate a security monitoring system, and how to creatively discover security incidents through log analysis and playbook development. With your well-oiled detection machine, you will discover incidents and new threats, while the team fields incident notifications from employees and external entities alike. Your analysts are researching and creating plays, investigating incidents, and sorting out false positives from confirmed malicious behavior, based on techniques from your playbook. However, an incident response playbook is more than just detection. It must also include instructions on *how to respond*.

We have discussed a structured approach to prepare for, detect, and analyze malicious behavior. Yet despite the effort involved in the detection phase, it is only the beginning of the incident response lifecycle process. After detecting an incident, the next most important step is to contain the problem and minimize the damage potential to your organization. After all, a key factor in an overall security strategy is to build a monitoring system and playbook to thwart security incidents as soon as possible to reduce downtime and data loss. After an incident has been triaged and the bleeding stopped, it's time to clean up the original problem. Remediation demands that you not only undo the work of the attacker (e.g., removing malware from a system, restoring a defaced website or files from backup), but that you also develop a plan to prevent similar incidents from happening in the future. Without a plan to prevent the same problems, you run the risk of repeat incidents and further complications to the organization, weakening your detection and prevention efforts.

For analysts to be successful in preventing computer security incidents from wreaking havoc with your network and data, it is imperative that you ensure consistent and thorough incident-handling procedures. A playbook for detection and analysis coupled with an incident response handbook for response methods provide consistent instructions and guidelines on how to act in the event of a security threat. Just as firefighters know not to turn their water hoses on a grease fire, your incident response team should know what to do, and what not to do, during a security incident.

In this chapter, we'll cover the response side of the playbook, specifically:

Preparation
> How to create and activate a threat response model.

Containment (mitigation)
> How to stop attacks after they have been detected, as well as how to pick up the pieces.

Remediation
> When to investigate the root cause, what to do once identified, and who is responsible for fixing it within the organization.

Long-term fixes
> How to use lessons learned to prevent future similar occurrences.

Shore Up the Defenses

In Figure 10-1, the hexagons on the right side of the diagram show the primary response functions of the incident response team once an incident becomes known. We also see that the source of an incident can come from many locations, like internal tools (the playbook) and employees or external entities. Measuring the number of incidents detected internally versus those reported by external groups offers a view into a team's response time and efficacy. There are external sources like MyNetwatchman, Spamhaus, SANS, and many others that will notify an organization if they are hosting compromised (and actively attacking) hosts. A higher ratio of internally detected incidents means the team is doing a better and faster job at detecting attacks. If you depend on external entities to inform you of security breaches, you are already far behind in the response process and need to improve your detection capabilities.

Additionally, long-term tasks such as patching vulnerabilities, fixing flawed code, and developing or amending policies to prevent future attacks are all part of the process. During a major incident, the response team's role is mitigation, coordination, consultation, and documentation:

Mitigation

Blocking the attack to stop any further problems for occurring as a result of the incident.

Coordination

Managing the entire incident response process, as well as ensuring each stakeholder understands the roles, responsibilities, and expectations.

Consultation

Providing technical analysis to relevant stakeholders (system owners, executives, PR, etc.) and suggesting long-term fixes leveraging any relevant IT experience.

Documentation

Incident reporting, tracking, and dissemination where appropriate.

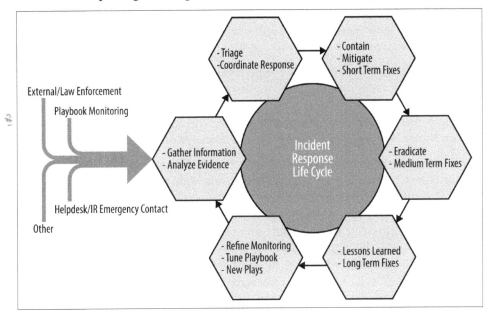

Figure 10-1. Incident response lifecycle

Organizations with small IT staff may find it easier to coordinate a response to a security incident. The closer an incident response team is to various IT organizations, the faster information can be shared and a long-term fix implemented. However, in a large organization, particularly those with various business units and partners, the response time can be much slower. While the InfoSec organization should have tight integration with all IT teams across an organization, unfortunately, this is not always the case. During the height of an incident, IT teams must trust and defer to the incident response team during the triage, short-term fix, and notification phases of the incident. However, the incident response team has to rely on the IT team—experts with their own systems and architecture—in order to solve bigger issues that may lead to additional incidents.

Major incidents require cooperation between those who are adept in handling a crisis and those who are in a position to understand the ramifications of any short- and long-term fixes. In Chapter 1, we discussed the various relationships that a CSIRT must maintain, and highlighted how relations with IT teams are paramount. Nothing is more certain than when IT infrastructure has been compromised.

Lockdown

A networked worm provides the perfect example of why containment is so important. If left unchecked, a worm, by design, will continue to spread to any and all vulnerable systems. If the "patient zero" system (and its subsequent victims) isn't cordoned off, it will attack as many other systems as possible, leading to exponential growth and intractable problems. This quickly spirals out of control from a single malware infection to a potential network meltdown.

In similar fashion, malware designed to perform DoS attacks can easily clog your network pipes with volumes of attack data destined toward external victims, not only creating problems for system resiliency, but also damaging your online reputation by making you complicit in attacks against your will. Additionally, you may find your organization as the target of a DoS or distributed denial of service (DDoS) attack.

Responding to these two types of attacks by blocking the source IP address or addresses has its place in your incident response toolkit, but it should be used with a word of caution. Blocking individual hosts is a tedious and potentially time-consuming process that may have no end. We refer to this as the *whack-a-mole approach*. For large-scale DDoS attacks, you may be the target of more attackers than you can reasonably block one-by-one, or a few at a time. Additionally, blocking all communications from an address or subnet may have the unintended consequence of also blocking legitimate traffic from the same addresses. Further, even if the attacks come from a finite number of source hosts that are manageable for you to block, the sources are often dynamic or pooled addresses that may in the future no longer be the source of malicious activity. Depending on the type of the attack, there may be better solutions by requesting blocking or rerouting assistance at the ISP level. In either case, you are faced with the questions: do you have a process to review or expire historical IP blocks, or will you continue to block unless you receive a complaint regarding service unavailability?

As mentioned in Chapters 8 and 9, the playbook's analysis section must include specific directives on how to interpret the result data, as well as how to properly respond to each event. Depending on the type of incident, it should include details on how to properly contain the problem. The methods for containment differ for incidents related to employee data theft or abuse, as opposed to malware outbreaks on networked systems. For insider threat incidents such as document smuggling, sabotage, and some abusive behaviors, the best remediation option may be to suspend or terminate account access and inform Human Resources or Employee Relations. Preventing disgruntled employees from logging in to their email, VPN, or other computer systems decreases their ability to cause damage or to steal additional confidential information.

The Fifth Estate

Responding to and containing security incidents is more than cleaning up after malware or disgruntled employees. This rings especially true if an incident deals with the loss of customer data and privacy. Not only does an organization have to deal with the court of public opinion in terms of loss of reputation, but there may be legal ramifications as well. Many countries and states have mandatory disclosure notification laws. To protect citizens, or at least inform them of their potential privacy loss at the hands of an organization, many laws demand that consumers and customers are notified in the event that their formerly private data has now been exposed.

Containing an incident that has gone public can be difficult and should only be done in concert with public relations, any legal entities representing the organization, and executive leadership. The role of the incident response team in a public-facing crisis means being able to provide irrefutable facts to people representing the organization. Don't let anyone other than public relations-vetted people speak with the media or external entities regarding the incident unless otherwise approved. Sharing too much detail or incorrect detail can lead to worse image problems than the original incident.

After his job was terminated, a network administrator for the city of San Francisco held hostage the root passwords to the entire city's networking infrastructure (*http://www.wired.com/2008/07/sf-city-charged/*). Being the *only* person with the correct password meant that the IT infrastructure was completely frozen by this disgruntled employee, and at his mercy, until either he revealed the passwords, or the network was rebuilt—an option more expensive and complex than imaginable. From a detection standpoint, a play for monitoring password changes of admin accounts, unusually timed logins, or authentication to critical systems, might have tipped off the incident response team that something was afoul. However, in this case, the admin never changed passwords—he was simply the sole proprietor of them. Had the incident response team been notified in advance that the network administrator was on notice or soon to be let go, the team could have immediately suspended his accounts before too much damage was done. For incidents relating to the members of your organization, a partnership with human resources allows the incident response team to (hopefully) proactively mitigate a threat, rather than reactively address a preventable incident.

Advanced and targeted attacks by their nature are much harder to contain. This makes them the most important attacks to focus on. Containment options for advanced attacks range from removing network connectivity from a compromised system or remote host, to locking out users and resetting passwords for known affected accounts, to blocking protocols or even shutting down the entire organization's Internet connection. Remember that it's not possible to block 100% of the attacks 100% of the time. Advanced attackers may successfully intrude your network undetected—at least initially—until you discover them and then update your plays with fresh indicators. The important thing to remember is that even though you will not discover every incident, you still need to be prepared to respond to the worst-case scenario.

These targeted attacks can also be difficult to control and contain if they have been exposed publicly. The public exposure of private details, or *doxing*, of an organization's employees or leadership can be disastrous, and could be exploited or abused in a number of ways. If the news of the attack on your organization is trending on Twitter, or regularly covered by the mainstream or tech press, it will be hard to put the genie back in the bottle. If the attack is high profile, it is also possible that an organization may call in additional resources to assist in the investigation and containment. This can relieve some of the pressure from the incident response team who can focus on the root causes, the extent and type of damage, active containment, business continuity, and improved security architecture.

No Route for You

When it comes to networked systems, the containment problem may be a little easier to solve. There are numerous options to mitigate an incident at the network and system level. In most cases, blocking network connectivity is the best option to allow for further forensic activity and may often be the only option for a non-IT managed system. Adding a MAC address to a quarantined VLAN or network segment can prevent any damage to the rest of the organization. A new 802.1x access control policy, firewall policy, or a simple extended network ACL can also limit the connectivity of a misbehaving device. However, this approach can present challenges. Most organizations adhere to some type of change control policy, meaning that modifications to critical infrastructure like routers, switches, and firewalls are only permitted during designated and recognized change windows. These windows limit the available time during which a routine ACL modification can be made. Additionally, new access control entries or firewall deny statements can potentially introduce instability if there are errors on entry (e.g., wrong subnet or other typo), or if a compromised host's traffic is so voluminous that packet filtering devices like firewalls and routers are under heavy CPU loads already and stagger under the increased CPU load of applying the new ACL.

Null routing, or blackholing, offers a more palatable immediate mitigation option that can be introduced without concern for further network degradation. There are two types of blackholing—source and destination. Destination blackholing works well in situations like cutting off reply traffic to Internet C2 servers by dropping traffic destined *to* a particular IP address. With destination blackholing, a router sets the next-hop for a host to a static route that points to null0, or a hardware void. Any connections destined to the blackholed host will be dropped when it reaches a routing device with the null route.

 Source blackholing, on the other hand, works well for incidents like worm outbreaks or DoS attacks, where you need to block all traffic *from* an IP address, either internal or external, regardless of the destination. Because routers are inherently poor at verifying connection sources, you can spoof TCP and UDP packets and create major problems. Unicast Reverse Path Forwarding (uRPF) (*http://www.cisco.com/c/dam/en/us/products/collateral/security/ios-network-foundation-protection-nfp/prod_white_paper0900aecd80313fac.pdf*), a type of reverse path forwarding (RPF), is a required solution to the source verification problem. When a routing device receives a packet, uRPF verifies that the device has a route to the source of the connection from the receiving interface (strict mode uRPF (*http://www.cisco.com/web/about/security/intelligence/unicast-rpf.html*)), or in a network with asymmetric routing, from the routing table (loose mode uRPF).

If the routing device doesn't have a route to the source (e.g., spoofed addresses) or if the return route to the source is to null0 (blackhole), the packet will be dropped. In this way, a loose mode uRPF blackholed address provides a feasible way to drop traffic both to and from the address.

The effect of a blackhole can be quickly propagated throughout your network using iBGP and a Remotely Triggered Blackhole (RTBH) router. By peering via iBGP with other routers in your network from a trigger router, you can announce the new null0 from the RTBH, and within a few seconds, blackhole an address across the organization (Figures 10-2 and 10-3). Because a packet will be routed in your network until it matches the null route, and because iBGP is not used on every routing device in a network, you should be aware where in your network topography the null route is applied.

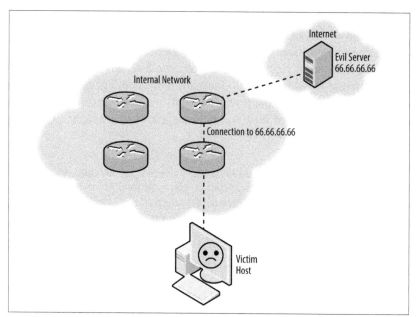

Figure 10-2. Malicious communication without black hole route

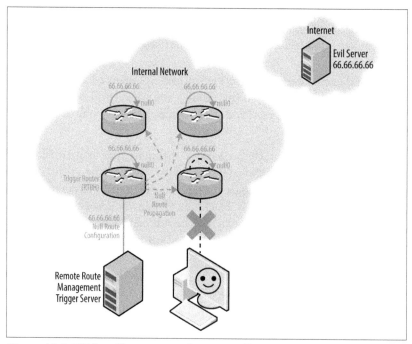

Figure 10-3. With null routing, malicious traffic can be blocked quickly without the hassle or scaling limitations associated with ACL management

Not Your Bailiwick

Another option for containing an infected host relies upon the foundational Internet protocol of the DNS. As discussed in Chapter 7, collecting DNS traffic can be a boon to your security monitoring operations. However, DNS can also be useful from a mitigation standpoint. RPZ can help you create the equivalent of a DNS firewall. This DNS firewall gives you four different types of policy triggers for controlling what domains can be resolved by your clients. If blocking external C2 systems by IP address isn't flexible enough, you can define a policy based on the name being queried by clients (QNAME policy trigger) to control how your recursive name servers handle the query. If policies based on the QNAME aren't enough, DNS RPZ also gives you more powerful policy controls, like blocking all domains that resolve to a certain IP address (IP address policy trigger). If you need to target a malicious name server itself, RPZ offers policy triggers either by the name server's name (NSDNAME policy trigger), or even the name server's IP address (NSIP policy trigger). RPZ policies go into a special zone that allows you to be authoritative for any domain in an easy-to-manage way. RPZ is especially powerful because of the response flexibility. Standard blocking by returning NXDOMAIN records is possible, but RPZ also allows forged responses that can redirect your clients to internal names if you need to capture more information about their activities to external domains.

Lastly, RPZ is only supported in the BIND DNS server, and does not work with Microsoft DNS Services. Microsoft DNS servers can point to authoritative BIND DNS servers to use RPZ capabilities; however, there's no current method to add hosts to a response zone on the Microsoft DNS server itself.

One Potato, Two Potato, Three Potato, Yours

Knowing when and why to hand off an incident relies on a common understanding in your organization of roles and responsibilities. While often a football defender may advance to the goal area for a scoring opportunity, the team ultimately needs that player back on defense before the next offensive play by the opposing team. A player's skillset should match the position they play, and stretching their talents into other roles affects the quality and capacity to do efficient work in their primary role. Even though a security investigator may have many of the same skills as a security architect, they cannot assume the responsibility of the long-term remediation plan for every incident.

Yet, one of the outputs of successful incident response is tangible: written evidence of architecture gaps and failures. A CSIRT should be able to understand the underlying problem and advise any security architects and engineers on appropriate and acceptable solutions based on incident details. Like the players on a football team, these security individuals must communicate about current threat landscapes, trends, and incidents. Only when all individual contributors are participating and performing the roles to which they are assigned, can an incident successfully move through the incident lifecycle, ultimately being remediated both in the short and long term.

Get to the Point

Handing off an incident or even closing one demands that an investigator decide whether or not to perform an exhaustive root cause analysis (RCA) to determine precisely why an incident occurred. In many cases, an RCA is simply mandatory. If a critical system is compromised, it's imperative to discover precisely what conditions allowed the attack to succeed so they can be avoided in the future. However, there are other situations where dedicating significant time to RCA is deleterious to other work. For example, if your organization has been scanned and exploit attempts have been launched by external organizations toward your web presence, it's not necessary to follow up on every "attack" if there is no additional evidence indicating that it was successful. The incident response team could spend a lot of time attempting to perform threat actor attribution to these types of attacks, but everyone knows that being on the Internet means you will be portscanned and attacked. Proper attribution isn't even reliable, given that attackers can come in from other hacked systems, proxies, or VPN addresses, masking their true origin.

For most organizations, knowing exactly *who* scanned your website, or sent a commonly used trojan via phishing doesn't necessarily yield any actionable results and may not even be considered incidents. Don't be flattered or concerned if you get scanned—it may not be targeted. We have to accept that malware is ubiquitous and ranges from annoying adware to sophisticated remote control and spying software. Researching every exploit attempt, probe, or malware sample doesn't justify the time investment required. Of course, malware that's *not* initially detected or deleted by host-based controls, is clearly targeted, or has other peculiar and unique characteristics will be worth investigating to discover additional indicators.

Portable computer systems (e.g., laptops, smartphones, and tablets) will join all types of uncontrolled external networks, from home LANs to coffee shops, bars, airplanes, or any number of public or private places. Without proper host controls like "always-on" HIPS, it can be difficult to even understand the source of a compromise outside the borders of your security monitoring. Not knowing the source of an attack or malware obfuscates the ability to block it in the future from within the organization, and makes determining the root cause extremely difficult, if not impossible. Additionally, there may not be log data available to accurately track each step leading up to a security incident. Most security event sources only alert on anomalous activity, while not reporting normal behaviors. If a series of normal behaviors led up to an eventual incident, understanding what created the conditions leading to the compromise will go unnoticed and unlogged.

Many RCAs come to dead ends simply due to insufficient details when revisiting the full attack and compromise cycle. This is why attempting to determine the source of every malicious binary dropped on a host often requires more effort than it's worth.

Lessons Learned

In the end, after the dust has settled on the incident and the bleeding has stopped, it will be time to develop a long-term strategy for avoiding similar issues. It's also the best time to refine your monitoring techniques and responses. Mistakes or inadequacies uncovered in the course of the incident response process will yield opportunities to improve in the future.

Consider this plausible, if not extreme, example. It's the middle of the day, and you're on call again when the incident response team receives an internal notification from an application developer regarding a newly discovered and unknown web application in a production web app server's webroot directory. Browsing to the web application, you're presented with a simple text box and a run button. Entering random text and hitting run surprisingly displays the text `-bash: asdf: command not found`. Bash? On the external web server? Quickly, you try a process listing, and the app generates a full `ps` output. Among system daemons in the process listing are Apache and Tomcat processes. Dreadfully, this output shows the web server processes are running as `root`. Fearing the worst, you run `whoami` through the web application only to have those fears confirmed when the output displays `root`.

The scope of the issue hits you—unauthenticated Internet-facing root access to one of your production web servers. You'll remediate the issue by taking the service offline, contain the issue after quantifying the scope of affected hosts, and perform RCA to determine how the hosts were compromised and who executed what commands via the shell. During the post-mortem, you ask yourselves what happened during this incident that had we known about it previously we could have detected, mitigated, or contained the incident sooner?

From a detection standpoint, you might identify the availability and usefulness of logs generated from any of the application, the web app server, the web server, or the operating system itself. It would be reasonable for the web app server to generate an event when a new web application is deployed, or for the web server to provide attacker attribution information identifying when the shell was accessed and by whom.

During the incident investigation, you learned about many longer-term infrastructure improvements that will likely require dedicated resources, tracking, and commitment to appropriately fix. If, in the previous example, your entire infrastructure runs the Tomcat systems as root, then you need to harden the systems, change the build process, and QA your applications on the now lower privilege application server. In a rush-to-market environment, these incident findings will require much more time and many more people to implement than is feasible to manage in your incident. Security architecture, system administration, and application development engineering all play a part to fully address the identified weaknesses, none of which reside solely in the domain of security monitoring or incident response. As an incident responder, how do you identify the responsible parties in your organization, get commitment from those parties that they will address weaknesses in their domain, and then ensure follow-through on the commitments?

By further analyzing this example against the incident lifecycle, you may learn of other weaknesses that need attention. Were you able to attribute the application or system to an actual owner via an asset management system? Could you quickly determine the scope of the incident via comprehensive vulnerability scanning? Does your organization have a scalable method of containing the incident when the problem exists across hundreds of hosts in the production environment? While your incident response team may have unearthed the issues and have a stake in their resolution, managing the issues to completion is not a core function of monitoring or response and therefore should be handled by the appropriate team within your organization.

Incidents that have already been resolved provide a wealth of detail within their documentation. Keeping accurate and useful records when investigating an incident will pay off in the future with newer team members, as well as providing historical and verified information that can help affect positive change for security architecture enhancements. Beyond this, any new procedures you used, contacts you required, or old processes you found to be inefficient or unusable should make their way into the incident response handbook. Keeping the incident response handbook alive with updated information will speed up responses to future incidents that demand similar tactics. Depending on the type of incident and how it was detected, there may also be a place for updating the analysis section of your playbook to more effectively respond to future incidents.

Chapter Summary

- After detection, the incident response team's role is to mitigate, coordinate, consult, and document.
- Having a reliable playbook and effective operations will lead to incident discovery.
- You need to ensure your response processes are well tested and agile in the event of a major incident.

- Mitigation systems are crucial for containing incidents and preventing further damage. DNS RPZ and BGP blackholing are excellent tools for cutting off basic network connectivity.

- An incident can be over in a few minutes or can take weeks to resolve. Long-term fixes may be part of the solution, but the incident response team should be prepared to consult and assist, rather than drive systematic and architectural changes.

CHAPTER 11

How to Stay Relevant

"Who controls the past, controls the future..."
—George Orwell

In 1983, the first mobile phone became available for consumer purchase (Figure 11-1). More than 30 years later, there are over seven billion wireless subscriptions globally, and almost half of the human population owns at least one mobile phone. Anyone in the early 1980s thinking about the first mobile phones would have difficulty imagining how much the tiny portable devices (now used everywhere by most people, for a significant part of their day) would permanently change human society and culture. No longer is a phone just a way to speak with another person. You have a constantly available record of your communications with anyone in your address book or otherwise. It is a news source, a radio, a television, a camera, a GPS, and a means of interacting with your money, to name only a few uses. Civilization is rapidly evolving toward ubiquitous computing, and discovering all the challenges that come with it—not the least of which are privacy and information security. The mobile phone phenomenon is one of many technology shifts throughout history from which we can learn, in order to reasonably anticipate future trends, problems, and challenges.

Figure 11-1. DynaTAC 8000X circa 1984

Computing trends are often cyclical, coming into, going out of, and coming back into favor. For instance, computing resources were previously centralized in shared mainframe computers. As hardware prices (and sizes) shrunk and new computing models developed, organizations moved toward on-premise solutions. Eventually, virtualization was able to scale to a point where most organizations have reverted to a centralized infrastructure, allowing a third party to manage virtualized network, compute, and storage layers. From a security monitoring perspective, each environment presents its own challenges. Though the variables and environments may change, a repeatable process of identifying what threats to monitor and how to detect and respond to those threats must be well founded in your security monitoring methodology. The medium and hardware may have changed, but many of the attacks, motives, and asset types you must protect have not. The playbook methodology helps you keep up with the pace of change. Technology and environments are only variables in the overall approach. As times and trends change, the playbook remains the framework you need to evolve your security monitoring and incident response processes. By reflecting on the past to prepare for the future, defenders can ready themselves and their networks for inevitable attacks.

In this chapter, we'll discuss some of the social and cultural components that drive technology change; how the expansion of technology throughout our daily lives affects security response; and how the playbook approach keeps your incident response and security monitoring processes relevant in the future.

Oh, What a Tangled Web We Weave, When First We Practice to Deceive!

If you are reading this text, chances are that technology is a significant influence in your life. It's even likely you're reading this on a computing device, be it a laptop, phone, or other ereader. At the same time, devices around you are connected through cellular networks, local wireless IP networks, personal area networks, Bluetooth connections, and any number of other radio protocols. We use these connected technologies to communicate with others via audio, video, and text, and to consume media, get directions, order and pay for food and other items, access our banks, lock our doors, change environmental settings in our homes, play games, meet new friends, and countless other daily tasks that are now commonplace. As networks continue to grow, the potential information they can maintain and create expands. Look no further than Metcalfe's law, which concludes that the value of a telecommunications network is proportional to the square of the number of connected users of the system. In other words, the more people that are interconnected on a network, the more valuable and desirable that network becomes to them.

Network connectivity is a foundational component to these activities. So foundational, in fact, that the President of the United States decreed the Internet be protected as a utility (*http://www.washingtonpost.com/blogs/the-switch/wp/2014/11/10/ obama-to-the-fcc-adopt-the-strongest-possible-rules-on-net-neutrality-including-title-ii/*), as common and necessary to the people as water or electricity. Just as Moore's law predicts the growth of computing power in hardware, Edholm's Law postulates that eventually network bandwidth will reach a convergence between all current methods of network access (wireless, mobile, and local area networks). Everyone with a networked device can transmit data from anywhere at any time, regardless of their connection type. This is one of the main benefits of layered networking: no matter what layer you change, the other layers still function. With regards to user experience, watching a video online doesn't change whether you are connecting through IPv4 or IPv6, or if your frames are forwarded over LTE, IEEE 802.3, or 802.11 links. More people with more devices only increases the network bandwidth necessary to handle the additional traffic, which in turn stimulates more innovative networked applications. However, additional networked users are not the only driving force in the throughput supply and demand equation. When bandwidth was so low that we could only transmit text, the idea of transmitting a decent resolution image did not occur to most people. When bandwidth allowed acceptable transmission of images, the idea of sending video didn't occur to most. The past has demonstrated that every time you try to satisfy the needs of today, you end up enabling the technology of tomorrow. In the process of increasing bandwidth and access, you're actually enabling the exponential growth of ideas and new uses for the technology. Always keep in mind, though, that higher throughput demands that monitoring devices and storage can keep pace with the additional traffic and log data.

Cheaper disk storage and faster network throughput also creates a ripe environment for online backup and file hosting services. Local backups to physical storage can save you headaches in the event of data loss. But during a catastrophic event where even your local backups are destroyed, hosted services allow you to retrieve your data and files over the Internet. Naturally, entrusting your data to someone else assumes a certain loss of control in the event of a data breach. As a consumer of the service, you expect that the hosting company secures the infrastructure on which your data resides.

The influx of technology in daily lives has had and will have multiple effects on the attack surface. The first is an increase in the scale of available devices. Increasing markets for mobile devices, networked automobiles, smart meters, wireless light bulbs and lamps, and wearables (*http://www.forbes.com/sites/gilpress/2014/08/22/internet-of-things-by-the-numbers-market-estimates-and-forecasts/*) will add millions of nodes to the Internet, many of which will require constant connectivity. Industrial control systems and municipal systems like traffic monitoring and utility measurement also add to the mix of network-connected devices. Logistical industries like shipping, freight, and trucking rely on Internet connectivity to track, plan, and reroute their shipments. In addition to the sheer number of nodes, each device will have its own network stack and common and custom applications. Applications will invariably have bugs, and bugs introduce vulnerabilities that an attacker can exploit. As with the current vulnerabilities on your network, you'll need to identify, detect, and mitigate issues resulting from these newly networked devices. By applying the playbook methodology to the new attack surfaces, you will identify different or new log sources, remediation processes, and mitigation capabilities to support the monitoring and incident response that results from the new devices.

The increase in devices will also affect attacker motivations. We've seen an explosion of growth in the criminal hacking and malware "industry" over the last decade because bad guys have finally started figuring out ways to monetize their exploits (pun intended). It used to be that virus writing was a digital version of graffiti, and provided a way to show off your skills and gain underground credibility. Now that there is real money in it, the hobbyist aspect no longer dominates, and monetary rewards attract more profiteers and criminal organizations. Any computing resource that can be exploited for money will be. There have always been ways to make money with CPU power, but cryptocurrency made the link so close that it became extremely easy to monetize the resource. Online advertising and syndication networks made it easy to monetize network connectivity via click fraud. Always-on networking also made DoS as a service easy (e.g., shakedowns via booter services). The rise in mobile devices led to abuse of premium SMS messaging services legitimately used for things like ringtone downloads or mobile payments. The point is, any time a link between a resource and a way to monetize that resource is made, bad guys will find a way to fill that niche.

Allowing digital devices to control the physical world in more ways only adds to the potential attack surface. Clever hackers are demonstrating how to steal cars over the Internet and clone RFIDs or other tokens for additional thefts or impersonation. Attackers have already compromised and controlled trains, buses, and traffic control systems. Imagine losing control of a building's power, fire suppression, or heating and cooling systems. Critical industrial controls modified by attackers might lead to serious consequences. How long would it take for your datacenter to melt down after the air conditioning has been disabled? How long until your nuclear plant runs out of fuel and shuts down after your centrifuges explode?

The Rise of Encryption

Law enforcement agencies have forever been interested in the dual-use nature of encryption. As a means of protecting information and communications, it has practical applications for everyone from governments and militaries to corporations and individuals. As a means of evasion and obfuscation, it provides a sense of security for miscreants. Governments have historically tried to regulate the use, distribution, and exportation of cryptographic technologies, in some cases labeling encryption algorithms as "munitions." The prohibited publishing of encryption techniques has even been challenged in American courts on the basis of free speech (*https://epic.org/crypto/export_controls/bernstein_decision_9_cir.html*). On a global scale, the Wassenaar Arrangement (*http://www.wassenaar.org/controllists/*) is a multinational agreement that aims to regulate the export of dual-use technologies, including encryption.

In some cases, governments and law enforcement agencies have influenced and/or infiltrated encryption development due to fears of impotency in cases of crimes with computer-based evidence.

 A fantastic example of government interference in encryption technology was the Clipper chip. This chipset designed for encrypted telecommunications included a key escrow system with an intentional backdoor. The backlash was harsh.

The U.S. Federal Bureau of Investigation (FBI) is suspected to have convinced Microsoft to leave some investigative techniques available in its Bitlocker full disk encryption software. The Dual Elliptic Curve Deterministic Random Bit Generator

(Dual_EC_DRBG) was also backdoored by the NSA to allow for cleartext extraction of any algorithm seeded by the pseudorandom number generator. The Dual_EC_DRBG algorithm has a curious property in that it's possible to have a secret key that makes the algorithm trivially breakable to anyone with the key, and completely strong for anyone without it. The NSA never mentioned that this secret key backdoor capability existed, but someone in the public eventually found that the algorithm could have this "feature." The NSA was even able to push the American National Institute of Standards and Technology (NIST) to standardize it even with this as public knowledge, and the International Organization for Standardization (ISO) also eventually standardized the algorithm. It wasn't until the leaked classified documents came out that there was essentially proof that the NSA intentionally designed the algorithm in this way.

Law enforcement is concerned with the use of encryption because they lose another technique for collecting evidence. Consider this quote from FBI Director James Comey's remarks at the Brookings Institute on default encryption on smartphones:

> Encryption isn't just a technical feature; it's a marketing pitch. But it will have very serious consequences for law enforcement and national security agencies at all levels. Sophisticated criminals will come to count on these means of evading detection. It's the equivalent of a closet that can't be opened. A safe that can't be cracked. And my question is, at what cost?

False equivalency and false dilemma fallacies aside, the FBI director is highlighting the double-edged sword of encryption and all technology in general. With more encryption can come better privacy, but potentially less overall security. The unfortunate caveat is that not all encrypted communications or data are completely innocent and cannot be known if everyone is to benefit from mobile phone encryption. In general, technology moves faster than law enforcement can adapt. Evidence is unavailable when agencies are unable to defeat digital protections. In those cases, other tried and tested investigative techniques and police work can still ferret out tangible evidence.

The proliferation of the Internet and its millions of networked devices, along with a propensity, if not incentive, for storing personal data on Internet-hosted systems, has set the stage for potentially disastrous data loss. Massive data breaches and leaks from well-known corporations and organizations have had a profound effect on the average Internet user. An educated user base has demanded an increased usage of encryption for personal means, and the expectation that personal data is protected against criminals, governments, and military alike. People want encryption now because their whole lives are online. We expect that transferring money from credit cards or mobile phones should be encrypted and secure. We expect that information we believe to be private should be kept private, and more so, that we should have control over who can access our information.

Encrypt Everything?

The specter of pervasive encryption has kept some security monitoring professionals from sleeping at night. Having all files and network transmissions encrypted to and from attackers seems like a nightmare scenario that yields little fruitful investigations. After all, if you can't see precisely what's in the traffic leaving your organization, how can you know for sure what might have been lost? In the security monitoring context, there are only two practical options for handling encryption: intercept, decrypt, inspect, and re-encrypt (known as man-in-the-middle, or MITM), or ignore encrypted traffic payloads. If MITM is unacceptable or impossible, there is still plenty of data to go around. Metadata from network traffic and other security event sources can create additional investigative paths and still solve problems.

Recall the Conficker worm that's likely still running through the unpatched backwaters of the Internet, impotent and headless after numerous, coordinated takedown efforts. The worm encrypted its payloads, eventually to key lengths of 4096 bits in later variants eventually leading to millions of dollars in damages for many organizations, including military and government. It also generated a random list of domains to retrieve for the bot check-in component with a domain name generation algorithm (DGA). This last component (among others in the C2 protocol) is detectable with IPS, or even with web proxy logs or passive DNS (pDNS) data. Conficker also uses a UDP based peer-to-peer protocol communication that's easily identifiable with IPS or other monitoring tools. The encrypted contents of the Conficker payload are irrelevant as long as you can detect its traffic patterns on the network and shut it down.

Correctly deploying end-to-end encryption (E2EE) is difficult, which can leave unencrypted data at risk to attack. Consider a point-of-sale (POS) terminal. For full E2EE, at a minimum, data (i.e., credit card information) would need to be encrypted on the card itself, at the hardware terminal scanning the card, the POS application processing the transaction, at the disk level for any locally stored artifacts, at the network transport layer back to a centralized POS server, and at the data storage layer in the centralized POS system. It's a difficult enough process that U.S. retailer Target suffered a $148 million loss (*http://www.forbes.com/sites/samanthasharf/2014/08/05/target-shares-tumble-as-retailer-reveals-cost-of-data-breach/*) in part as a result of hackers scraping unencrypted credit card transactions from memory on their POS terminals.

For the same reasons that it's difficult to implement encryption in a corporate setting, it's difficult for attackers to do so in their software and infrastructure. Advanced adversaries and campaigns often encrypt C2 communications (e.g., screenshots, keylogger data, etc.), but less sophisticated attacks rarely encrypt command and control. This fact can lead to a detectable anomaly in and of itself. The cost of implementing and maintaining encryption outweighs the profits in the malware industry. If phishing and malware campaigns are highly lucrative without running complicated PKI infrastructures, or running and supporting more advanced cryptographic algorithms and key management systems, why would criminals bother? If an attacker requires confidentiality, then they should encrypt. If the goal is to not be detected, encryption is largely unimportant.

Some attackers use encryption not to protect their own data, but to block access to yours, as discussed in Chapter 3. The ransomware Trojan Cryptolocker (among others) uses both AES encryption and 2048-bit RSA keys to encrypt victim files it holds hostage.

Catching the Ghost

If you monitor an organization's network, you will eventually need to deal with encrypted data on the wire or "at rest" on a host. If you deploy a web proxy, you'll need to assess the feasibility in your environment of MITM secure HTTP connections. From a monitoring perspective, it's technically possible to monitor some encrypted communications. From a policy perspective, it's a different story. Does your Internet access policy allow communications to external email, banking, or social media sites that may inadvertently MITM your user's personal credentials? Depending on your organization's network usage policies, you may be required to whitelist certain sites from decryption. For performance reasons, it can be in your best interest to inspect only encrypted traffic streams to sites or applications with which you do not have an implicit trust.

Remember that even if data cannot be decrypted on the wire, all hope is not lost. There are numerous metadata components such as IP addresses, hostnames, TCP ports, URLs, and bytes transferred that can yield invaluable clues to an investigation. Intrusion detection may not be able to record the payloads, but if the packet structure from a particular malware campaign is predictable or expressible, the IPS can detect or block the attack. Metadata like NetFlow can provide context to the communications. Agents can be installed to decrypt network communications directly on the host. DNS queries can provide further investigative clues for you to trace to transitive closure. System, network, or application logs can identify different portions of the encrypted communications. CSIRTs have gone for years without full packet inspection and still discover security incidents.

As described in Chapter 4, metadata and log mining can still uncover the details that can be used to resolve problems, even if you can't read the full contents of a packet. It's always nice to have the full breakdown of all the communications, but even without encryption, having that data is often not available simply due to storage restrictions. Triggers can still fire for suspicious sequences of metadata, hosts, and applications, and people can be profiled by their data patterns and their outliers.

Technology evolves at a tremendous pace, yet we're still able to keep up and respond. Undeniably, technology will continue to evolve, but there is no reason to believe it will change or will be capable of changing in such a way that monitoring and responding to security incidents is impossible. Remember that even as technology and IT trends change, the playbook approach holds fast as a reliable framework to plug in new variables and inputs with consistent results.

TL;DR

There are millions more computers on the way, along with millions of new applications, services, and technological phenomena. Along with the future generations of computers and technology, there will be more connectivity, more data, more capability, and more encryption and obfuscation. However, as long as there are computer networks, there should always be ways to monitor them, regardless of how big they become. As long as there are applications, there will be the possibility for helpful log data. In the end, security investigations boil down to asking the right people the right questions about the right data, and then analyzing any logs you can get for evidence. Even if the content of log data isn't readable, the data *about the data* will certainly exist.

Staying relevant in InfoSec not only means knowing how to defend what you have, but also knowing how to predict what's coming. Technology clearly moves in trends based largely on computing capabilities, and given the infinite ingenuity of human innovation, things can change quickly. Talk to most people that have been in IT for years, and they can all tell you about the things they used to be experts in but are now irrelevant or completely obsolete. You will also hear of the various trends over the years and their impact (whether positive or negative) on the current state of operations. The technology industry and the InfoSec industry in particular are accelerating rapidly. As crime adapts to the digital landscape, the pace of development forces criminals and network defenders to constantly try and gain an edge over one another, at an ever-increasing pace. Given the complexity of the computing environments and networks of today, the possibilities for attackers is seemingly limitless, while defenders must stay on top of the latest techniques and methods to remain relevant.

In Chapter 2, we introduced four core questions to guide our playbook methodology:

- What are we trying to protect?
- What are the threats?
- How do we detect them?
- How do we respond?

Though the environments in which those questions are asked and answered may change over time, the underlying methodology ensures a repeatable process that can adapt with changing technologies, vendors, and products. At a micro level, the playbook allows for constructive adjustments, revision, replacement, or even retirement for any given monitoring objective. At a macro level, the playbook allows new plays and methods to be introduced, no matter what tools you are using, what threats you are facing, what network you are monitoring, or what trends you are following. As we mentioned in Chapter 6, even if you were somehow able to defend all your systems and detect all of the threats you face today, the pace of technology ensures that you will face something new tomorrow. A successful CSIRT will have, at its core, a solid foundational playbook and the ability to apply that living model to a rapidly changing security landscape.

Index

IRT (see CSIRT (computer security incident response team))
Israel, adversarial attacks on, 42
IT policies, 25
IT team, 5

J

Java attacks, 32, 67, 180-183
Jflow (see NetFlow)

K

kill chain model, 111-112
knowledge, evolution of, 66
Krebs, Brian, 37

L

law enforcement support, 9
legal department, 7
linked charts, 217-219
LinkedIn information, 42
lockdown (see containment)
Lockheed Martin, 46
log data
    fields, 55-62
    filtering, 50-54
    normalization, 54-55
log exploration, 189
log management systems, 113-116
long-term fixes, 233
lost hosts, 20
lost/hidden servers, 17

M

malware campaigns, 36-42
    business of, 36-37
    disrupting, 36
    state-sponsored, 41-42
malware detection (see queries)
Markov chains, 211
media and PR issues, 227
metadata, 62-68
    content-free, 129
    context enrichment, 66-68
    defining, 62
    NSA leak of, 63
metadata attribution, 19
Metcalfe's law, 239
Microsoft, 20, 33, 125, 241

Microsoft Active Directory , 137
misconfiguration errors, 40
mitigation (see incident containment)
monetizing attacks, 37-39, 240
Moore's law, 239

N

nameserver query distribution, 199
NASA, 46, 62
National Security Agency (NSA), 63, 242
NetFlow, 66, 129-135, 196
    application identification, 130
    deployment considerations, 129
    detecting port scanning behavior, 206-207
    device support, 134
    and directionality, 133
    examples, 131-132
    and expiration, 132
    limitations of, 132
    1:1 versus sampled, 129
    pros and cons, 135
    and UDP data transfer, 135
Netstream (see NetFlow)
Network Address Translation (NAT), 19
network monitoring, 33
network operations team, 5
Network Time Protocol (NTP), 19
null routing, 229-231

O

objective statement, 75
Open Systems Interconnection (OSI) reference model, 110
Operation Aurora, 42
operational errors, 40
operationalizing, 81-108
    analysis team, 85-91
    automation limitations, 83-85
    case tracking systems, 105-106
    continuation and reliability, 106
    core metrics development, 91-92
    event query system, 98-99
    human element requirement, 83-87
    incident handling and remediation systems, 103-104
    questions to ask, 81-83
    result presentation system, 99-103
    systematic approach, 91-92
    updating, 107-108

organized crime, 40
outsourcing InfoSec, 12

P

packet capture programs, 157-158
   deployment considerations, 157
   examples, 157
   limitations of, 158
   pros and cons, 158
passive detection versus inline blocking, 118-120
patterns, as report cues, 179, 182
Payment Card Industry Data Security Standards (PCI DSS), 25
Pearson's chi-squared test, 209
personal information access, 37-40
phishing, 24, 37, 112, 151, 162
playbook, 3, 10, 13
   action plan (see operationalizing)
   benefits of, 71
   reports, 72-79
      (see also report framework; reports)
   South Park analogy, 82
   uniqueness of, 28
playbook management system, 92-98
   key points, 102
   quality assurance process, 94
   report guidelines, 95-97
   reviewing reports, 97-98
policies, traditional IT and InfoSec, 25
port scanning behavior, 206-207
privacy breaches, 227-228
product security, 8
product vendors, 9
public relations (PR), 7, 227

Q

queries, 77, 98-99, 115
   (see also reports)
   ad-hoc searches, 115, 183-190
   advanced strategies, 193-221
   basic versus advanced, 193-195
   and beaconing, 207-209
   blocking (see DNS RPZ)
   breadth-first search (BFS), 220
   correlation through contingent data, 212-217
   data sources, 196
   distribution among nameservers, 199

DNS capture of, 138
event aggregation, 203-205
false positives, 177, 195-196
feature lists for, 181
finding commonalities, 197-199
finding deviant host behavior, 199-202
finding patterns for, 176-179
generic/specific balance, 180-183
graph-based, 217-221
on historical data, 196
IDS signatures and, 203
pattern detection, 182
port scanning behavior, 206-207
positive versus negative features in, 183
random behavior, 209-212
simplicity in, 190
statistical analysis, 202
subverting, 140

R

ransomware attack example, 29-31
regulation, 241
regulatory compliance standards, 25-27
relevance of data, 50-54
remediation, 231-233
remediation systems, 103-104
report framework
   analyst comments/notes, 78
   category, 74
   data query/code, 77
   description, 75
   event source, 74
   ID numbering system, 72
   objective statement, 75
   result analysis, 76-77
   type, 73-74
reports, 167-191
   (see also queries)
   accuracy checklist, 95-97
   attack detection, 171-173
   automation limitations, 83-85
   cost-benefit analysis, 169, 171
   examples-based, 171-183
   false positives, 168
   getting started creating, 174
   high-fidelity, 170, 174
   hunch-based, 183-190
   intel-based, 189
   investigative, 170

U

User Datagram Protocol (UDP), 32, 135

V

vendor support, 9
vertical scanning, 206
viewing results data, 100
virtual machine (VM) attribution, 20
Volumetric DDoS (VDDoS) attacks, 32
VPN, 19

W

watering hole attacks, 24, 113, 151
Web Cache Communication Protocol (WCCP),
   147, 156

web proxies, 145-157
   blocking abilities, 146
   deployment considerations, 146-151
   examples, 151-155
   exploit kits, 151-155
   limitations of, 155-157
   pros and cons, 156
   threat prevention, 151
whitelisting, 125, 198
Windows XP, 32
worms, 31, 176-179

Z

ZeuS Tracker service, 175
Zeus Trojan, 151

About the Authors

With over ten years of information security experience, **Jeff Bollinger** has worked as a security architect and incident responder for both academic and corporate networks. Specializing in investigations, network security monitoring, and intrusion detection, he currently works as an information security investigator, and has built and operated one of the world's largest corporate security monitoring infrastructures. Jeff regularly speaks at international FIRST conferences, and writes for the Cisco Security Blog. His recent work includes log mining, search optimization, threat research, and security investigations.

Brandon Enright is a senior information security investigator with Cisco Systems. Brandon has a bachelor's degree in computer science from UC San Diego where he did research in the Systems and Networking group. Brandon has coauthored several papers on the infrastructure and economics of malware botnets and a paper on the impact of low entropy seeds on the generation of SSL certificates. Some of his work in cryptography includes presenting weaknesses in some of the NIST SHA3 competition candidates, fatally knocking one out of the competition, and authoring the Password Hashing Competition proposal OmegaCrypt. Brandon is a long-time contributor to the Nmap project, a fast and featureful port scanner and security tool. In his free time, Brandon enjoys mathematical puzzles and logic games.

Matthew Valites is a senior investigator and site lead on Cisco's Computer Security Incident Response Team (CSIRT). He provides expertise building an Incident Response and monitoring program for cloud and hosted service enterprises, with a focus on targeted and high-value assets. A hobbyist Breaker and Maker for as long as he can recall, his current professional responsibilities include security investigations, mining security-centric alerts from large data sets, operationalizing CSIRT's detection logic, and mobile device hacking. Matt enjoys speaking at international conferences, and is keen to share CSIRT's knowledge, best practices, and lessons learned.

Colophon

The animal on the cover of *Crafting the InfoSec Playbook* is an American crocodile (*Crocodylus acutus*), the most widespread crocodile species in the Americas. It prefers tropical coastal habitats near brackish or salty water, and is found in the Caribbean, the state of Florida, Mexico, Central America, and parts of South America. The name *crocodylus* comes from the Greek for "pebble worm," because of this animal's bumpy scaled skin and typical crawling motion.

This species of crocodile is one of the largest reptiles—males can grow up to 20 feet long and weigh 2,000 pounds. Females are smaller, around 12 feet long on average. Though they are formidable predators, the American crocodile does not often attack large animals (or humans, though it is not unheard of). The bulk of its diet is made up of fish, reptiles, birds, and small mammals, with an occasional deer or cow on the menu. They are not capable of running long distances, and rely on an ambush technique to catch land prey. Within the water, their olive brown skin camouflages them well; when another animal comes close, they lunge forward and grab their victim with exceptionally strong jaws.

Interestingly, while crocodiles have one of the strongest bite forces of any animal (more than seven times stronger than a great white shark), the muscles for opening their jaw are extremely weak compared to those for closing it. Thus, their mouth can be held shut with duct tape.

From the 1930s to the 1960s, American crocodiles were overhunted due to high demand for their hides in leather goods such as shoes and handbags. Though many countries began protecting them in the 1970s, they are still endangered by illegal hunting and coastal development that destroys their nesting grounds.

Many of the animals on O'Reilly covers are endangered; all of them are important to the world. To learn more about how you can help, go to *animals.oreilly.com*.

The cover image is from Lydekker's *Royal Natural History*. The cover fonts are URW Typewriter and Guardian Sans. The text font is Adobe Minion Pro; the heading font is Adobe Myriad Condensed; and the code font is Dalton Maag's Ubuntu Mono.

Have it your way.

Get even more for your money.

Join the O'Reilly Community, and register the O'Reilly books you own. It's free, and you'll get:

- $4.99 ebook upgrade offer
- 40% upgrade offer on O'Reilly print books
- Membership discounts on books and events
- Free lifetime updates to ebooks and videos
- Multiple ebook formats, DRM FREE
- Participation in the O'Reilly community
- Newsletters
- Account management
- 100% Satisfaction Guarantee

Signing up is easy:

1. Go to: oreilly.com/go/register
2. Create an O'Reilly login.
3. Provide your address.
4. Register your books.

Note: English-language books only

To order books online:
oreilly.com/store

For questions about products or an order:
orders@oreilly.com

To sign up to get topic-specific email announcements and/or news about upcoming books, conferences, special offers, and new technologies:
elists@oreilly.com

For technical questions about book content:
booktech@oreilly.com

To submit new book proposals to our editors:
proposals@oreilly.com

O'Reilly books are available in multiple DRM-free ebook formats. For more information:
oreilly.com/ebooks